D1006589

·EXPLORING·

SCIENCE AND MEDICAL DISCOVERIES

Vaccines

·EXPLORING·

SCIENCE AND MEDICAL DISCOVERIES

Vaccines

Other books in the
Exploring Science and Medical Discoveries series:

Antibiotics
Cloning
Gene Therapy

SCIENCE AND MEDICAL DISCOVERIES

◆ Vaccines

Clay Farris Naff, *Book Editor*

Bruce Glassman, *Vice President*
Bonnie Szumski, *Publisher*
Helen Cothran, *Managing Editor*
David M. Haugen, *Series Editor*

GREENHAVEN PRESS
An imprint of Thomson Gale, a part of The Thomson Corporation

THOMSON
━━━✳━━━ ™
GALE

Detroit • New York • San Francisco • San Diego • New Haven, Conn.
Waterville, Maine • London • Munich

© 2005 Thomson Gale, a part of The Thomson Corporation.

Thomson and Star Logo are trademarks and Gale and Greenhaven Press are registered trademarks used herein under license.

For more information, contact
Greenhaven Press
27500 Drake Rd.
Farmington Hills, MI 48331-3535
Or you can visit our Internet site at http://www.gale.com

ALL RIGHTS RESERVED.
No part of this work covered by the copyright hereon may be reproduced or used in any form or by any means—graphic, electronic, or mechanical, including photocopying, recording, taping, Web distribution or information storage retrieval systems—without the written permission of the publisher.

Every effort has been made to trace the owners of copyrighted material.

Cover credit: © Hulton/Archive by Getty Images
Library of Congress, 89
National Archives, 27

LIBRARY OF CONGRESS CATALOGING-IN-PUBLICATION DATA

Vaccines / Clay Farris Naff, book editor.
p. cm. — (Exploring science and medical discoveries)
Includes bibliographical references and index.
ISBN 0-7377-1969-9 (lib. : alk. paper) — ISBN 0-7377-1970-2 (pbk. : alk. paper)
1. Vaccines—Popular works. I. Naff, Clay Farris. II. Series.
QR189.V2682   2005
615'.372—dc22
                                                2004047406

Printed in the United States of America

CONTENTS

LIBRARY
DEXTER MUNICIPAL SCHOOLS
DEXTER, NEW MEXICO 88230

$29⁰⁰

GaleGroup / Bond Money

12-17-04.

smallpox by inoculating with a related disease known as variola or cowpox.

Chapter 2: Milestones in Disease Prevention

of the team that guided its eradication in 1980 recalls
the steps that led to his involvement in that successful
global campaign.

Chapter 3: Setbacks and Controversies

against bioweapons. Not everyone, however, is convinced of the vaccine's effectiveness or its safety.

Chapter 4: Future Prospects and Challenges

spreads easily—cannot afford the expensive vaccines manufactured by wealthier nations.

FOREWORD

Most great science and medical discoveries emerge slowly from the work of generations of scientists. In their laboratories, far removed from the public eye, scientists seek cures for human diseases, explore more efficient methods to feed the world's hungry, and develop technologies to improve quality of life. A scientist, trained in the scientific method, may spend his or her entire career doggedly pursuing a goal such as a cure for cancer or the invention of a new drug. In the pursuit of these goals, most scientists are single-minded, rarely thinking about the moral and ethical issues that might arise once their new ideas come into the public view. Indeed, it could be argued that scientific inquiry requires just that type of objectivity.

Moral and ethical assessments of scientific discoveries are quite often made by the unscientific—the public—sometimes for good, sometimes for ill. When a discovery is unveiled to society, intense scrutiny often ensues. The media report on it, politicians debate how it should be regulated, ethicists analyze its impact on society, authors vilify or glorify it, and the public struggles to determine whether the new development is friend or foe. Even without fully understanding the discovery or its potential impact, the public will often demand that further inquiry be stopped. Despite such negative reactions, however, scientists rarely quit their pursuits; they merely find ways around the roadblocks.

Embryonic stem cell research, for example, illustrates this tension between science and public response. Scientists engage in embryonic stem cell research in an effort to treat diseases such as Parkinson's and diabetes that are the result of cellular dysfunction. Embryonic stem cells can be derived from early-stage embryos, or blastocysts, and coaxed to form any kind of human cell or tissue. These can then be used to replace damaged or diseased tissues in those suffering from intractable diseases. Many researchers believe that the use of embryonic stem cells to treat human diseases promises to be one of the most important advancements in medicine.

However, embryonic stem cell experiments are highly controversial in the public sphere. At the center of the tumult is the fact that in order to create embryonic stem cell lines, human embryos must be destroyed. Blastocysts often come from fertilized eggs that are left over from fertility treatments. Critics argue that since blastocysts have the capacity to grow into human beings, they should be granted the full range of rights given to all humans, including the right not to be experimented on. These analysts contend, therefore, that destroying embryos is unethical. This argument received attention in the highest office of the United States. President George W. Bush agreed with the critics, and in August 2001 he announced that scientists using federal funds to conduct embryonic stem cell research would be restricted to using existing cell lines. He argued that limiting research to existing lines would prevent any new blastocysts from being destroyed for research.

Scientists have criticized Bush's decision, saying that restricting research to existing cell lines severely limits the number and types of experiments that can be conducted. Despite this considerable roadblock, however, scientists quickly set to work trying to figure out a way to continue their valuable research. Unsurprisingly, as the regulatory environment in the United States becomes restrictive, advancements occur elsewhere. A good example concerns the latest development in the field. On February 12, 2004, professor Hwang Yoon-Young of Hanyang University in Seoul, South Korea, announced that he was the first to clone a human embryo and then extract embryonic stem cells from it. Hwang's research means that scientists may no longer need to use blastocysts to perform stem cell research. Scientists around the world extol the achievement as a major step in treating human diseases.

The debate surrounding embryonic stem cell research illustrates the moral and ethical pressure that the public brings to bear on the scientific community. However, while nonexperts often criticize scientists for not considering the potential negative impact of their work, ironically the public's reaction against such discoveries can produce harmful results as well. For example, although the outcry against embryonic stem cell research in the United States has resulted in fewer embryos being destroyed, those with Parkinson's, such as actor Michael J. Fox, have argued that prohibiting the development of new stem cell lines ultimately will prevent a timely cure for the disease that is killing Fox and thousands of others.

Greenhaven Press's Exploring Science and Medical Discoveries series explores the public uproar that often follows the disclosure of scientific advances in fields such as stem cell research. Each anthology traces the history of one major scientific or medical discovery, investigates society's reaction to the breakthrough, and explores potential new applications and avenues of research. Primary sources provide readers with eyewitness accounts of crucial moments in the discovery process, and secondary sources offer historical perspectives on the scientific achievement and society's reaction to it. Volumes also contain useful research tools, including an introductory essay providing important context, and an annotated table of contents enabling students to quickly locate selections of interest. A thorough index helps readers locate content easily, a detailed chronology helps students trace the history of the discovery, and an extensive bibliography guides readers interested in pursuing further research.

Greenhaven Press's Exploring Science and Medical Discoveries series provides readers with inspiring accounts of how generations of scientists made the world's great discoveries possible and investigates the tremendous impact those innovations have had on the world.

Vaccines: Preventing Disease but Not Controversy

Humanity has struggled for many thousands of years against infectious diseases. In the premodern era doctors lacked both an understanding of such diseases and the means to treat them. Until vaccines became widely used in the twentieth century, infectious diseases made life for most people, as seventeenth-century British philosopher Thomas Hobbes famously observed, "nasty, brutish, and short."[1]

Yet, even after they had demonstrated great potential for preventing disease, vaccines were treated with suspicion. Implementation of universal vaccination campaigns proved slow and difficult. To this day, vaccines continue to be a source of great controversy, misunderstanding, and popular resistance.

Before widespread vaccination erected barriers against infectious diseases, contagion respected neither social position nor national borders. In medieval Europe, epidemics of bubonic plague and of smallpox killed as many as one in three people. Well into the twentieth century, every American family faced the prospect of losing one or more children to communicable disease. When diseases did not kill, they often left permanent disability. Franklin Delano Roosevelt, president of the United States from 1932 until his death in 1945, had earlier been crippled by polio, making him the only wheelchair-bound chief executive in history.

Roosevelt was not, however, the only president to be afflicted by infectious disease. Presidents William Henry Harrison (1841) and Zachary Taylor (1849–1850) both died of illness while in office. Even the man considered by many historians to have been America's greatest president faced domestic tragedy from infectious disease. In the midst of the Civil War, Abraham Lincoln and his wife Mary had to endure the loss of their beloved son Willie at the age of eleven. He died on February 20, 1862, of typhoid fever, a disease now virtually unknown in America thanks to vaccines. One of Lincoln's military advisers, General Jessie Fremont, noted, "A sadder face than that of the President I have rarely seen."[2]

Lincoln's tragic loss was a hardship familiar to millions of ordinary people. In nineteenth century America, infectious disease struck nearly every home. For example, according to the National Institute of Allergy and Infectious Diseases: "Tuberculosis was so prevalent that encountering a family who had escaped the disease entirely was almost unimaginable. Remarking upon the swath cut by tuberculosis, an American epidemiologist in 1849 wrote, 'any facts regarding a disease that destroys one-seventh to one-fourth of all that die, cannot but be interesting.'"[3]

Interest, however, did not translate immediately into effective action. Vaccines would have to fight an uphill battle for acceptance, first in the medical community and then with the public. Once they did, the results were astonishing.

Public Health Revolution

The U.S. government's Centers for Disease Control (CDC) report that over the course of the twentieth century widespread vaccination in America achieved better than a 99 percent reduction in the annual occurrences of eight notorious childhood diseases. Among these scourges are such familiar names as measles, mumps, rubella, polio, and, of course, smallpox. Other potentially deadly diseases, such as tuberculosis, tetanus, whooping cough, and influenza have been dramatically curbed by the same means.

Contrary to widespread belief, however, vaccines do not directly prevent disease. Instead, they owe their success to their ability to prime the body's immune system for a particular disease. Vaccines do this by introducing relatively harmless antigens into the body. An antigen is anything that stimulates an immune response. It may be a virus or a bacterium similar to the one that causes a particular disease. It may be a killed or disabled germ of the type that causes a disease. It might even be fragments of protein or DNA extracted from the germ.

Whatever type of antigen is introduced, the immune system will remember its key features and recognize them if a germ with similar features invades. It is a marvelous and still somewhat mysterious system, according to biological theorist Mihaela Oprea of Rockefeller University: "Subsequent encounters with an antigen

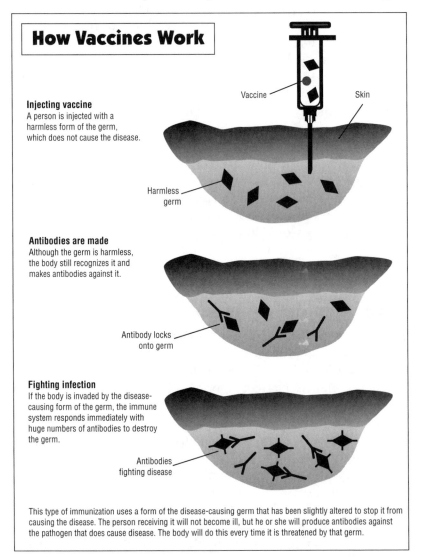

How Vaccines Work

Vaccine   Skin

Injecting vaccine
A person is injected with a harmless form of the germ, which does not cause the disease.

Harmless germ

Antibodies are made
Although the germ is harmless, the body still recognizes it and makes antibodies against it.

Antibody locks onto germ

Fighting infection
If the body is invaded by the disease-causing form of the germ, the immune system responds immediately with huge numbers of antibodies to destroy the germ.

Antibodies fighting disease

This type of immunization uses a form of the disease-causing germ that has been slightly altered to stop it from causing the disease. The person receiving it will not become ill, but he or she will produce antibodies against the pathogen that does cause disease. The body will do this every time it is threatened by that germ.

trigger a faster, more efficient elimination of it, to the extent that the second infection may not even be clinically apparent. This is the essence of immune memory, although the mechanisms that underlie it are not completely understood. It is also what makes vaccination so efficient."[4]

The body responds to a familiar antigen by producing a variety of antibodies tailor-made to track down and kill a particular kind of invading microorganism. Antibodies are cells that specialize in defeating diseases. They come in different varieties of so-called T and B cells and perform various roles. Some mark invaders for destruction by roaming killer cells. Others carry out the demolition job themselves. Still others block viruses from entering cells, thereby preventing them from reproducing.

Grudging Acceptance

Thanks in large part to the effectiveness of vaccines, the life expectancy of Americans rose by 50 percent during the twentieth century. Similar results were achieved in western Europe and Japan and have begun to be seen in the developing world. Yet, these achievements have been slow in coming. According to the CDC: "Although the first vaccine against smallpox was developed in 1796, greater than 100 years later its use had not been widespread enough to fully control the disease. Four other vaccines—against rabies, typhoid, cholera, and plague—had been developed late in the 19th century but were not used widely by 1900."[5]

At every stage, public health vaccination campaigns have had to overcome patches of strong resistance. Although there are fresh developments in each generation, to really understand the controversy that dogs vaccines, it is necessary to go back to a period that predates the scientific understanding of disease.

Coming to Grips with Germs

It is a curious fact that vaccines arose before the causes of infectious disease were understood. For many centuries before germ theory took hold in the late 1800s, traditional medicine in China, Turkey, and some other nations had achieved some minor success in smallpox prevention by inoculating people with the scabs of smallpox victims. Bacteria had been regularly observed since 1683, when Dutch inventor Antoni van Leeuwenhoek spotted them through his two-lens microscope. Yet most of the medical profession regarded them as harmless little entertainments. Even after physician Edward Jenner published his 1798 report of success in vaccinating against smallpox, the response in the West was spotty. Two leading scholars of public health law note: "Dr. Jenner's discovery of the smallpox vaccine did not instantly result in government-led immunization efforts in Europe. For some time, public distrust and a general lack of governmental action stood in the way of compulsory vaccination laws."[6]

Early Efforts at Vaccination

There were sporadic attempts at widespread vaccination. The French emperor Napoléon Bonaparte had his troops vaccinated against smallpox in 1805 before marching them off to war. In 1818 the tiny German principality of Wittenberg began requiring children to be vaccinated before entering school or apprenticeships. On the whole, however, throughout the first half of the nineteenth century smallpox vaccination remained a privilege of Europe's aristocracy. In the United States, Congress authorized a national smallpox vaccination effort in 1813 but repealed the law less than ten years later after the campaign not only failed to prove effective due to poor quality control but even led, in one case, to an outbreak of the disease it was meant to prevent.

A major problem was that no one understood how vaccinations worked. Lacking knowledge of the causes of communicable disease, European and American medical establishments took conflicting positions on the value of vaccines compared with other medical practices of the time. This confusion continued for many decades. By the mid–nineteenth century, Jenner's fellow British physicians continued to be utterly mystified by contagious illnesses. In 1853 Thomas Wakely, editor of Britain's most prestigious medical journal, the *Lancet*, wrote in that publication's editorial page concerning an epidemic of cholera: "All is darkness and confusion, vague theory, and a vain speculation. Is it a fungus, an insect, a miasma, an electrical disturbance, a deficiency of ozone, a morbid off-scouring from the intestinal canal? We know nothing; we are at sea in a whirlpool of conjecture."[7]

French scientist Louis Pasteur did much to clear away the mystery. In a series of brilliant experiments conducted from the 1850s through the 1880s, he demonstrated that microorganisms were self-reproducing, were responsible for infection, and could be blocked by vaccination. Yet, although his work attracted wide attention, it was not universally accepted.

Even those who agreed that germs caused disease were left with big questions about vaccination. So complex are the body's defenses that although Pasteur could clearly demonstrate that germs caused infection and that vaccines prevented it, he could not explain the underlying mechanisms of immunology. A detailed understanding of antibodies, for example, would not begin to take shape in the scientific community until the 1930s. Thus, vaccines went into use long before a scientific understanding of both germs and the immune system had been acquired. This may be one of the key reasons why vaccines faced so much resistance.

Roots of Resistance

However, opposition was not entirely due to a lack of full medical understanding. It also sprang from conflicts of interest, from religious beliefs, and from libertarian political sentiments. All three fanned public distrust of vaccination throughout the nineteenth century. As compulsory education took hold throughout America and Europe, legislatures passed smallpox vaccination requirements. These met fierce resistance in many communities.

By 1892 a British antivaccination league had persuaded more than 90 percent of the parents in the city of Leicester to refuse to have their children vaccinated, despite the risk of fines. During a smallpox outbreak in New York City in 1894, police had to be called out to protect vaccinators from angry residents.

Conflicts of Interest

Within the medical community vaccines faced stiff competition throughout the nineteenth century. The scientific method, with its controlled experiments and statistical checks on error, had yet to be implemented in medicine. The positive results of vaccination persuaded some physicians, yet numerous others in the medical establishment were reluctant to accept it. Speculative theories of healing had gained large followings, and many physicians made a living by committing their practices to patent medicines, sanatoriums, extreme diets, and other dubious treatments. They were loath to give these up in favor of a new and only partially understood method of disease prevention.

Even some of those committed to what is now considered mainstream medicine had private reasons to withhold their support from germ theory and its implications. Plunging into vaccination might be risky to their practices, some thought. Indeed, vaccination, because it introduces germs or parts of germs into the body, always carries risk of causing disease. That risk was far greater in the nineteenth century, before modern techniques of weakening germs were developed.

Some worried about offending powerful religious leaders or feared a public backlash. Above all, many physicians may have been reluctant to admit that by not washing their hands, they themselves could well have infected many of their patients by transferring disease from one to the next. As summed up on the Timelinescience Web site, some physicians

> thought that childbed fever was God's punishment to women for the act of giving birth. To change their point of view would mean accepting that the deadly disease was caused by an invisible something which could be transferred from patient to patient. But more than that, it was hard for doctors to admit that they themselves had spread the disease and killed their patients instead of curing them.[8]

Threat to Livelihood

For practitioners outside the mainstream, there was another motive for their rejection of vaccines. To accept germ theory would have discredited the entire basis of their claims to perform cures. Vaccines, and the theory that underlay them, represented a mortal threat to such practices as chiropractic healing, which assumes that all disease arises from misalignment of the spine, and naturopathy, which presumes that disease arises from a holistic violation of "natural laws." These competing theories, though without scientific merit, grew rapidly at the end of the nineteenth century and beyond. Their leaders were not about to alienate the clientele by accepting germ theory.

In 1918, more than three decades after Pasteur's anthrax and rabies vaccines had proven effective, America's leading naturopath, Benedict Lust, showed not only a disdain for vaccines but a profound ignorance of their role in preventing (rather than curing) infections: "The contemporary fashion of healing disease is that of serums, inoculations and vaccines, which, instead of being an improvement on the fake medicines of former ages are of no value in the cure of disease, but on the contrary introduce lesions into the human body of the most distressing and deadly import."[9]

Just as vehement a rejection of immunization arose in the chiropractic community. Its founder, D.D. Palmer, had been a "magnetic healer" for some years when he hit upon a new approach to cures: manipulation of the spine. In 1897 he founded a school dedicated to the proposition that all disease arises from "subluxations," or distortions of the spine. Its exclusive-cause theory was later made unmistakably clear by his son and successor, B.J. Palmer: "If we had one hundred cases of small-pox, I can prove to you where, in one, you *will* find a subluxation and you will find the *same conditions* in the other ninety-nine. I adjust one and return his functions to normal. . . . There is no contagious disease. . . . There is no infection."[10]

Religious and Political Opposition

Another source of nineteenth-century opposition to vaccines lay in religion. Although many church leaders took a dim view of medical interference with what they viewed as God's will, none was more adamant or popular in this position than Mary Baker Eddy (1821–1910), founder of the Church of Christ, Scientist. Having founded Christian Science in 1879 in a suburb of Boston, she energetically spread the view that disease is a spiritual condition that can be cured only through prayer and religious study. The new religion grew rapidly, and its adherents became some of the most determined resisters of vaccination.

Wealthy American Protestants also had their share of religiously inspired antivaccination views. As the nineteenth century neared its end, a peculiar fusion of social Darwinism and Calvinist religion took shape among the elite. Adherents came to feel that their success in life was proof of God's blessing on the "survival of the fittest." This view expressed itself in opposition to vaccines based on the belief that epidemics were God's way of maintaining a "wholesome balance between the blessed and the damned."[11]

In view of America's national ideals of individual rights, it comes as no surprise that the libertarian resistance to vaccination policy has been strongest in the United States. From the start, the idea that the government could compel its people to undergo vac-

cination has ignited outrage in many Americans. Resistance to
vaccination was portrayed as a heroic act by the citizenry against
a tyrannical government. An early twentieth-century petition calling for the abolition of compulsory vaccination employed typically inflammatory rhetoric: "We have seen men, calling themselves doctors, claiming the right to force dangerous medical
operations on school children and soldiers without their free will
and consent . . . as they might do with dangerous beasts."[12]

Contemporary Controversies

Despite such denunciations, by the end of the twentieth century
childhood vaccination had become routine for most Americans.
The success of vaccines, especially in the second half of the century, convinced most voters to support them, and courts increasingly ruled in favor of compulsory programs.

By school age, more than 90 percent of children have received
the recommended vaccinations. To judge from the much lower immunization rate for preschool children (78 percent in 1997), this is
mainly due to state laws that require families to provide documen-
tation of vaccination for children entering school. Whether the
school-entering laws will remain effective cannot be ascertained,
because renewed opposition to vaccination has again grown into a
politically potent force. Interestingly, contemporary opposition
springs from much the same sources as its historical forebears.

Suspicion of government continues to play a strong role. Libertarian opponents question the safety and efficacy of vaccines as well
as the right of the government to compel citizens to undergo vaccination. A 2002 editorial column published in an Idaho libertarian
monthly typifies these views: "Historically, vaccination policy has
been a conflict between the 'thought police' who profit financially
from this medical fraud and evidence-based humanitarians who
subscribe to the precautionary principle: 'First do no harm.'"[13]

Political movements against universal vaccination are by no
means confined to the fringe. Legislatures with libertarian-leaning
majorities have in recent years debated bills to expand and sim-
plify the process for parents to exempt their children from vaccination. Texas has already passed such a bill. This has raised grave
concerns among public health officials. The level of protection
that vaccines offer differs from person to person, and several require multiple doses over a long period before immunity is se-

cured. Officials say that unless high levels of participation in vaccination programs can be maintained, outbreaks of disease in schools are likely to occur even among vaccinated children.

Some Religious Opposition Continues

Although the Christian Science movement has been on the wane since the middle of the twentieth century, its members continue to be among the staunchest of religiously motivated vaccine opponents. The resistance continues despite calls by modern Christian Scientist church leaders for its members to accept vaccination where required. The CDC reports, for example, that some of the largest U.S outbreaks of measles since 1993 have occurred in Christian Scientist schools in Missouri and Illinois.

Some Catholics have expressed reservations about vaccines based on moral concerns about the alleged use of fetal tissue in their production. However, the Catholic Church as a whole endorses vaccination. Most other religious denominations also support vaccination, and some have begun to challenge its opponents.

New Age Contrarians

The nineteenth century's love affair with quack cures, holistic healing, and spiritual medicine enjoyed a surprising revival at the close of the twentieth century. A broad range of unproven practices under the general heading of "alternative medicine" gained such popularity that Congress responded by exempting herbal supplements from pharmaceutical regulations and creating an office to study "complementary and alternative medicine" (CAM) within the National Institutes of Health. A Harvard Medical School study indicates that seven of ten people under the age of thirty-three have made use of CAM.

Like its nineteenth-century predecessors, much of the alternative medicine movement rejects (at least in part) the idea that germs cause disease, and therefore the idea that vaccines are effective in preventing it. Some alternative medicine advocates and religious groups have formed alliances against vaccination. As nurse Cindy Province of the advocacy group Christians Investigating New Age Medicine, notes:

The "antivaccine" movement has gained momentum. . . . More recent religious opposition has come from groups that tend to eschew medical treatment, such as Christian Scientists and the Amish, whose members also tend to reject vaccines. . . . Opposition to vaccines has also come from some "alternative" health care interests, most notably chiropractic and homeopathy . . . along with a curious mix of political interests and advocacy groups.[14]

The chiropractic industry continues to be an influential player in the opposition movement. Although not all chiropractors endorse antivaccination, their international association has adopted a policy on vaccines that states in part:

The International Chiropractors Association recognizes that the use of vaccines is not without risk, and questions the wisdom of mass vaccination programs. Chiropractic principles favor the enhancement of natural immunity over artificial immunizations. . . . In accordance with such principles and based upon the individual's right to freedom of choice, the ICA is opposed to compulsory programs which infringe upon such rights.[15]

Difficulties in the Developing World

A new channel of resistance to vaccines has arisen in the context of international vaccination campaigns. Opposition by Islamic leaders in developing countries threatens the success of a campaign to eliminate polio and could undermine other vaccination efforts.

Vaccines remained rare in the developing world during much of the twentieth century. After World War II, when the Cold War arose, U.S.-Soviet conflicts were offset to some degree by "vaccine diplomacy." This began in 1956 with cooperation on the testing of an oral polio vaccine. A few years later the two superpowers were cooperating in a worldwide campaign that resulted in 1981 in the eradication of smallpox. Working through the World Health Organization, they also contributed to reducing the global incidence of measles by 90 percent. The extent of Cold War cooperation on vaccines is still being investigated by scholars. The chair of microbiology at George Washington University comments: "It may never be fully learned how this international scientific collaboration contributed to a partial Cold War thaw and might even have reduced the likelihood of nuclear holocaust. However, the health and humanitarian impact of the joint American-

Soviet scientific war on [disease] was impressive."[16]

An ironic effect of the collapse of the Soviet Union is that it has become more difficult in some respects to extend the benefits of vaccination into the developing world. One problem is that numerous regional and civil wars broke out in the decade following the collapse of the Soviet Union in 1991. That made it more difficult for field teams to get vaccines out to the developing world.

More recently, deep suspicion of the West in the Islamic world has given rise to a new wave of resistance. A stronghold of oppo-

Dr. Albert Sabin administers an oral polio vaccine. He developed the "live" vaccine, which was given on a lump of sugar or in a teaspoonful of syrup.

sition has been the West African nation of Nigeria, particularly in its Muslim-majority northern states. While the World Health Organization struggled to eradicate polio in West Africa in 2003 and 2004, rumors took hold in Nigeria's Islamic communities that the vaccine had been intentionally altered to make Muslim children sterile. Those rumors prompted fierce resistance, even while the crippling disease made a comeback in the region.

It is not clear whether such opposition will spread to other countries with large Muslim populations. Public health officials are concerned, however, because they consider children in developing Islamic countries to be at the greatest risk of infectious disease.

Military and Medical Doubters

To observe that many opponents of vaccination are motivated by political, religious, or even unscientific medical views is not to discredit their concerns. Nor are all skeptics of vaccination associated with such viewpoints.

Two vaccines in particular have stirred intense and widespread controversy in recent years. The first is the anthrax vaccine administered to all members of the U.S. military. Numerous refusals (estimates vary wildly) by servicemen and servicewomen have led to demotions, punishments, and dishonorable discharges. Yet, according to the *Washington Post*, following the invasion of Iraq the failure to find any biological weapons has led to renewed resistance by military personnel. A lawsuit by six anonymous armed forces members forced a brief halt to the vaccination program late in 2003.

Objections to this vaccine, some from within the medical community, center on two concerns. The first has to do with the quality and safety of the vaccine. Unlike most such preventatives, the military's anthrax vaccine has never been reviewed by the U.S. Food and Drug Administration. Furthermore, it is produced by only one company under conditions of military secrecy. Some military personnel and veterans claim to have been seriously harmed by the anthrax vaccine.

The second objection concerns its effectiveness. Although many vaccines have proven effective against naturally occurring diseases, some critics doubt that a single vaccine can protect against all forms of *weaponized* anthrax. After all, they reason, anyone who develops anthrax with the intention of using it to kill will certainly do whatever they can to work around a vaccine. The Pentagon, however, says that an independent study finds that the vaccine is effective "for the protection of humans against anthrax, including inhalation anthrax, caused by all known or plausible engineered strains of *Bacillus anthracis* [the anthrax bacterium]."[17] It appears that a prolonged battle in the courts will be necessary to settle the question.

Uproar over MMR

The other big controversy arose from published claims that measles-mumps-rubella (MMR) vaccine causes autism in some children. The furor began in 1998 when British physician Andrew Wakefield and a dozen colleagues published a study in the *Lancet* suggesting that the measles component of MMR was linked to the development of autism, a mysterious behavioral disease that afflicts a small percentage of children.

In public statements, Wakefield expressed no doubt about his hypothesis that the inactivated measles virus contained in MMR was behind a bowel inflammation he blames for autism: "Parents came to us with questions that we were obliged to answer, and the studies that we have done have borne out their concerns. Not only that the children have had bowel disease that had gone undetected, but we have now confirmed the presence of the measles virus within the bowel."[18]

As the apparent implications of the study spread, worried parents began to refuse to allow their children to be inoculated with MMR. In 2000 Congress held hearings into the issue, strengthening the impression that something was wrong with the vaccine. In Britain, where the study had been published, the percentage of children receiving MMR vaccinations plummeted from 90 percent to under 80 percent—below the threshold believed necessary to prevent an outbreak.

Meantime, other articles alleging a link between vaccines and autism appeared in professional journals. Some blamed a mercury-based preservative called thimerosal. Wakefield continued to blame the viral component of the vaccination.

Case Closed

However, in April 2001 the National Academy of Science's Institute of Medicine released a report that rejected the hypothesis. Prepared by the institute's Committee on Immunization Safety Review, the report said that there was no statistical pattern among the millions of children vaccinated that could support the link between MMR and autism. It also said that theoretical models were fragmentary and that animal studies failed to support the hypothesis. The American Academy of Pediatrics conducted its own review and vigorously rejected claims of a connection between vaccines and autism.

As the medical and scientific establishments continued to review the evidence, a consensus took hold: No connection had been established. In an unusual turnabout, ten of the thirteen authors of the 1998 study announced in the March 6, 2004, issue of the *Lancet*, where the original paper appeared, that they reject the implication that a causal link exists between the MMR vaccine and autism. The retraction came amid charges that their lead author had engaged in unprofessional conduct during the research. Wakefield denied the allegations and continued to defend his stance.

For the scientific community the six-year controversy has likely ended, but there is no telling how long it will persist among members of the public. It illustrates how difficult it can be for science to investigate and refute unfounded allegations of danger in vaccines.

At the same time, scientists and medical professionals have a duty to inform the public about real dangers that indeed lurk in vaccines. No medicine, and certainly no vaccine, comes without risk. So predictable are the rare injuries from vaccines that a system of standardized compensation has been created in response.

Rising Challenges

However, fresh controversies are on the boil as nations struggle to prepare against the possibility of bioterrorism. The wisdom of widely vaccinating against smallpox, a disease no longer found in nature, has been hotly debated. In the meantime, unprecedented rates of migration are bringing significant numbers of unvaccinated people into the United States and other developed countries. Since no vaccine is 100 percent effective for all people, public health officials worry about maintaining high enough rates of immunization to prevent an outbreak.

Still other new challenges are at hand. The AIDS virus has so far frustrated all attempts to create a successful vaccine. Previously rare viruses, such as West Nile, hantavirus, and SARS, call out for new vaccines. Tuberculosis, once suppressed by vaccination and antibiotics, has mutated into new and more dangerous forms.

In the face of such challenges, promising new technologies, such as DNA-based vaccines, and promising new approaches, such as evolutionary medicine, give cause for hope. In the balance hangs a question: Will the twenty-first century mark continued progress in eradicating infectious disease, or will it herald a return to the misery of epidemics? Public support for research and development of new vaccines and cooperation in immunization campaigns may be crucial to the outcome. To judge from past and recent events, however, public support may be difficult to sustain.

Notes

1. Thomas Hobbes, *Leviathan.* New York: Penguin, 1994 (originally published in 1651), p. 18.

2. Quoted in The Lincoln Institute, "Redecoration and Willie's Death," www.mrlincolnswhitehouse.org/templates/display.search.cfm?ID=208.

3. National Institute of Allergy and Infectious Diseases, "Tuberculosis: Ancient Enemy, Present Threat," www.niaid.nih.gov/newsroom/focuson/tb02/story.htm.

4. Mihaela Oprea, trans. www.santafe.edu/~mihaela/thesis/node5.html.

5. Centers for Disease Control and Prevention, *CDC Morbidity and Mortality Weekly Report*, April 2, 1999, pp. 243–48. www.cdc.gov/mmwr/preview/mmwrhtml/00056803.htm#top.

6. James G. Hodge and Lawrence O. Gostin, *School Vaccination Requirements: Historical, Social, and Legal Perspectives.* Baltimore, MD: Center for Law and the Public's Health, February 2002, p. 14.

7. Quoted in UCLA Department of Epidemiology, "Brief History During the Snow Era (1813–58)," www.ph.ucla.edu/epi/snow/1859map/cholera_prevailingtheories_a2.html.

8. Timelinescience, "The Germ Theory of Disease," www.timelinescience.org/resource/students/penicilin/germ_th.htm.

9. Quoted in Kimball C. Atwood IV and Stephen Barrett, "Naturopathic Opposition to Immunization," *Quackwatch*, December 29, 2001. www.quackwatch.org/01QuackeryRelatedTopics/Naturopathy/immu.html.

10. Quoted in James B. Campbell, Jason W. Busse, and H. Stephen Injeyan, "Chiropractors and Vaccination: A Historical Perspective," *Pediatrics*, April 2000, pp. 105–109.

11. Hodge and Gostin, *School Vaccination Requirements*, p. 23.

12. Charles M. Higgins, quoted in Rupel Piuto, final draft of paper for His-

tory of Science Junior Research Seminar, Harvard University, 2001.

13. Barbara Flynn, "Smallpox Vaccinations at Gunpoint?" *Idaho Observer*, April 2002. http://proliberty.com/observer/20020408.htm.

14. Cindy Province, "Shot . . . or Not? What to Make of the Anti-vaccination Information," www.cinam.net/son1-1-cp.html.

15. *Chiropractic Choice*, "The National Vaccine Information Center (NVIC), an Ally for Freedom of Choice," June 2002. www.thechiropracticchoice. com/TCC_June_2002/national_vaccine_information_cen.htm.

16. Peter Hotez, "Appeasing Wilson's Ghost: The Expanded Role of the New Vaccines in International Diplomacy," occasional paper 3. Washington, DC: Chemical and Biological Arms Control Institute, 2002, pp. 1–2.

17. U.S. Department of Defense, "Anthrax Vaccine Immunization Program," 2004. www.anthrax.osd.mil/vaccine/facts.asp.

18. Quoted in Kate Foster, "Expert Says MMR Autism Link Will Be Proved This Year," *Scotsman*, March 18, 2002. http://thescotsman.scotsman.com/ index.cfm?id=298322002.

CHAPTER 1

The Development of Vaccines

LIBRARY
DEXTER MUNICIPAL SCHOOLS
DEXTER, NEW MEXICO 88230

A Brief History of the War Against Infectious Disease

By Joshua Lederberg

Contagion—the spread of a disease from one person to another—was understood long before the discovery of germs, Joshua Lederberg explains. The distinguished microbiologist notes that even during the terrible European plagues of the Middle Ages, people had some grasp of the spread of disease, but being helpless to stop it they acted out their fury by blaming "witches," Jews, and others. As neither prayer nor sacrifice availed, an estimated one of every three Europeans died. Nearly four centuries later, in 1796, the first steps toward vaccination began. It would take nearly another century for scientists to come up with an explanation for the spread of germs. From that point, late in the nineteenth century, Lederberg notes the increasing tempo of discovery, prevention, and cure right up to the current era. Today's fight against disease calls for a new strategy, he says. Humanity can never win a "war" against microorganisms, because their ability to evolve around medical defenses is inexhaustible. Instead, Lederberg suggests the aim should be for peaceful coexistence. The least harmful versions of germs should be encouraged, with scientific help, to outcompete their more harmful cousins. Lederberg is a Nobel laureate biomedical researcher and former president of Rockefeller University, where he heads the Laboratory of Molecular Genetics and Informatics.

In 1530, to express his ideas on the origin of syphilis, the Italian physician Girolamo Fracastoro penned *Syphilis, sive morbus Gallicus* (*Syphilis, or the French disease*) in verse. In it he

Joshua Lederberg, "Infectious History," *Science*, vol. 287, April 14, 2000, pp. 287–90. Copyright © 2000 by the American Association for the Advancement of Science. Reproduced by permission of the publisher and the author.

taught that this sexually transmitted disease was spread by "seeds" distributed by intimate contact. In later writings, he expanded this early "contagionist" theory. Besides contagion by personal contact, he described contagion by indirect contact, such as the handling or wearing of clothes, and even contagion at a distance, that is, the spread of disease by something in the air.

Fracastoro was anticipating, by nearly 350 years, one of the most important turning points in biological and medical history—the consolidation of the germ theory of disease by Louis Pasteur and Robert Koch in the late 1870s. As we enter the 21st century, infectious disease is fated to remain a crucial research challenge, one of conceptual intricacy and of global consequence.

The Incubation of a Scientific Discipline

Many people laid the groundwork for the germ theory. Even the terrified masses touched by the Black Death (bubonic plague) in Europe after 1346 had some intimation of a contagion at work. But they lived within a cognitive framework in which scapegoating, say, of witches and Jews, could more "naturally" account for their woes. Breaking that mindset would take many innovations, including microscopy in the hands of Antoni van Leeuwenhoek. In 1683, with one of his new microscopes in hand, he visualized bacteria among the animalcules harvested from his own teeth. That opened the way to visualize some of the dreaded microbial agents eliciting contagious diseases.

There were pre-germ-theory advances in therapy, too. Jesuit missionaries in malaria-ridden Peru had noted the native Indians' use of Cinchona bark. In 1627, the Jesuits imported the bark (harboring quinine, its anti-infective ingredient) to Europe for treating malaria. Quinine thereby joined the ratified pharmacopoeia—including opium, digitalis, willow (Salix) bark with its analgesic salicylates, and little else—that prior to the modern era afforded patients any benefit beyond placebo.

Beginning in 1796, Edward Jenner took another major therapeutic step—the development of vaccination—after observing that milkmaids exposed to cowpox didn't contract smallpox. He had no theoretical insight into the biological mechanism of resistance to the disease, but vaccination became a lasting prophylactic technique on purely empirical grounds. Jenner's discovery had precursors. "Hair of the dog" is an ancient trope for countering injury and may go back to legends of the emperor Mithridates, who habituated himself to lethal doses of poisons by gradually increasing the dose. We now understand more about a host's immunological response to a cross-reacting virus variant.

Sanitary reforms also helped. Arising out of revulsion over the squalor and stink of urban slums in England and the United States, a hygienic movement tried to scrub up dirt and put an end to sewer stenches. The effort had some health impact in the mid-19th century, but it failed to counter diseases spread by fleas and mosquitoes or by personal contact, and it often even failed to keep sewage and drinking water supplies separated.

It was the germ theory—which is credited to Pasteur (a chemist by training) and Koch (ultimately a German professor of public health)—that set a new course for studying and contending with infectious disease. Over the second half of the 19th century, these scientists independently synthesized historical evidence with their own research into the germ theory of disease.

Pasteur helped reveal the vastness of the microbial word and its many practical applications. He found microbes to be behind the fermentation of sugar into alcohol and the souring of milk. He developed a heat treatment (pasteurization, that is) that killed microorganisms in milk, which then no longer transmitted tuberculosis or typhoid. And he too developed new vaccines. One was a veterinary vaccine against anthrax. Another was against rabies and was first used in humans in 1885 to treat a young boy who had been bitten by a rabid dog.

One of Koch's most important advances was procedural. He articulated a set of logical and experimental criteria, later restated as "Koch's Postulates," as a standard of proof for researchers' assertions that a particular bacterium caused a particular malady. In 1882, he identified the bacterium that causes tuberculosis; a year later he did the same for cholera. Koch also left a legacy of students (and rivals) who began the systematic search for disease-causing microbes: The golden age of microbiology had begun.

Discovery of Viruses

Just as the 19th century was ending, the growing world of microbes mushroomed beyond bacteria. In 1892, the Russian microbiologist Dmitri Ivanowski, and in 1898, the Dutch botanist Martinus Beijerinck, discovered exquisitely tiny infectious agents that could pass through bacteria-stopping filters. Too small to be seen with the conventional microscope, these agents were described as "filtrable [sic] viruses."

With a foundation of germ theory in place even before the 20th century, the study of infectious disease was ready to enter a new phase. Microbe hunting became institutionalized, and armies of researchers systematically applied scientific analyses to understanding disease processes and developing therapies.

During the early acme of microbe hunting, from about 1880 to 1940, however, microbes were all but ignored by mainstream biologists. Medical microbiology had a life of its own, but it was almost totally divorced from general biological studies. Pasteur and Koch were scarcely mentioned by the founders of cell biology and genetics. Instead, bacteriology was taught as a specialty in medicine, outside the schools of basic zoology and botany. Conversely, bacteriologists scarcely heard of the conceptual revolutions in genetic and evolutionary theory.

Bacteriology's slow acceptance was partly due to the minuscule dimensions of microbes. The microscopes of the 19th and early 20th centuries could not resolve internal microbial anatomy with any detail. Only with the advent of electron microscopy in the 1930s did these structures (nucleoids, ribosomes, cell walls and membranes, flagella) become discernible. Prior to that instrumental breakthrough, most biologists had little, if anything, to do with bacteria and viruses. When they did, they viewed such organisms as mysteriously precellular. It was still an audacious leap for René Dubos to entitle his famous 1945 monograph "The Bacterial Cell."

The Path to DNA

The early segregation of bacteriology and biology per se hampered the scientific community in recognizing the prospects of conducting genetic investigation with bacteria. So it is ironic that the pivotal discovery of molecular genetics—that genetic information resides in the nucleotide sequence of DNA—arose from studies on serological types of pneumococcus, studies needed to monitor the epidemic spread of pneumonia.

This key discovery was initiated in 1928 by the British physician Frederick Griffith. He found that extracts of a pathogenic strain of pneumococcus could transform a harmless strain into a pathogenic one. The hunt was then on to identify the "transforming factor" in the extracts. In 1944, Oswald Avery, Colin MacLeod, and Maclyn McCarty reported in the Journal of Experimental Medicine that DNA was the transforming factor. Within a few years, they and others ruled out skeptics' objections that protein coextracted with the DNA might actually be the transforming factor.

Those findings rekindled interest in what was really going on in the life cycle of bacteria. In particular, they led to my own work in 1946 on sexual conjugation in Escherichia coli and to the construction of chromosome maps emulating what had been going on in the study of the genetics of fruit flies, maize, and mice for the prior 45 years. Bacteria and bacterial viruses quickly supplanted fruit flies as the test-bed for many of the subsequent developments of molecular genetics and the biotechnology that followed. Ironically, during this time, we were becoming nonchalant about microbes as etiological agents of disease.

Despite its slow emergence, bacteriology was already having a large impact. Its success is most obviously evidenced by the graying of the population. That public health has been improving—due to many factors, especially our better understanding of infectious agents—is graphically shown by the vital statistics. These began to be diligently recorded in the United States after 1900 in order to guide research and apply it to improving public health. The U.S. experience stands out in charts depicting life expectancy at birth through the century. The average life-span lengthened dramatically: from 47 years in 1900 to today's expectation of 77 years (74 years for males and 80 for females). Similar trends are seen in most other industrialized countries, but the gains have been smaller in economically and socially depressed countries.

Other statistics reveal that the decline in mortality ascribable to infectious disease accounted for almost all of the improvement in longevity up to 1950, when life expectancy had reached 68. The additional decade of life expectancy for babies born today took the rest of the century to gain. Further improvements now appear to be on an asymptotic trajectory: Each new gain is ever harder to come by, at least pending unpredictable breakthroughs in the biology of aging.

The mortality statistics fluctuated considerably during the first half of the [twentieth] century. Much of this instability was due to sporadic outbreaks of infections such as typhoid fever, tuberculosis, and scarlet fever, which no longer have much statistical impact. Most outstanding is the spike due to the great influenza pandemic of 1918–19 that killed 25 million people worldwide—comparable to the number of deaths in the Great War. Childhood immunization and other science-based medical interventions have played a significant role in the statistical trends also. So have public health measures, among them protection of food and water supplies, segregation of coughing patients, and personal hygiene. Overall economic growth has also helped by contributing to less crowded housing, improved working conditions (including sick leave), and better nutrition.

As infectious diseases have assumed lower rankings in mortality statistics, other killers—mostly diseases of old age, affluence, and civilization—have moved up the ladder. Heart disease and cancer, for example, have loomed as larger threats over the past few decades. Healthier lifestyles, including less smoking, sparer diets, more exercise, and better hygiene, have been important countermeasures. Prophylactic medications such as aspirin, as well as medical and surgical interventions, have also kept people alive longer.

The 1950s were notable for the "wonder drugs"—the new antibiotics penicillin, streptomycin, chloramphenicol, and a growing list of others that at times promised an end to bacteria-based disease. Viral pathogens have offered fewer routes to remedies, except for vaccines, such as Jonas Salk's and Albert Sabin's polio vaccines. These worked by priming immune systems for later challenges by the infectious agents. Old vaccines, including Jenner's smallpox vaccine, also were mobilized in massive public health campaigns, sometimes with fantastic results. By the end of the 1970s, smallpox became the first disease to be eradicated from the human experience.

Confidence about medicine's ability to fight infectious disease had grown so high by the mid-1960s that some optimists were portraying infectious microbes as largely conquered. They suggested that researchers shift their attention to constitutional scourges of heart disease, cancer, and psychiatric disorders. These views were reflected in the priorities for research funding and pharmaceutical development. President Nixon's 1971 launch of a national crusade against cancer, which tacitly implied that cancer could be conquered by the bicentennial celebrations of 1976, was an example. Few people now sustain the illusion that audacious medical goals like conquering cancer or infectious disease can be achieved by short-term campaigns.

Wake-Up Calls

The overoptimism and complacency of the 1960s and 1970s was shattered in 1981 with the recognition of AIDS. Since then, the spreading pandemic has overtaken one continent after another with terrible costs. Its spread has been coincident with another wake-up call—the looming problem of antibiotic-resistant microbes. This was a predictable consequence of the evolutionary process operating on microbes challenged by the new selection pressure of antibiotics, arising in part from medical prescriptions and in part from unregulated sales and use in feed for crop animals.

AIDS's causative agent, the human immunodeficiency virus (HIV), is a member of the retrovirus family. These viruses had been laboratory curiosities since 1911, when Francis Peyton Rous discovered the Rous sarcoma virus (RSV) in chickens. Early basic research on retroviruses later helped speed advances in HIV research. By the time AIDS began to spread, RSV had been studied for years as a model for cancer biology, because it could serve as a vector for transferring oncogenes into cells. That work accelerated the characterization of HIV as a retrovirus, and it also helped guide our first steps toward medications that slow HIV infection.

AIDS and HIV have spurred the most concentrated program of biomedical research in history, yet they still defy our counterattacks. And our focus on extirpating the virus may have deflected less ambitious, though more pragmatic, aims, including learning to live with the virus by nurturing in equal measure the immune system that HIV erodes. After all, natural history points to analogous infections in simians that have long since achieved a mutually tolerable state of equilibrium.

Costly experiences with AIDS and other infectious agents have led to widespread reexamination of our cohabitation with microbes. Increased monitoring and surveillance by organizations such as the U.S. Centers for Disease Control and Prevention (CDC) and the World Health Organization (WHO) have revealed a stream of outbreaks of exotic diseases. Some have been due to the new importation of microbes (such as cholera in the Southern Hemisphere); some to older parasites (such as Legionella) that have been newly recognized as pathogenic; and some to newly evolved antibiotic-resistant pneumonia strains.

Surprising Discoveries

Even maladies that had never before been associated with infectious agents recently have been revealed as having microbial bases. Prominent among these are gastric ulcers, which previously had been attributed almost entirely to stress and other psychosomatic causes. Closer study, however, has shown a Helicobacter to be the major culprit. Researchers are now directing their speculations away from stress and toward Chlamydia infection as a cause of atherosclerosis and coronary disease.

The litany of wake-up calls goes on. Four million Americans are estimated to be infected with hepatitis C, mainly by transfusion of contaminated blood products. This population now is at significant risk for developing liver cancer. Those harboring hepatitis C must be warned to avoid alcohol and other hepatotoxins, and they must not donate blood.

Smaller but lethal outbreaks of dramatic, hypervirulent viruses have been raising public fear. Among these are the Ebola virus outbreak in Africa in 1976 and again in 1995 and the hantavirus outbreak in the U.S. Southwest in 1993. In hindsight, these posed less of a public health risk than the publicity they received might have suggested. Still, studying them and uncovering ecological factors that favor or thwart their proliferation is imperative because of their potential to mutate into more diffusible forms.

Our vigilance is mandated also by the facts of life: The processes of gene reassortment in flu viruses, which are poorly confined to their canonical hosts (birds, swine, and people), goes on relentlessly and is sure to regenerate human-lethal variants. Those thoughts were central in 1997 when the avian flu H5N1 transferred into a score of Hong Kong citizens, a third of whom died. It is likely that the resolute actions of the Hong Kong health authorities, which destroyed 2 million chickens, stemmed that outbreak and averted the possibility of a worldwide spread of H5N1.

Complacency is not an option in these cases, as other vectors, including wildfowl, could become carriers. In Malaysia, a new infectious entity, the Nipah virus, killed up to 100 people last year; authorities there killed a million livestock to help contain the outbreak. New York had a smaller scale scare last summer with the unprecedented appearance of bird- and mosquito-borne West Nile encephalitis, although the mortality rate was only a few percent of those infected. We need not wonder whether we will see outbreaks like these again. The only questions are when and where?

These multiple wake-up calls to the infectious disease problem have left marks in vital statistics. From midcentury to 1982, the U.S. mortality index (annual deaths per 100,000) attributable to infection had been steady at about 30. But from 1982 to 1994, the rate doubled to 60. (Keep in mind that the index was 500 in 1900 and up to 850 in 1918–19 due to the Spanish flu epidemic.) About half of the recent rise in deaths is attributable to AIDS; much of the rest is due to respiratory disease, antibiotic resistance, and hospital-acquired infection.

New Questions Arising

As our awareness of the microbial environment has intensified, important questions have emerged. What puts us at risk? What precautions can and should we be taking? Are we more or less vulnerable to infectious agents today than in the past? What are the origins of pathogenesis? And how can we use deeper knowledge to develop better medical and public health strategies? Conversely, how much more can the natural history of disease teach us about fundamental biological and evolutionary mechanisms?

An axiomatic starting point for further progress is the simple recognition that humans, animals, plants, and microbes are cohabitants of the planet. That leads to refined questions that focus on the origin and dynamics of instabilities within this context of cohabitation. These instabilities arise from two main sources loosely definable as ecological and evolutionary.

Ecological instabilities arise from the ways we alter the physical and biological environment, the microbial and animal tenants (humans included) of these environments, and our interactions (including hygienic and therapeutic interventions) with the parasites. The future of humanity and microbes likely will unfold as episodes of a suspense thriller that could be titled *Our Wits Versus Their Genes*. . . .

Medical defense against the interchange of infectious disease did not exist in the 16th century. In the 21st century, however, new medical technologies will be key parts of an armamentarium that reinforces our own immunological defenses. This dependence on technology is beginning to be recognized at high levels of national and international policy-making. With the portent of nearly instant global transmission of pathogenic agents, it is ever more important to work with international organizations like WHO for global health improvement. After all, the spread of AIDS in America and Europe in the 1980s and 1990s was due, in part, to an earlier phase of near obliviousness to the frightful health conditions in Africa. One harbinger of the kind of high-tech wit we will need for defending against outbreaks of infectious disease is the use of cutting-edge communications technology and the Internet, which already have been harnessed to post prompt global alerts of emerging diseases.

The Role of Evolution

"Germs" have long been recognized as living entities, but the realization that they must inexorably be evolving and changing has been slow to sink in to the ideology and practice of the public health sector. This lag has early roots. In the 19th century, Koch was convinced that rigorous experiments would support the doctrine of monomorphism: that each disease was caused by a single invariant microbial species rather than by the many that often showed up in culture. He argued that most purported "variants" were probably alien bacteria that had floated into the petri dishes from the atmosphere.

Koch's rigor was an essential riposte to careless claims of interconvertibility—for example, that yeasts could be converted into bacteria. It also helped untangle confusing claims of complex morphogenesis and life cycles among common bacteria. But strict monomorphism was too rigid, and even Koch eventually relented, admitting the possibility of some intrinsic variation rather than contamination. Still, for him and his contemporaries, variation remained a phenomenological and experimental nuisance rather than the essence of microbes' competence as pathogens. The multitude of isolable species was confusing enough to the epidemic tracker; it would have been almost too much to bear to have to cope with constantly emerging variants with altered serological specificity, host affinity, or virulence.

Even today it would be near heresy to balk at the identification of the great plague of the 14th century with today's Yersinia pestis; but we cannot readily account for its pneumonic transmission without guessing at some intrinsic adaptation at the time to aerosol conveyance. Exhumations of ancient remains might still furnish DNA evidence to test such ideas.

We now know and accept that evolutionary processes elicit changes in the genotypes of germs and of their hosts. The idea that infection might play an important role in natural selection sank in after 1949 when John B.S. Haldane conjectured that the prevalence of hemoglobin disorders in Mediterranean peoples might be a defense against malaria. That idea developed into the first concrete example of a hereditary adaptation to infectious disease. . . .

The human race evidently has withstood the pathogenic challenges encountered so far, albeit with episodes of incalculable tragedy. But the rules of encounter and engagement have been changing, the same record of survival may not necessarily hold for the future. If our collective immune systems fail to keep pace with microbial innovations in the altered contexts we have created, we will have to rely still more on our wits. . . .

Taming the Enemy

Microbes indeed have a knack for making us ill, killing us, and even recycling our remains to the geosphere. But in the long run microbes have a shared interest in their hosts' survival: A dead host is a dead end for most invaders too. Domesticating the host is the better long-term strategy for pathogens. . . .

It helps for them to have aggressive means of entering the body surfaces and radiating some local toxicity to counter the hosts' defenses, but once established they also do themselves (and their hosts) well by moderating their virulence. Better understanding of this balancing act awaits further research. And that may take a shift in priorities. . . .

I suggest that a successful parasite (one that will be able to remain infectious for a long time) tends to display just those epitopes (antigen fragments that stimulate the immune system) as will provoke host responses that a) moderate but do not extinguish the primary infection, and b) inhibit other infections by competing strains of the same species or of other species. According to this speculative framework, the symptoms of influenza evolved as they have in part to ward off other viral infections.

Research into infectious diseases, including tuberculosis, schistosomiasis, and even AIDS, is providing evidence for this view.

So are studies of Helicobacter, which has been found to secrete antibacterial peptides that inhibit other enteric infections. We need also to look more closely at earlier stages of chronic infection and search for cross-protective factors by which microbes engage one another. HIV, for one, ultimately fails from the microbial perspective when opportunistic infections supervene to kill its host. That result, which is tragic from the human point of view, is a byproduct of the virus's protracted duel with the host's cellular immune system. The HIV envelope and those of related viruses also produce antimicrobials, although their significance for the natural history of disease remains unknown.

Now genomics is entering the picture. Within the past decade, the genomes of many microbes have been completely sequenced. New evidence for the web of genetic interchange is permeating the evolutionary charts. The functional analyses of innumerable genes now emerging are an unexplored mine of new therapeutic targets. It has already shown many intricate intertwinings of hosts' and parasites' physiological pathways. Together with wiser insight into the ground rules of pathogenic evolution, we are developing a versatile platform for developing new responses to infectious disease. Many new vaccines, antibiotics, and immune modulators will emerge from the growing wealth of genomic data.

The lessons of HIV and other emerging infections also have begun taking hold in government and in commercial circles, where the market opportunities these threats offer have invigorated the biotechnology industry. If we do the hard work and never take success for granted (as we did for a while during the last century), we may be able to preempt infectious disasters such as the influenza outbreak of 1918–19 and the more recent and ongoing HIV pandemic.

Perhaps one of the most important changes we can make is to supercede the 20th-century metaphor of war for describing the relationship between people and infectious agents. A more ecologically informed metaphor, which includes the germs'-eye view of infection, might be more fruitful. Consider that microbes occupy all of our body surfaces. Besides the disease-engendering colonizers of our skin, gut, and mucous membranes, we are host to a poorly cataloged ensemble of symbionts to which we pay scant attention. Yet they are equally part of the superorganism genome with which we engage the rest of the biosphere.

Life Before Preventative Medicine

By Christine A. Smith

Even with the slow-burning AIDS epidemic as a contemporary exception, it is difficult for twenty-first-century Americans to imagine life when plagues could—and frequently did—wipe out a third or more of the population of whole cities or towns in a matter of weeks. In the selection that follows, student historian Christine A. Smith brings that reality into focus with an examination of the writings of eyewitnesses to ancient plagues. Smith draws on sources that range from the ancient Greek historian Thucydides, best known for his history of the Peloponnesian War of 431 to 404 B.C., to early Christian writers including the Roman author Procopius, who as secretary to a general had a chance to witness the Justinian plague that swept the Roman Empire starting around 541 A.D. Author Christine A. Smith served as president of the *Student Historical Journal* from 1996 to 1997. She was then a student at Loyola University of New Orleans.

Throughout history, humans have been faced with disastrous catastrophes which must be endured in order to survive. One of the most incomprehensible disasters for humanity has been the plague. This term in Greek can refer to any kind of sickness; in Latin, the terms are *plaga* and *pestis*. In antiquity, two of the most devastating plagues were the Athenian plague of 430 B.C. and the Justinianic plague of 542 A.D. . . .

The Athenian plague occurred in 430–26 B.C. during the Peloponnesian War, which was fought between Athens and Sparta from 431 to 404 B.C. Because of overcrowded wartime conditions

Christine A. Smith, "Plague in the Ancient World: A Study from Thucydides to Justinian," *The Loyola University Student Historical Journal*, vol. 28, 1996–1997. Copyright © 1997 by Loyola University, New Orleans. Reproduced by permission.

in the city, the plague spread quickly, killing tens of thousands. Included among its victims was Pericles, the former leader of Athens. The only surviving source for the Athenian plague is the first-hand account of Thucydides in his *History of the Peloponnesian War.* Thucydides, who lived from c. 460 to c. 400 B.C., was an Athenian general and political critic.

In his *History of the Peloponnesian War*, Thucydides employed a carefully developed structure to investigate the meaning and causes of historical events. His writing, which evolved from Sophistic thought, reflected a constant conscious analysis of grammar and rhetoric. History, according to Thucydides, was a process of human nature; and as such, it was highly influenced by mass movements. He, therefore, stressed physical reality, and did not allow for the active intervention by the gods. This is most evident in his account of the Athenian plague, since plagues were traditionally attributed to the wrath of the gods, as evidenced in Herodotus, as well as in the Book of Exodus and the *Iliad* of Homer. Through this work, Thucydides began an historiographical tradition which would become the model for many future historians.

Writing from Experience

Having suffered from the plague himself, Thucydides presented a very systematic account of the symptoms. His aim was merely to "describe what it was like, and set down the symptoms, knowledge of which will enable it to be recognized, if it should ever break out again." The Athenian plague originated in Ethiopia, and from there spread throughout Egypt and Greece. Thucydides, however, remarked that the city of Athens suffered the greatest toll from the disease. Initial symptoms of the plague included headaches, conjunctivitis, a rash which covered the body, and fever. The victims then coughed up blood, and suffered from extremely painful stomach cramping, followed by vomiting and attacks of "ineffectual retching." Many people also experienced insomnia and restlessness. Thucydides also related that victims had such an unquenchable thirst that it drove them to throw themselves into the wells. Infected individuals generally died by the seventh or eighth day. If anyone managed to survive this long, however, s/he was then stricken by uncontrollable diarrhea, which frequently caused death. Those who survived this stage might suffer from partial paralysis, amnesia, or blindness for the rest of their lives. Fortunately, infection of the plague provided immunity; that is, few caught the disease twice, and if this occurred, the second attack was never fatal.

Thucydides' description also included the social consequences of the Athenian plague, which he conceived within the context of the war. Doctors and other caregivers frequently caught the disease, and died with those whom they had been attempting to heal. Spartans besieging the city, however, were not affected by the disease spreading through Athens. The despair caused by the plague within the city led the people to be indifferent to the laws of men and gods, and many cast themselves into self-indulgence. In particular, Thucydides mentioned that no one observed the customary funerary rites. With the fall of civic duty and religion, superstition reigned, especially in the recollection of old oracles. During the first century B.C., Lucretius would use this section of Thucydides' account of the Athenian plague to support the doctrines of Epicurus. To him, the plague illustrated not only human vulnerability, but also the futility of religion and belief in the gods.

Although many disastrous epidemics probably occurred between the Athenian and Justinianic plagues, few sources detailing these plagues have survived. Unfortunately, the accounts which do exist, are meager; and because of this, the microbial origins of the described plagues cannot be diagnosed. These sources frequently copy the literary style of Thucydides; however, they do not generally adhere to his belief regarding the noninvolvement of the gods.

Antonine and Justinianic Plagues

One such disease, known as the Antonine plague, occurred during the reign of Marcus Aurelius (161–180 A.D.). It was brought back by soldiers returning from Seleucia, and before it abated, it had affected Asia Minor, Egypt, Greece, and Italy. The plague destroyed as much as one-third of the population in some areas, and decimated the Roman army. In 180, Marcus Aurelius caught some type of infection and died in his army camp. There has been some speculation that this infection was the plague. Another plague occurred during the reigns of Decius (249–251 A.D.) and Gallus (251–253 A.D.). This pestilence broke out in Egypt in 251, and from there infected the entire empire. Its mortality rate severely depleted the ranks of the army, and caused massive labor shortages. The plague was still raging in 270, when it caused the death of the emperor Claudius Gothicus (268–270).

After the third century, there is not another well-documented plague until the Justinianic plague in the mid-sixth century. . . .

From the description provided by Procopius it is known that in the spring of 542, the bubonic plague reached Constantinople. Modern scholars are uncertain as to its exact origins, which may have been the plague reservoir of the modern central African countries of Kenya, Uganda, and Zaire. Still others believe the plague originated in the central Asian steppes and spread along the trade routes with the Far East, as did the Black Death of 1348. The sources contemporary with the plague also disagree over where the disease began. Procopius claimed the plague originated in Egypt near Pelusium; yet Evagrius stated that the plague began in Axum (modern day Ethiopia and eastern Sudan). Evagrius' thesis may have stemmed from a traditional prejudice of the time that diseases came from warm areas. At any rate, it certainly emerged in Egypt in 541; and following its sojourn in Constantinople, it spread throughout the empire along trade and military routes, always moving from the coastal cities to the interior provinces. The plague then surfaced in Italy in 543, and reached Syria and Palestine in the same year. From there, the contagion migrated to Persia, where it infected the Persian army and King Khusro himself, causing them to retreat east of the Tigris to the plague-free highlands of Luristan. Gregory of Tours related how St. Gall saved the people of Clermont-Ferrand in Gaul from the disease in 543, and there is some speculation that the plague may have spread to Ireland by 544. Moreover, like the Black Death, the Justinianic plague was recurrent, with the bacteria remaining endemic in the population for 250–300 years. Agathias, writing of a second outbreak in the capital in 558, related that since the first epidemic, the plague had never completely abated, rather it simply moved from one place to another.

This was the first known pandemic of bubonic plague to affect Europe. While it is less famous than the Black Death of the fourteenth century, the Justinianic plague was certainly quite as deadly. Bubonic plague is spread by the bite of fleas which find their home on rodents. The black rat carried the Black Death, and there is no reason to believe that it was not an active carrier in the sixth century. It probably was not the only carrier; the dogs which are described as dying in Constantinople almost certainly carried fleas as well. Once trading brought the plague to a city, rats found urban areas, which were overcrowded with a stationary population, conducive to their lifestyle. This assessment agrees with the evidence in that although the disease overwhelmed the Roman and Persian Empires, the nomadic Berbers of Africa and the Arab peoples were not greatly affected by the plague.

The plague itself actually occurs in three forms: bubonic, pneumonic (also called pulmonary), and septicaemic. The bubonic variety, which must exist before the other two strains can become active, will be described in detail; this form is not directly contagious unless the patient harbors fleas. Since Procopius did not state that those who cared for the sick necessarily contracted the disease, it is inferred that the bubonic form was most active in the Justinianic plague. Pneumonic plague occurs when the disease bacilli, called *Yersinia pestis*, invade the lungs. This variety is highly contagious from one person to another, and is spread by airborne droplets. Due to Procopius' observation that the plague was not directly contagious, and the absence of the major symptoms of pneumonic plague in the accounts, namely shallow breathing and tightness in the chest, this form was probably not very active. Septicaemia occurs when the infection enters the bloodstream, and death is swift, usually before buboes [telltale swellings] are able to form. In his account, Agathias reported some victims dying as if by an attack of apoplexy. This seems to indicate that the septicaemic form did exist during the sixth century outbreak. Bubonic plague results in death in roughly 70 percent of cases; pneumonic plague has over a 90 percent mortality rate. Septicaemic plague leaves no survivors. Although all three forms probably existed during the Justinianic plague, clearly the bubonic form predominated.

Hellish Visions

During the Justinianic plague, many victims experienced hallucinations previous to the outbreak of illness. The first symptoms of the plague followed closely behind these hallucinations though; they included fever and fatigue, neither of which seemed life-threatening. Evagrius described facial inflammation, followed by a sore throat, as an introductory symptom. Some victims also initially suffered from diarrhea. Soon however, buboes appeared in the groin area or armpits, or occasionally beside the ears. Following this symptom, the disease progressed rapidly; infected individuals usually died within two to three days. The victim generally entered a semi-conscious, lethargic state, and would not wish to eat or drink. Following this stage, the victims would be seized by madness, causing great difficulties to those who attempted to care for them. Many people died painfully when their buboes gangrened. A number of victims broke out with black blisters covering their bodies, and these individuals died swiftly. Still others died vomiting blood. Pregnant women who contracted the disease generally died through miscarriage or in childbirth, but curiously, Agathias reports that young males suffered the heaviest toll overall. There were also cases, however, in which the buboes grew to great size, and then ruptured and suppurated. If this occurred, the patient usually recovered, although s/he would often suffer afterwards from muscular tremors. Doctors, noticing this trend and not knowing how else to fight the disease, sometimes lanced the buboes of those infected to discover that carbuncles had formed. Those individuals who did survive infection usually had to live with withered thighs and tongues, classic aftereffects of the plague. One interesting fact to note here is that humans were not the only victims of this contagion. Animals, including dogs, mice, and even snakes, contracted the disease.

John of Ephesus recounted a long, somewhat rhetorical description of the plague and its effects in Palestine and within the city of Constantinople. As a Christian writer who clearly stated that the end of the world was at hand, he related many of the more grotesque elements of the epidemic. To him, the plague was a manifestation of divine wrath, and a call for repentance. His account vividly detailed scenes of havoc in which men collapsed in agony within the public quarters. The fear of being left unburied, or of falling prey to scavengers, led many individuals to wear identification tags, and when possible, to avoid leaving their homes at all. In a related description, John of Ephesus described a house which men avoided because of its foul odor. When it was finally entered, they found over twenty corpses decaying. Many men also saw apparitions and terrible visions both before and after the disease produced symptoms in them. In typical apocalyptic literature style, John of Ephesus did not see these "apparitions" and "visions" as hallucinations; to him, they offered a glimpse of the otherworldly realm. As previously mentioned, the plague spread along trade routes infecting port cities. John of Ephesus reported in his account that many ships would float aimlessly at sea, later washing up to shore with all of their crew dead from plague. He also described sailors reporting sightings of a spectral bronze ship with headless oarsmen, and monsters which appeared in the sea off the Palestine coast.

Contending with the Plague

Although the emperor Justinian contracted the disease himself, he nevertheless attempted to minimize the disaster. Following the outbreak within Constantinople, Justinian commanded Theodore and the palace guard to dispose of the corpses. By this time all gravesites were beyond capacity, and the living resorted to throwing the bodies of victims out into the streets or piling them along the seashore to rot. Theodore responded to this problem by having huge pits dug across the Golden Horn in Sycae (Galata) and then hiring men to collect the dead. Although these pits reportedly held 70,000 corpses each, they soon overflowed. Bodies were then placed inside the towers in the walls, causing a stench which pervaded the entire city.

The plague left a severe impact on urban life. Although the urban poor were the first to suffer from the devastating effects, the pestilence soon spread to the wealthier districts. As if the threat of disease was not problem enough, bread became scarce, and some of the sick may actually have died of starvation, rather than disease. Many houses became tombs, as whole families died from the plague without anyone from the outside world even knowing. Streets were deserted, and all trades were abandoned. Inflation soared. In 544, Justinian's legislation of price controls was partly successful, but the scarcity of food persisted, especially in the capital. As the taxation base shrank dramatically, financial pressure on the cities also increased. In an effort to economize, civic governments curtailed salaries for teachers and physicians and slashed the budgets for public entertainment.

Although many rural areas were spared from the plague, those areas infected were crippled. This, in turn, affected the urban areas, since a reasonable harvest was essential to ensure that the cities would not experience food shortages. . . .

To modern readers, the accounts of the plague, even those of the Christian writers, seem strikingly sober, given the magnitude of the disaster. Procopius and Agathias, like Thucydides before them, employed a detached, almost agnostic, stance, while the Christian writers accepted the plague as a just punishment from God. Unlike the Black Death, the Justinianic plague appears not to have been accompanied by mass hysteria, flagellant processions, or persecutions of the Jews. The general populace seems almost accepting of the calamity.

Early Efforts to Inoculate

By Christopher S.W. Koehler

Modern science-based medicine is often referred to as "Western medicine," in contrast to what is sometimes called "traditional medicine." However, as author Christopher S.W. Koehler makes clear in the following selection, these terms can give a misleading impression. In the struggle to combat infectious disease, he writes, the first successes came in China, and the inspiration for the inoculation procedure originated in Turkey. Nevertheless, it remains true that a distinctive chain of rapid medical progress can be traced, link by link, through notable researchers in western Europe from the eighteenth century until the modern era, in which the scientific enterprise becomes truly global. Koehler takes readers on a voyage of discovery that begins in the Orient, goes through England and Europe, and then broadens out again to include a notable Japanese researcher. Along the way, he points out the important role played by aristocratic sponsors, who were just as vulnerable to infectious disease as the lowly commoner. Koehler holds a doctorate in the history of science from the University of Florida. He writes and teaches in northern California.

The earliest known attempts to produce artificial immunity to disease involved smallpox, one of the great diseases of history. It disfigured or killed people of all social classes, from kings to commoners; and many cultures tried to stop it by inducing immunity. In [seventeenth-century] China, powdered smallpox scabs were blown into the sinuses, and a century before Edward Jenner, Chinese physicians prepared pills made from the fleas of cows in an effort to prevent the disease. In India, physicians conferred immunity by applying scabs to the scarified skin

Christopher S.W. Koehler, "Science, Society, and Immunity," *Modern Drug Discovery*, vol. 4, October 2001, pp. 59–60. Copyright © 2001 by the American Chemical Society. Reproduced by permission.

of the healthy. The technique spread west along the silk road to Istanbul, where it came to Western attention.

Wisdom from the East

The story of smallpox and inoculation is really two stories that converged. The first strand of the story is that of a British aristocrat, Lady Mary Wortley Montague (1689–1762), herself a survivor of smallpox. In 1717, Lady Montague's husband was appointed British ambassador to Turkey, and it was there that she encountered a practice called "variolation". An uninfected person would be exposed to material from smallpox pustules. In a letter to a friend, Lady Montague described seeing old women make a small number of scratches or punctures to introduce smallpox from someone who had suffered a light case. She called it "ingrafting". Given her own experiences, she insisted that the embassy surgeon variolate her son.

On her return to London in 1721, Lady Montague had the surgeon, Charles Maitland, inoculate her daughter before the physicians of the royal court. This caught the attention of the Princess of Wales, who later had Maitland treat her own children. Because it was not just any mothers who had their children treated to prevent smallpox, but two aristocratic women, including the wife of the heir to the throne, this significantly publicized the new practice and its possibilities.

Maitland went on to perform experiments on orphans and on prisoners (who received full pardons for their risk) with the blessings of the English crown. Prisoners and orphans alike survived and proved immune to smallpox.

Despite the risks of infection from variolation, the number of cases of smallpox plummeted. The mortality rate in uninoculated children was 1:14, but 1:91 in children who had been inoculated. Thus variolation spread throughout Europe, spurred by the inoculation of many of Europe's ruling dynasties. In the United States, although happening independently and without a clear-cut aristocracy, the role requirement for a famous and respected public figure was similar.

The Role of Edward Jenner

The second strand of the smallpox story likewise involved simple medical technology within a complicated social milieu. Later in the 18th century, the work of Edward Jenner (1749–1823) aroused controversy similar to that faced in the Americas. Had he not surmounted this debate, his breakthrough might have been relegated to footnotes and postponed by decades.

It was a staple of rural lore that milkmaids who had contracted cowpox from the cows they tended did not contract smallpox. Cowpox, to cows, is a relatively minor infection of the udder, leading to a slight decrease in milk production. It also led to a case of pox in humans that might scar, but not nearly to the extent of smallpox, and it was not fatal. That was a small price to pay for immunity to the "speckled monster".

Over the years, observant people, from farmers to physicians, had noted that contraction of cowpox conferred smallpox immunity. Jenner, who had success with variolation, became obsessed with this connection between a minor disease in cows and the possibility of freedom from one of the great scourges of human health. By 1788, he was convinced that the folk belief was also scientific truth, and an outbreak of cowpox in 1796 allowed him to experiment. He extracted fluid from the milkmaid Sarah Nelmes's hand and used it to inoculate 8-year-old James Phipps. Phipps later proved resistant to not only cowpox but also smallpox.

Yet Jenner's paper detailing the experiment and its success was rejected for publication by the Royal Society. In fact, he was warned against publishing it anywhere out of concern for his reputation. Perhaps Lady Montague and the Princess of Wales had succeeded too well in publicizing variolation, for medical authorities were at first unwilling to credit Jenner's technique, which he called *vaccination* (from the Latin for cow). After all, how could the reputation of a milkmaid compare with that of the Princess of Wales?

Nonetheless, Jenner's findings were subsequently verified by other physicians, including William Woodville of London's Smallpox and Inoculation Hospital. Just as with variolation, Jenner's technique spread because it was rapidly espoused by Europe's ruling families. By 1800, it had been adopted in most European countries.

Pasteur Makes a Breakthrough

The late 19th century saw further development of the modern tools needed to induce "active" immunity. Active immunity is that developed by the body's own immune system against a pathogenic organism. Obviously, the normal pathogen itself is inappropriate for a vaccine, because it would cause the very disease it was intended to treat; instead, a debilitated or dead pathogen, or only part of the pathogen, is used. Variolation and cowpox inoculation unwittingly took advantage of this technique, by using a natural debilitated strain in the first case and a related but "safe" virus in the second.

Louis Pasteur developed the first modern vaccine in 1885 in his attempt to prevent the onset of rabies. Rabies, a disease of the nervous system, is characterized by encephalitis and, in the absence of treatment, death. But how could Pasteur make a vaccine from a pathogen that was a sure death sentence in its native state?

The answer came to Pasteur through his work with chicken cholera. Healthy birds inoculated with cholera quickly contracted it. However, by accident he noted that although a given culture would lose its efficacy, a bird dosed with that culture would resist infections from fresh cultures. Pasteur thus found a way of producing resistance without the initial disease by using an attenuated, or weakened, form of a pathogen. But devising an experimental vaccine through a weakened form of a deadly pathogen is one thing, testing it quite another. On July 6, 1885, a boy, Joseph Meister, was bitten by a rabid dog. Pasteur tested his novel vaccine on a human for the first time, and Meister did not develop rabies.

Scientists, inspired by Pasteur's success, realized that if other pathogens could be weakened through this strategy, an entirely new frontier of preventions would be available to medicine. This breakthrough and those that rapidly followed drove late-19th-century medical science in a grand quest for knowledge about microbiology.

In 1890, five years after Pasteur's breakthrough in vaccines, Emil von Behring and Shibasaburo Kitasato (who would later demonstrate that the bacillus *Pasteurella pestis* caused bubonic plague), isolated the first of the antitoxins. What these researchers called "antitoxins" were actually antibodies to specific disease substances—in this case the toxins produced by the pathogens.

The efficacy of antitoxins in disease therapeutics was discovered through work on diphtheria and tetanus. Startlingly, von Behring and Kitasato noted that blood from animals already immune to specific diseases could be used to heal other infected animals. Between 1893 and 1895, antitoxin experiments were successfully conducted in humans; and in 1901, von Behring won the first Nobel Prize in Physiology or Medicine (such prizes would go far in creating a scientific social elite in the future) for his development of the first "reliable weapon" against diphtheria.

But this new technology was not embraced without controversy either. According to James H. Cassedy, organized protests flared up in the United States against the adoption of the diphtheria antitoxin in the 1890s, and violent reactions also occurred among immigrants of the same period who were forced to take smallpox vaccinations.

Today, as in Pasteur's era, the production of artificial immunity still involves the isolation of the infectious agent (or a part thereof) to spark an immune response without causing the disease. And as in Cotton Mather's time, distrust of inoculations, including vaccines given to military personnel against biological warfare agents (claimed by some to have caused various veterans' ailments), is currently rampant among certain public sectors. Similarly, many parents recently have been upset by reports of possible correlations between multiple vaccinations and autism.

So perhaps a role still exists, at least in some cases, for trusted elites like Lady Montague, Mather, and Pasteur to help allay the public's natural fears of a technology so intimately associated with deadly and terrible diseases. And as for the role of social elites, especially royalty, in the promulgation of medical science in the modern world—well, the King of Sweden still hands out the Nobels every year.

Inoculating Against Smallpox

By Edward Jenner

Smallpox was once among the most devastating of infectious diseases. It killed most of its victims and left the survivors permanently disfigured. A landmark development in the fight against smallpox came in the career of British surgeon Edward Jenner. Born in 1749 in Glouscestershire, England, Jenner became an apprentice to a famed London surgeon and anatomist and gained a lifelong interest in a scientific approach to medical challenges. A keen observer, he noticed that milkmaids frequently caught a mild disease known as cowpox and thereafter gained immunity to smallpox. In 1796, he experimented by inoculating a boy with cowpox and then exposing him to smallpox. Such an experiment would never be permitted today, but fortunately it worked and the boy proved immune. In the following extracts from Jenner's papers, it is interesting to note how much the eighteenth-century physician was able to accurately infer about the disease, considering that the virus was completely unobserved at that time. In fact, nearly a century would pass before a theoretical understanding of germs and contagion became firmly established. Theory aside, Jenner's methods, while crude by contemporary standards, clearly bear a strong resemblance to modern vaccination.

The deviation of man from the state in which he was originally placed by nature seems to have proved to him a prolific source of diseases. From the love of splendour, from the indulgences of luxury, and from his fondness for amusement he has familiarised himself with a great number of animals, which may not originally have been intended for his associates.

The wolf, disarmed of ferocity, is now pillowed in the lady's

Edward Jenner, *An Inquiry into the Causes and Effects of Variolae Vaccinae*, 1798.

lap. The cat, the little tiger of our island, whose natural home is the forest, is equally domesticated and caressed. The cow, the hog, the sheep, and the horse, are all, for a variety of purposes, brought under his care and dominion. . . .

The Risk of Milking

In this dairy country a great number of cows are kept, and the office of milking is performed indiscriminately by men and maid servants. One of the former having been appointed to apply dressings to the heels of a horse affected with the grease, and not paying due attention to cleanliness, incautiously bears his part in milking the cows, with some particles of the infectious matter adhering to his fingers. When this is the case, it commonly happens that a disease is communicated to the cows, and from the cows to the dairymaids, which spreads through the farm until the most of the cattle and domestics feel its unpleasant consequences. This disease has obtained the name of the cow-pox. It appears on the nipples of the cows in the form of irregular pustules. At their first appearance they are commonly of a palish blue, or rather of a colour somewhat approaching to livid, and are surrounded by an erysipelatous inflammation. These pustules, unless a timely remedy be applied, frequently degenerate into phagedenic ulcers, which prove extremely troublesome. The animals become indisposed, and the secretion of milk is much lessened. Inflamed spots now begin to appear on different parts of the hands of the domestics employed in milking, and sometimes on the wrists, which quickly run on to suppuration, first assuming the appearance of the small vesications produced by a burn. Most commonly they appear about the joints of the fingers and at their extremities; but whatever parts are affected, if the situation will admit, these superficial suppurations put on a circular form, with their edges more elevated than their centre, and of a colour distantly approaching to blue. . . .

Morbid matter of various kinds, when absorbed into the system, may produce effects in some degree similar; but what renders the cow-pox virus so extremely singular is that the person who has been thus affected is forever after secure from the infection of the smallpox; neither exposure to the variolous effluvia, nor the insertion of the matter into the skin, producing this distemper.

In support of so extraordinary a fact, I shall lay before my reader a great number of instances. . . .

Case II.—Sarah Portlock, of this place, was infected with the cow-pox when a servant at a farmer's in the neighbourhood, twenty-seven years ago.

In the year 1792, conceiving herself, from this circumstance, secure from the infection of the smallpox, she nursed one of her own children who had accidentally caught the disease, but no indisposition ensued. During the time she remained in the infected room, variolous matter was inserted into both her arms, but without any further effect than in the preceding case.

Case III.—John Phillips, a tradesman of this town, had the cow-pox at so early a period as nine years of age. At the age of sixty-two I inoculated him, and was very careful in selecting matter in its most active state. It was taken from the arm of a boy just before the commencement of the eruptive fever, and instantly inserted. It very speedily produced a sting-like feel in the part. An efflorescence appeared, which on the fourth day was rather extensive, and some degree of pain and stiffness were felt about the shoulder: but on the fifth day these symptoms began to disappear, and in a day or two after went entirely off, without producing any effect on the system.

Case IV.—Mary Barge, of Woodford, in this parish, was inoculated with variolous matter in the year 1791. An efflorescence of a palish red colour soon appeared about the parts where the matter was inserted, and spread itself rather extensively, but died away in a few days without producing any variolous symptoms. She has since been repeatedly employed as a nurse to smallpox patients, without experiencing any ill consequences. This woman had the cow-pox when she lived in the service of a farmer in this parish thirty-one years before. . . .

Vaccination's Power Proven

Although I presume it may be unnecessary to produce further testimony in support of my assertion "that the cow-pox protects the human constitution from the infection of the smallpox," yet it affords me considerable satisfaction to say that Lord Somerville, the President of the Board of Agriculture, to whom this paper was shewn by Sir Joseph Banks, has found upon inquiry that the statements were confirmed by the concurring testimony of Mr. Dolland, a surgeon, who resides in a dairy country remote from this, in which these observations were made. . . .

It is singular to observe that the cow-pox virus, although it renders the constitution unsusceptible of the variolous, should nevertheless, leave it unchanged with respect to its own action. I have already produced an instance to point out this, and shall now corroborate it with another.

Elizabeth Wynne, who had the cow-pox in the year 1759, was inoculated with variolous matter, without effect, in the year 1797, and again caught the cow-pox in the year 1798. When I saw her, which was on the eighth day after she received the infection, I found her affected with general lassitude, shiverings, alternating with heat, coldness of the extremities, and a quick and irregular pulse. . . .

It is curious also to observe that the virus, which with respect to its effects is undetermined and uncertain previously to its passing from the horse through the medium of the cow, should then not only become more active, but should invariably and completely possess those specific properties which induce in the human constitution symptoms similar to those of the variolous fever, and effect in it that peculiar change which for ever renders it unsusceptible of the variolous contagion.

May it not then be reasonably conjectured that the source of the smallpox is morbid matter of a peculiar kind, generated by a disease in the horse, and that accidental circumstances may have again and again arisen, still working new changes upon it until it has acquired the contagious and malignant form under which we now commonly see it making its devastations amongst us? And, from a consideration of the change which the infectious matter undergoes from producing a disease on the cow, may we not conceive that many contagious diseases, now prevalent among us, may owe their present appearance not to a simple, but to a compound, origin? For example, is it difficult to imagine that the measles, the scarlet fever, and the ulcerous sore throat with a spotted skin have all sprung from the same source, assuming some variety in their forms according to the nature of their new combinations? The same question will apply respecting the origin of many other contagious diseases which bear a strong analogy to each other.

A Mild Variant

There are certainly more forms than one, without considering the common variation between the confluent and distinct, in which the smallpox appears in what is called the natural way. About seven years ago a species of smallpox spread through many of the towns and villages of this part of Gloucestershire: it was of so mild a nature that a fatal instance was scarcely ever heard of, and consequently so little dreaded by the lower orders of the community that they scrupled not to hold the same intercourse with each other as if no infectious disease had been present among them. I never saw nor heard of an instance of its being confluent. The most accurate manner, perhaps, in which I can convey an idea of it is by saying that had fifty individuals been taken promiscuously and infected by exposure to this contagion, they would have had as mild and light a disease as if they had been inoculated with variolous matter in the usual way. The harmless manner in which it shewed itself could not arise from any peculiarity either in the season or the weather, for I watched its progress upwards of a year without perceiving any variation in its general appearance. I consider it then as a variety of the smallpox.

Means of Inoculation

In some of the preceding cases I have noticed the attention that was paid to the state of the variolous matter previous to the experiment of inserting it into the arms of those who had gone through the cow-pox. This I conceived to be of great importance in conducting these experiments, and, were it always properly attended to by those who inoculate for the smallpox, it might prevent much subsequent mischief and confusion. With the view of enforcing so necessary a precaution I shall take the liberty of digressing so far as to point out some unpleasant facts relative to mismanagement in this particular, which have fallen under my own observation.

A medical gentleman (now no more), who for many years inoculated in this neighbourhood, frequently preserved the variolous matter intended for his use on a piece of lint or cotton, which, in its fluid state, was put into a vial, corked, and conveyed into a warm pocket; a situation certainly favourable for speedily producing putrefaction in it. In this state (not unfrequently after it had been taken several days from the pustules) it was inserted into the arms of his patients, and brought on inflammation of the incised parts, swellings of the axillary glands, fever, and sometimes eruptions. But what was this disease? Certainly not the smallpox; for the matter having from putrefaction lost or suffered a derangement in its specific properties, was no longer capable of producing that malady, those who had been inoculated in this manner being as much subject to the contagion of the smallpox as if they had never been under the influence of this artificial disease; and many, unfortunately, fell victims to it, who thought themselves in perfect security. . . .

The "Modern" Approach

A very respectable friend of mine, Dr. Hardwicke, of Sodbury in this country, inoculated great numbers of patients previous to the introduction of the more modern method by Sutton, and with such success that a fatal instance occurred as rarely as since that method has been adopted. It was the doctor's practice to make as slight an incision as possible upon the skin, and there to lodge a thread saturated with the variolous matter. When his patients became indisposed, agreeably to the custom then prevailing, they were directed to go to bed and were kept moderately warm. Is it not probable then that the success of the modern practice may depend more upon the method of invariably depositing the virus in or upon the skin, than on the subsequent treatment of the disease? . . .

As the cases of inoculation multiply, I am more and more convinced of the extreme mildness of the symptoms arising merely from the primary action of the virus on the constitution, and that those symptoms which, as in the accidental cow-pox, affect the patient with severity, are entirely secondary, excited by the irritating processes of inflammation and ulceration; and it appears to me that this singular virus possesses an irritating quality of a peculiar kind, but as a single cow-pox pustule is all that is necessary to render the variolous virus ineffectual, and as we possess the means of allaying the irritation, should any arise, it becomes of little or no consequence. . . .

In the present early stage of the inquiry (for early it certainly must be deemed), before we know for an absolute certainty how soon the virus of the cow-pox may suffer a change in its specific properties, after it has quitted the limpid state it possesses when forming a pustule, it would be prudent for those who have been inoculated with it to submit to variolous inoculation. No injury or inconvenience can accrue from this. . . .

The Value of Doubt

Some there are who suppose the security from the smallpox obtained through the cow-pox will be of a temporary nature only. This supposition is refuted not only by analogy with respect to the habits of diseases of a similar nature, but by incontrovertible facts, which appear in great numbers against it. To those already adduced in the former part of my first treatise many more might be adduced were it deemed necessary; but among the cases I refer to, one will be found of a person who had the cow-pox fifty-three years before the effect of the smallpox was tried upon him. As he completely resisted it, the intervening period I conceive must necessarily satisfy any reasonable mind. . . .

The scepticism that appeared, even among the most enlightened of medical men when my sentiments on the important subject of the cow-pox were first promulgated, was highly laudable. To have admitted the truth of a doctrine, at once so novel and so unlike any thing that ever had appeared in the annals of medicine, without the test of the most rigid scrutiny, would have bordered upon temerity; but now, when that scrutiny has taken place, not only among ourselves, but in the first professional circles in Europe, and when it has been uniformly found in such abundant instances that the human frame, when once it has felt the influence of the genuine cow-pox in the way that has been described, is never afterwards at any period of its existence assailable by the smallpox, may I not with perfect confidence congratulate my country and society at large on their beholding, in the mild form of the cow-pox, an antidote that is capable of extirpating from the earth a disease which is every hour devouring its victims; a disease that has ever been considered as the severest scourge of the human race!

Louis Pasteur and the Causes of Infection

By René Dubos

Until the middle of the nineteenth century people had no clear idea what caused infectious diseases or how they spread. Even though bacteria had been discovered centuries before (in 1683 by the Dutch naturalist Antoni van Leeuwenhoek using a microscope he had built himself), no one had forged a conclusive chain of causal links from the tiny, wriggling creatures in a drop of water to the devastating epidemics that took so many lives in Europe. The common belief was that microorganisms were harmless little specks that appeared spontaneously out of nothing. It took a French scientist named Louis Pasteur (1822–1895) many years of painstaking work to prove them wrong. As his countryman and fellow microbiologist René Dubos shows in the following selection, Pasteur had an exceptionally rigorous mind. His experiments with swan-necked flasks showed beyond all doubt that germs do not arise spontaneously but instead grow and spread from host to host. That proof led to the nearly universal acceptance of germ theory. Pasteur contributed much more than the foundation of modern infectious disease prevention, however. He also created an effective vaccine against anthrax, and went on to discover and defeat the virus that causes rabies. René Dubos (1901–1982), was born in France but trained as a microbiologist in the United States. After receiving his PhD from Rutgers University in 1927, he made his career at the Rockefeller Institute for Medical Research.

René Dubos, *Pasteur and Modern Science*. Madison, WI: Science Tech Publishers, 1960. Copyright © 1960 by Science Tech Publishers. Reproduced by permission.

Among the many other types of experiments that Pasteur designed to rule out spontaneous generation, one is worth some emphasis by virtue of its very simplicity and decisiveness and because it finally silenced his opponents and settled the issue—at least for the time being. A fermentable fluid was put into a flask, the long neck of which was then heated and drawn into the form of an S tube (hence the name "swan-neck flask"). When the liquid was boiled, the vapor forced the air out through the orifice of the neck. As the fluid became cool again, the air slowly returned to the flask, but was washed in the moisture that condensed in the curves of the neck after heating was interrupted. Under these conditions, any dust or particle carried by the air was trapped in the neck, and the fluid in the flask remained clear, sterile. However, when the neck of the flask was broken, and the unwashed air allowed to come into contact with the fluid, then microscopic life immediately began to develop.

Despite the spectacular success of these experiments, there were still unforeseen difficulties to overcome. They arose from the fact, then unknown but now well understood, that certain species of bacteria form *heat-resistant spores.* In some of the early experiments these spores persisted in the fluid that was presumed to have been sterilized by heating, and when they germinated, they gave rise to bacterial growth even though access to outside air had been prevented. These difficulties arising from the presence of heat-resistant spores were eventually overcome, and Pasteur was able to prepare his swan-neck flasks in such a manner that the broth remained sterile in them all. Some of these flasks prepared over 100 years ago can still be seen today at the Pasteur Institute in Paris, the fluid as limpid as the day it was sterilized. . . .

Identifying Killer Germs

We are now in a better situation to evaluate the events of 1877 when Pasteur began his work on anthrax. Contrary to general belief, the year does not deserve a place in history for the first demonstration that microbes can cause disease. This had been shown for the potato blight in 1850 and for the *pébrine* of silkworms in 1868. What does make the years 1876–77 a landmark in the history of medicine is the fact that for the first time a microbe was shown to be capable of causing an important disease affecting higher animals and humans. The disease was anthrax, then very common on farms all over Europe. Strangely enough, it turned out that just as Pasteur was beginning to work on anthrax, its microbial origin was also being studied by a young German physician who was soon to become immensely famous, Robert Koch. Let us salute in passing this great German scientist who shares with Pasteur the honor of having founded medical microbiology. To symbolize the magnitude of Koch's discoveries, we need only mention that shortly after the completion of his studies on anthrax he electrified the world by discovering the microbes responsible for *cholera* and for *tuberculosis*—two of the most destructive enemies of humankind.

In reality, several veterinarians and physicians had suspected long before Pasteur and Koch that bacteria were responsible for anthrax. They had seen bacteria in the blood and organs of sick animals, and, furthermore, they had transferred the disease by injecting into healthy animals a few drops of infected blood. But, for a number of technical reasons . . . these observations were far from convincing, and it took the experimental genius of Koch and Pasteur to demonstrate once and for all what the observation of their predecessors had merely suggested.

Koch's great experiment was to sow fragments of tissues from sick animals into a drop of blood serum of normal rabbits. He saw that bacteria similar to those originally present in the organs multiplied extensively in the serum and with the culture thus obtained he inoculated another drop of serum. After repeating the process eight times he found to his great satisfaction that the last culture injected into a healthy mouse was as capable of producing anthrax as was blood taken directly from an animal just dead of the disease. Koch also made the important discovery that the bacterium associated with anthrax produced heat-resistant spores and that these spores were part of the life cycle of the organism. These experiments appeared convincing, but despite their thoroughness and elegance, they still left a loophole for those who believed that there was in the blood something other than the bacteria capable of inducing anthrax. Although Koch had transferred his cultures eight times in succession, this was not sufficient to rule out the possibility that some hypothetical component of the blood had been carried over from the original drop and was responsible, instead of the bacteria, for transmitting the infection to the inoculated animal. It was this debatable point that Pasteur's experiments were designed to settle.

Proof by Experiment

Pasteur knew from his earlier studies on spontaneous generation that the blood of a healthy animal, taken aseptically during life and added to any kind of nutrient fluid, would not putrefy or give rise to any living microorganism. He expected, therefore, that the blood of an anthrax animal handled with aseptic precautions should give cultures containing only the anthrax bacillus. Experiment soon showed this to be so, and showed also that rapid and abundant growth of the bacillus could be obtained by cultivating it in neutral urine; these cultures could be readily maintained through many generations by transfers in the same medium. Pasteur added one drop of blood to fifty cubic centimeters (nearly two ounces) of sterile urine and then, after incubation and multiplication of the bacilli, transferred one drop of this culture into a new flask containing fifty cubic centimeters of urine. After repeating this process one hundred times in succession, he arrived at a culture in which the dilution of the original blood was so great—of the order of 1 part in 100^{100}—that not even one molecule of it was left in the final material. Only the bacteria could escape the dilution, because they continued to multiply with each transfer. And yet, a drop of the hundredth culture killed a guinea pig or a rabbit as rapidly as a drop of the original infected blood, thus demonstrating that the "virulence principle" rested in the bacterium, or was produced by it.

Pasteur devised many other ingenious experiments to secure additional evidence that the anthrax bacillus was the cause of disease. He filtered cultures through membranes fine enough to hold back the bacteria and showed that the clear filtrate injected into a rabbit did not make it sick. He allowed flasks of culture to rest undisturbed in places at low and constant temperature, until the bacteria had settled to the bottom; again the clear supernatant fluid was found incapable of establishing the disease in experimental animals, but a drop of the deposit, containing the bacterial bodies, killed them with anthrax. These results constituted the strongest possible evidence that the anthrax bacillus itself was responsible for the infection. The germ theory of disease was now firmly established.

Discovery of Viruses

The three decades that followed the original studies on anthrax saw the discovery of many other bacterial agents of disease by

Pasteur, Koch, their associates, and their followers. The spectacular achievements of this period, which has been called the "golden age of microbiology," had great import for the welfare of the human race. Startling as they were, these discoveries constitute merely the technical exploitation of the fundamental methods established by Koch and Pasteur, methods which rapidly became standard practice in the bacteriological laboratories of the world. It is of extraordinary interest, however, that the next great theoretical advance in the germ theory of disease was to be made by Pasteur himself when he discovered that disease can be caused by agents so small as to be invisible under the microscope and able to pass through filters, and so peculiar as to fail to grow in the ordinary culture media of the bacteriologists. These agents of disease are now known as *filterable viruses* or simply, *viruses.*

The new discovery came from the study of *rabies.* Rabies was then known as a disease contracted by humans or a few species of animals from the bite of rabid dogs or wolves. Bacteriological studies—and this must have been very disheartening—failed to reveal to Pasteur a bacterial cause for rabies. Attempts were made to cultivate a microorganism in spinal fluid, and even in fresh nerve substance obtained from normal animals, but all in vain. His failure is not to be wondered at, for it is now known that rabies is caused by a filterable virus, which cannot be seen by ordinary microscopy, and which cannot be cultivated in lifeless bacteriological media. With an uncommon and truly admirable intellectual agility, Pasteur then gave up the *in vitro* cultural techniques [that is, growing cultures in a lab, not in a living creature], to the development of which he had contributed so much. Heretofore, he had emphasized the necessity of discovering for each type of microorganism the nutrient medium most selectively adapted to its cultivation. He now conceived the idea of using the susceptible tissues of experimental animals, instead of sterile nutrient solutions, to cultivate the virus of the disease; the concept of selectivity of cultural conditions was thus simply carried over from lifeless media to receptive living cells.

Live Animal Experiments

The general symptoms of rabies suggested that the nervous system was attacked during the disease. Nerve tissue seemed to be an ideal medium for the virus of rabies, and to fulfill the condition of

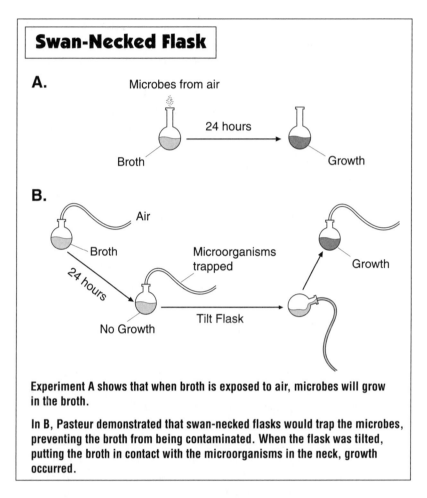

Swan-Necked Flask

A.

Microbes from air

Broth — 24 hours → Growth

B.

Air

Broth

24 hours

No Growth

Microorganisms trapped

Tilt Flask

Growth

Experiment A shows that when broth is exposed to air, microbes will grow in the broth.

In B, Pasteur demonstrated that swan-necked flasks would trap the microbes, preventing the broth from being contaminated. When the flask was tilted, putting the broth in contact with the microorganisms in the neck, growth occurred.

selectivity, which was the foundation of the cultural method. As the main problem was to gain access to this tissue under aseptic conditions, the surest way was to attempt to inoculate dogs under the dura mater (the fibrous membrane surrounding the brain), by boring a hole through the skull (a technique called *trephining*). "The thought that the skull of a dog was to be perforated was disagreeable to him," wrote his assistant, Emile Roux. "He desired intensely that the experiment be made, but he dreaded to see it undertaken. I performed it one day in his absence; the next day, when I told him that the intracranial inoculation presented no difficulty, he was moved with pity for the dog: 'Poor beast. Its brain is certainly badly wounded. It must be paralyzed.' Without replying, I went below to look for the animal and had him brought into the laboratory. Pasteur did not love dogs; but when he saw this one full of life, curiously ferreting about everywhere he showed the greatest satisfaction and straightaway lavished upon him the kindest words."

The dog inoculated by trephination developed rabies fourteen days later, and all the dogs treated in the same fashion behaved in a similar manner. Now that the cultivation of the virus in the animal body was possible the work could progress at a rapid pace, as in the case of anthrax, and other bacterial diseases.

Thus was discovered a technique for the cultivation of an unknown infectious agent in the receptive tissues of a susceptible animal. This technique has permitted the study of those agents of disease that are not cultivable in lifeless media, and has brought them within the fold of the germ theory of disease. The demonstration that invisible viruses could be handled almost as readily as cultivable bacteria was a great technical feat. . . .

Inventing Modern Vaccination

One of the first bacterial diseases that Pasteur undertook to study after anthrax was *fowl cholera*. He had no difficulty isolating its causative agent, and there would be no reason to single out this disease for particular discussion, if it were not for the fact that its study led to the discovery of vaccination—an achievement as remarkable in its practical consequences as in its theoretical implications.

Pasteur had begun experiments on chickens infected with fowl cholera in the spring of 1879, but an unexpected difficulty interrupted the work after the summer vacation. The cultures of the chicken cholera bacillus that had been kept in the laboratory during the summer failed to produce disease when inoculated into chickens in the early fall. A new, virulent culture was obtained from a natural outbreak, and it was inoculated into new animals, as well as into the chickens which had resisted the old cultures. The new animals, just brought from the market, succumbed to the infection in the customary length of time, thus showing that the fresh culture was very active. But to everyone's astonishment, and the astonishment of Pasteur himself, almost all the chickens that had previously been infected with the nonvirulent culture survived the infection. According to the accounts left by one of his collaborators, Pasteur remained silent for a minute, then exclaimed as if he had seen a vision, "Don't you see that these animals have been *vaccinated*!"

The Origins of Vaccination

To the modern reader, there is nothing remarkable in the use of the word "vaccination," which has become part of everyday language. But this was over a century ago. Then the word *vaccination* was used only to refer to the special case of injection of *cowpox* material for inducing protection against *smallpox*. We must stop for a minute, therefore, to retrace the steps that led Pasteur to see a relation between the protective effect of cowpox against smallpox, and the survival of the chickens in his accidental experiment.

In eighteenth-century England some people believed that anyone who had had cowpox, a skin infection contracted by contact with an infected cow and somewhat similar to smallpox, was thereby rendered incapable of contracting the latter disease. It is reported that Edward Jenner (1749–1823) was led to study the matter by the statement of a Gloucestershire dairymaid who had come to him as a patient. When he suggested that she was suffering from smallpox, she immediately replied: "I cannot take the smallpox because I have had the cowpox." Jenner attempted to give scientific foundation to the popular belief by studying systematically the protective effect of cowpox injection in human beings, and he soon convinced himself, and the world, that this treatment did in fact give protection against exposure to virulent smallpox.

Thus was introduced into the Western world the practice of immunization against smallpox by the injection of material originating from skin lesions in the cow; the word "vaccination," under which the method came to be known, is derived from the Latin word *vacca*, a cow.

Jenner soon had many followers in England, but it was perhaps in America that the method received the most vigorous support. Benjamin Waterhouse in Boston took up the cudgels for vaccination, and, having received vaccine virus from England, he vaccinated his own family in July 1800 and dared expose his children to infection in the smallpox hospital in order to demonstrate that they were immune. In 1801 he sent some of Jenner's vaccine to President Thomas Jefferson, who had his own family vaccinated, as well as some of their neighbors and a few Indians.

Generalizing from Jenner

Pasteur was familiar with Jenner's work, of course, and with the practice of vaccination against smallpox. And soon after the beginning of his work on infectious diseases he became convinced that something similar to vaccination was the best approach to their control. It was this conviction that made him perceive immediately the meaning of the accidental experiment with chickens. By transferring to humans pox material from the cow, Jenner had so modified the human constitution as to render it no longer receptive to smallpox. Pasteur recognized that this effect was the manifestation of a general law, and that his odd cultures of fowl cholera bacteria, which had become "attenuated" during the summer, had brought about some transformation in the body of the inoculated chickens making them less receptive to the virulent form of the microorganism. Jenner's discovery was only a special case for developing attenuated cultures that could be used in immunization procedures. More generally, vaccination could be regarded as a technique for specifically increasing the resistance of the body to an inimical agent. To make more emphatic the analogy between his and Jenner's discoveries, Pasteur chose to describe the phenomenon that he had observed in chickens under the name "vaccination." Thus, as has happened to many words, the meaning of "vaccination" progressively evolved from the description of a concrete procedure (Jenner's procedure for smallpox) into the expression of an abstract scientific concept.

The discoveries of Jenner and Pasteur have implications which transcend immunological science. They reveal in what subtle manner and how profoundly the behavior of living things can be affected by influences that reach them from the external world. Humans or fowl, once having received a minute amount of material from cowpox or from the culture of a bacterium, are indelibly marked by this apparently trivial experience; they thereby become somewhat different living beings. Pasteur realized immediately that his observations of fowl cholera brought the phenomenon of immunity within the range of study by microbiological techniques. As he could cultivate the causative bacillus of fowl cholera *in vitro*, and as attenuation of the bacillus had occurred spontaneously in some of his cultures, Pasteur became convinced that it should be possible to produce vaccines at will in the laboratory. Instead of depending upon the chance finding of naturally occurring immunizing agents, as cowpox was for smallpox, vaccination could then become a general technique, applicable to all infectious diseases. Within the incredibly short period of four years, Pasteur succeeded in demonstrating the practical possibilities of this visionary concept for fowl cholera, anthrax, swine erysipelas, and rabies. I shall select a few of the aspects of the work on vaccination against anthrax and rabies to illustrate not the specialized techniques employed, but rather the amazing intellectual courage that Pasteur displayed in the prosecution of his work.

As soon as he had obtained an attenuated culture of the anthrax bacillus and worked out the technique of vaccination against the disease in his Paris laboratory, Pasteur expressed the desire to put the technique to the test in farm animals under field conditions. Anthrax was then a disease of great economic importance, and the possibility of finding a protection against it constituted a lively subject of discussion in veterinary circles. The germ theory of disease was still in its infancy, and few were the physicians and veterinarians who had any concept of the scientific meaning of immunization.

In the spring of 1881 a veterinarian named Rossignol succeeded in enlisting the support of many farmers of the Brie district, near Paris, to finance a large-scale test of anthrax immunization. Pasteur was well aware of the fact that many veterinarians and physicians were highly skeptical of his claims, and he recognized that many saw in the proposed test an occasion to cover the germ theory with ridicule. Nothing, therefore, could set in bolder relief his confidence and gameness of spirit than his acceptance of the incredibly drastic terms of the protocol submitted to him. Rossignol publicized the test widely, and the experiment thus became an event of international importance. It took place in the presence of a great assembly of people of all kinds, including the Paris correspondent of the *Times* of London, Mr. De Blowitz, who for a few days focused the eyes of his readers throughout the world on the farm at Pouilly le Fort, where the test was being conducted.

A Controlled Experiment

In the experiment twenty-four sheep, one goat, and six cows were inoculated on May 5 [1881] with five drops of a living attenuated culture of anthrax bacillus. On May 17 all these animals were revaccinated with a second dose of a less-attenuated culture. On May 31 all the immunized animals were then infected with a highly virulent anthrax culture, and the same culture was injected as well into twenty-nine normal animals: twenty-four sheep, one goat, and four cows. When Pasteur arrived on the field on the second day of June with his assistants Chamberland, Roux, and Thuillier, he was greeted with loud acclamation. All the vaccinated sheep were well. Twenty-one of the control sheep and the single goat were dead of anthrax, two other control sheep died in front of the spectators, and the last unprotected sheep died at the end of the day. The six vaccinated cows were well and showed no symptoms, whereas the four control cows had extensive swellings at the site of inoculation and febrile reactions. The triumph was complete. . . .

Taking on Rabies

It is, however, the antirabies treatment which is usually cited as Pasteur's greatest triumph and claim to immortality, and which established microbiological sciences in the popular mind and in the practice of medicine. Rabies had long had a firm hold on public imagination and was the epitome of terror and mystery. It was therefore well suited to satisfy Pasteur's longing for romantic problems. It combined a supreme challenge to the experimenter and his method, and the chance to capture the interest of the medical and lay public by a spectacular achievement. In fact, Pasteur was right in the selection of this seemingly hopeless problem. The Pouilly le Fort experiment on anthrax had rendered the public conversant with the doctrine of immunization, but it was the prophylaxis of rabies that made of microbiological science an established religion and surrounded its creator with the halo of sainthood.

In the first phase of the rabies work, Pasteur showed that the spinal cords of rabbits dead of the disease could be rendered almost nonvirulent by keeping them for two weeks in sterile dried air. Specifically, the technique consisted in keeping the spinal cord in a container with caustic potash to prevent putrefaction, and allowing penetration of oxygen to attenuate the virus. The famous portrait painted by Edelfeldt shows Pasteur absorbed in the contemplation of one of these flasks. By inoculating dogs with emulsions of progressively less attenuated cord, it was possible to protect the animal against inoculation with the most virulent form of virus. Under normal conditions of exposure rabies develops slowly in humans as well as in animals. For example, a person bitten by a mad dog ordinarily does not display symptoms of the disease until a month or more after the bite. This period of incubation therefore appeared long enough to suggest the possibility of establishing resistance by vaccinating even after the bite had been inflicted. Experiments made on dogs bitten by rabid animals, and then treated with the vaccine, gave promising results. Would the same method be applicable to human beings bitten by rabid animals and still in the incubation period of the disease?

A Human Subject

The story of the mental anguish Pasteur experienced before daring to proceed from animal experiments to the treatment of human disease has often been told. The decision to apply rabies vaccination to the human was forced upon him when a young boy, Joseph Meister, was brought from Alsace for treatment on July 6, 1885, suffering from rabid dog bites on the hands, legs, and thighs. After consulting with physicians who assured him that the boy was doomed, Pasteur reluctantly decided to administer the vaccine. On July 7, sixty hours after the accident, Joseph Meister was injected with rabbit spinal cord attenuated by fourteen days' drying. In twelve successive inoculations he received stronger and stronger virus until, on July 16, he received an inoculation of still fully virulent spinal cord which had been removed the day before from the body of a rabbit that had died following inoculation with the virus. Joseph Meister exhibited no symptom and returned to Alsace in good health. He later became gatekeeper of the Pasteur Institute. In 1940, fifty-five years after the accident that gave him a lasting place in medical history, he committed suicide rather than open Pasteur's burial crypt for the German invaders.

The second case treated by Pasteur was that of a shepherd, Jean Baptiste Jupille, aged fifteen. Seeing a dog about to attack some children, Jupille had seized his whip in an attempt to drive it away, but was severely bitten; he finally managed to wind his whip around the muzzle of the animal and to crush its skull with his wooden shoe. The dog was subsequently declared rabid, and Jupille was brought to Paris for treatment six days after being bitten. He survived, and his deed was commemorated in a statue which stands today in front of the Pasteur Institute in Paris.

The Modern Vista of Vaccines

By the National Immunization Program

The twentieth century witnessed many amazing developments in medicine, but none more dramatically changed the quality of life than the widespread introduction of vaccines. In the following selection, the National Immunization Program (NIP) offers many specific instances of the enormous difference vaccines have made. For example, according to the Centers for Disease Control and Prevention (CDC), during the twentieth century, the average lifespan of an American grew by some thirty years, to about seventy-five. The CDC attributes twenty-five of those thirty additional years of life to advances in public health, including vaccines. Much of the success came in the second half of the century, when immunization of children became routine. By the late 1990s, the NIP reports, more than 90 percent of young children were being immunized against the major preventable diseases. The National Immunization Program is part of the CDC. Based in Atlanta, Georgia, the NIP provides leadership for the planning, coordination, and conduct of immunization activities nationwide.

At the beginning of the 20th century, infectious diseases were widely prevalent in the United States and exacted an enormous toll on the population. For example, in 1900, 21,064 smallpox cases were reported, and 894 patients died. In 1920, 469,924 measles cases were reported, and 7575 patients died; 147,991 diphtheria cases were reported, and 13,170 patients died. In 1922, 107,473 pertussis cases were reported, and 5099 patients died.

In 1900, few effective treatment and preventive measures existed to prevent infectious diseases. Although the first vaccine

National Immunization Program, "Achievements in Public Health, 1900–1999: Impact of Vaccines Universally Recommended for Children—United States, 1990–1998," *CDC Morbidity and Mortality Weekly Report*, vol. 48, April 2, 1999, pp. 243–48.

against smallpox was developed in 1796, greater than 100 years later its use had not been widespread enough to fully control the disease. Four other vaccines—against rabies, typhoid, cholera, and plague—had been developed late in the 19th century but were not used widely by 1900.

Since 1900, vaccines have been developed or licensed against 21 other diseases. Ten of these vaccines have been recommended for use only in selected populations at high risk because of area of residence, age, medical condition, or risk behaviors. The other 11 have been recommended for use in all U.S. children.

During the 20th century, substantial achievements have been made in the control of many vaccine-preventable diseases. This report documents the decline in morbidity from nine vaccine-preventable diseases and their complications—smallpox, along with the eight diseases for which vaccines had been recommended for universal use in children as of 1990. Four of these diseases are detailed: smallpox has been eradicated, poliomyelitis caused by wild-type viruses has been eliminated, and measles and Haemophilus influenzae type b (Hib) invasive disease among children aged less than 5 years have been reduced to record low numbers of cases.

Information about disease and death during the 20th century was obtained from the MMWR [*Morbidity and Mortality Weekly Report*] annual summaries of notifiable diseases and reports by the U.S. Department of Health, Education, and Welfare. For smallpox, Hib, and congenital rubella syndrome (CRS), published studies were used.

Most Children Now Vaccinated

National efforts to promote vaccine use among all children began with the appropriation of federal funds for polio vaccination after introduction of the vaccine in 1955. Since then, federal, state, and local governments and public and private health-care providers have collaborated to develop and maintain the vaccine-delivery system in the United States.

Overall, U.S. vaccination coverage is at record high levels. In 1997, coverage among children aged 19–35 months (median age: 27 months) exceeded 90% for three or more doses of diphtheria and tetanus toxoids and pertussis vaccine (DTP), three or more doses of poliovirus vaccine, three or more doses of Hib vaccine, and one or more doses of measles-containing vaccine. Coverage with four doses of DTP was 81% and for three doses of hepatitis

B vaccine was 84%. Coverage was substantially lower for the recently introduced varicella [chicken pox] vaccine (26%) and for
the combined series of four DTP/three polio/one measles-
containing vaccine/three Hib (76%). Coverage for rotavirus vaccine, licensed in December 1998, has not yet been measured
among children aged 19–35 months. Coverage among children
aged 5–6 years has exceeded 95% each school year since 1980 for
DTP; polio; and measles, mumps, and rubella vaccines (CDC, unpublished data, 1998).

Prevention Works

Dramatic declines in morbidity have been reported for the nine
vaccine-preventable diseases for which vaccination was universally recommended for use in children before 1990 (excluding hepatitis B, rotavirus, and varicella). Morbidity associated with
smallpox and polio caused by wild-type viruses has declined
100% and nearly 100% for each of the other seven diseases.

Smallpox. Smallpox is the only disease that has been eradicated.
During 1900–1904, an average of 48,164 cases and 1528 deaths
caused by both the severe (variola major) and milder (variola minor) forms of smallpox were reported each year in the United
States. The pattern in the decline of smallpox was sporadic. Outbreaks of variola major occurred periodically in the first quarter of
the 1900s and then ceased abruptly in 1929. Outbreaks of variola
minor declined in the 1940s, and the last case in the United States
was reported in 1949. The eradication of smallpox in 1977 enabled
the discontinuation of prevention and treatment efforts, including
routine vaccination. As a result, in 1985 the United States recouped
its investment in worldwide eradication every 26 days.

Polio. Polio vaccine was licensed in the United States in 1955.
During 1951–1954, an average of 16,316 paralytic polio cases and
1879 deaths from polio were reported each year. Polio incidence
declined sharply following the introduction of vaccine to less than
1000 cases in 1962 and remained below 100 cases after that year.
In 1994, every dollar spent to administer oral poliovirus vaccine
saved $3.40 in direct medical costs and $2.74 in indirect societal
costs. The last documented indigenous transmission of wild poliovirus in the United States occurred in 1979. Since then, reported
cases have been either vaccine-associated or imported. As of 1991,
polio caused by wild-type viruses has been eliminated from the

Western Hemisphere. Enhanced use of the inactivated polio vaccine is expected to reduce the number of vaccine-associated cases, which averaged eight cases per year during 1980–1994.

Measles. Measles vaccine was licensed in the United States in 1963. During 1958–1962, an average of 503,282 measles cases and 432 measles-associated deaths were reported each year. Measles incidence and deaths began to decline in 1965 and continued a 33-year downward trend. This trend was interrupted by epidemics in 1970–1972, 1976–1978, and 1989–1991. In 1998, measles reached a provisional record low number of 89 cases with no measles-associated deaths. All cases in 1998 were either documented to be associated with international importations (69 cases) or believed to be associated with international importations (CDC, unpublished data, 1998). In 1994, every dollar spent to purchase measles-containing vaccine saved $10.30 in direct medical costs and $3.20 in indirect societal costs.

Hib. The first Hib vaccines were polysaccharide products licensed in 1985 for use in children aged 18–24 months. Polysaccharide-protein conjugate vaccines were licensed subsequently for use in children aged 18 months (in 1987) and later for use in children aged 2 months (in 1990). Before the first vaccine was licensed, an estimated 20,000 cases of Hib invasive disease occurred each year, and Hib was the leading cause of childhood bacterial meningitis and postnatal mental retardation. The incidence of disease declined slowly after licensure of the polysaccharide vaccine; the decline accelerated after the 1987 introduction of polysaccharide-protein conjugate vaccines for toddlers and the 1990 recommendation to vaccinate infants. In 1998, 125 cases of Hib disease and Haemophilis influenzae invasive disease of unknown serotype among children aged less than 5 years were provisionally reported: 54 were Hib and 71 were of unknown serotype (CDC, unpublished data, 1998). In less than a decade, the use of the Hib conjugate vaccines nearly eliminated Hib invasive disease among children.

Challenges Ahead

Vaccines are one of the greatest achievements of biomedical science and public health. Despite remarkable progress, several challenges face the U.S. vaccine-delivery system. The infrastructure of the system must be capable of successfully implementing an increasingly complex vaccination schedule. An estimated 11,000 children are born each day in the United States, each requiring 15–19 doses of vaccine by age 18 months to be protected against 11 childhood diseases. In addition, licensure of new vaccines is anticipated against pneumococcal and meningococcal infections, influenza, parainfluenza, respiratory, syncytial virus (RSV), and against chronic diseases (e.g., gastric ulcers, cancer caused by Helicobacter pylori, cervical cancer caused by human papilloma virus, and rheumatic heart disease that occurs as a sequela of group A streptococcal infection). Clinical trials are under way for vaccines to prevent human immunodeficiency virus infection, the cause of acquired immunodeficiency syndrome.

To achieve the full potential of vaccines, parents must recognize vaccines as a means of mobilizing the body's natural defenses and be better prepared to seek vaccinations for their children; health-care providers must be aware of the latest developments and recommendations; vaccine supplies and financing must be made more secure, especially for new vaccines; researchers must address increasingly complex questions about safety, efficacy, and vaccine delivery and pursue new approaches to vaccine administration more aggressively; and information technology to support timely vaccinations must be harnessed more effectively. In addition, the vaccine-delivery system must be extended to new populations of adolescents and adults. Each year, thousands of cases of potentially preventable influenza, pneumococcal disease, and hepatitis B occur in these populations. Many of the new vaccines will be targeted at these age groups. The U.S. vaccine-delivery system must routinely include these populations to optimally prevent disease, disability, and death.

Despite the dramatic declines in vaccine-preventable diseases, such diseases persist, particularly in developing countries. The United States has joined many international partners, including the World Health Organization and Rotary International, in seeking to eradicate polio by the end of 2000. Efforts to accelerate control of measles, which causes approximately one million deaths each year, and to expand rubella vaccination programs also are under way around the world. Efforts are needed to expand the use of existing vaccines in routine childhood vaccination programs worldwide and to successfully introduce new vaccines as they are developed. Such efforts can benefit the United States and other developed countries by decreasing disease importations from developing countries.

CHAPTER 2

Milestones in Disease Prevention

Conquering Polio

By Jane S. Smith

The late Jonas Salk (1914–1995) may not have achieved the lasting fame of Albert Einstein, but in his day Salk was among the most publicly revered and privately reviled of scientists. The reason for both feelings was his invention of a vaccine for polio. A viral disease now largely forgotten in the developed world, polio crippled or killed more than fifty thousand Americans a year as late as 1952. In the following extract from her prizewinning 1990 biography, author Jane S. Smith describes how Salk, building on the advances of others in isolating and culturing the polio virus, developed a killed-virus vaccine. Brushing aside concerns that it would not work and might even cause harm, he conducted secret tests of the vaccine on institutionalized children, some of whom had already suffered crippling episodes of the disease. Fortunately for the children and for Salk's reputation, the vaccine worked. Hailed as a hero, Salk pressed his advantage and quickly established large-scale field tests over the objections of colleagues. His vaccine soon became the national standard. However, the professional controversy did not fade, and within a decade his vaccine was largely supplanted by a live-virus version created by Salk's archrival, Albert Sabin. Jane S. Smith is an author and adjunct professor of the history of medicine and science at Northwestern University in Illinois. Her biography of Jonas Salk, *Patenting the Sun*, was nominated for a Pulitzer Prize and was awarded the *Los Angeles Times* Book Prize in 1990.

Translating possibility into fact was a tricky process that took a number of years, but by the mid-1930s several animal viruses had been cultured in laboratory flasks, as well as in the developing chicken embryos of fertile eggs. No one had succeeded in growing poliovirus, however, until 1936, when Albert Sabin and Peter Olitsky managed for the first time to cultivate po-

Jane S. Smith, *Patenting the Sun: Polio and the Salk Vaccine*. New York: William Morrow and Company, 1990. Copyright © 1990 by Jane S. Smith. All rights reserved. Reproduced by permission.

liovirus in test-tube cultures using human embryonic nervous tissue as their medium.

This was a dubious triumph, since their failure to culture the virus in other kinds of human tissue led to the erroneous but widely accepted conclusion that poliovirus multiplied only in the cells of the nervous system. It was a logical assumption, since polio damaged nervous-system tissue, but it raised major problems for vaccine research. Nervous-system tissue is notorious for provoking fatal allergic brain damage when injected into the human body. . . . Since there was no way to be sure that all nervous-tissue cells were removed when "harvesting" virus from the culture medium, Sabin and Olitsky's findings made it seem highly unlikely that tissue-culture methods could be used to produce the large quantities of poliovirus that would be needed to make a vaccine.

John Enders was not particularly interested in polio when, in 1948, he showed that Sabin and Olitsky had been wrong. . . .

Learning How to Culture Polio

In 1948 Enders had taken on two young associates, Tom Weller and Frederick C. Robbins, both graduates of the Harvard Medical School class of 1940 who had spent the war years as army bacteriologists. As so often happened in the small world of virus research, they had financial backing from the National Foundation for Infantile Paralysis. Enders' laboratory was supported in part by a National Foundation grant for basic research, and Robbins was paid through a National Research Council fellowship funded by the National Foundation. They were not working on polio, however, but on mumps and chickenpox, experimenting with the possibility of using tissue cultures to diagnose the many different infectious diseases their young patients carried. When Thomas Weller prepared a few too many tubes of culture medium for an experiment he was doing with chickenpox virus, Enders suggested he seed the extra tubes with some poliovirus he had in the laboratory freezer, sent by the National Foundation and shoved into storage some time ago. To everyone's intense interest, the virus grew even though the medium contained no nervous-system tissue cells. The exclusive affinity for nerve cells that Sabin and Olitsky had discovered would soon prove to have been a peculiarity of the type of poliovirus they had been using for their experiments. Using the advanced techniques of tissue culture Enders, Weller, and Robbins had developed, it would be feasible, for the first time, to produce enough poliovirus to make a vaccine.

Enders' tissue-culture techniques transformed virus production the same way John Deere's plow and Cyrus McCormick's reaper transformed agriculture. Before, polio researchers had to infect individual monkeys, coddle the animals until they achieved just the right degree of sickness, and then kill them to grind up their spinal columns and take the live virus within. A single monkey could provide enough virus to make only a few doses of vaccine, and there weren't enough monkeys on earth to produce sufficient virus for large-scale commercial production of vaccine. Now, however, laboratory workers would be able to prepare racks of tissue-culture tubes, each filled with a murky broth of tissue finely minced and suspended in a nutrient medium, "seed" the virus in the tubes, incubate them at a temperature between 96.8 and 98.6 degrees Fahrenheit, and "harvest" the entire crop at once. It took a fraction of the time and used only a small percentage of the monkeys required by the older methods.

Salk Foresees Vaccine

Everybody in the polio business saw that Enders' breakthrough was staggering news. Astonishingly, only Jonas Salk began immediately to equip a lab for the new production techniques, recognizing at once that it offered a way of speeding the completion of the virus-typing project while simultaneously developing the means to produce a potential polio vaccine.

In growing poliovirus in glass tubes instead of in monkeys, Salk saved both time and money. Two hundred culture tubes could be prepared from the kidneys of a single monkey, whereas before a monkey could be used to test, at most, three samples of virus. Salk learned the trick from Enders, who took a few days instead of a few weeks to type a set of virus samples Salk sent him: seed a tissue-culture tube with unknown virus, challenge it with blood serum from a monkey or a human being known to have antibodies to one of the three types, and see what happens. Attacked by antibodies that match its type, the virus will die. This is the way the immune system works, and it's very exciting to watch the immune system duplicated under a laboratory microscope. . . .

The question one asks now is why Enders himself did not proceed to make a polio vaccine, or why nobody else but Salk followed his lead. The answers are various, depending on the different circumstances of the careers of other people, but they all illustrate in one way or another the reason so many people in the academic research community resisted the applied science that making a vaccine entails.

Under the best of circumstances, making a vaccine is not a simple job. The object is to produce a form of the virus that will provoke a strong antibody response but not a powerful infection. The two basic strategies are either to kill the virus so it can no longer multiply or to weaken it until the infection it causes is so mild as to be harmless. Viruses are killed, or inactivated, by being heated, treated with radiation, or bathed in chemicals—most commonly formaldehyde—until they are no longer able to reproduce within the living cell. For a killed-virus vaccine, the idea is that the very presence of the foreign virus within the body will stimulate an antibody response, even without the galvanizing challenge of infection; the trick is to be sure that every single virus particle is really truly dead, and yet still have a product capable of causing immunity. By contrast, live-virus vaccines are made from viruses bred to be particularly weak. . . .

Free of any qualms about the use of a killed-virus vaccine, Salk still had a huge number of technical problems to overcome before he would have any vaccine ready. Killing a virus is just as intricate a process as growing it, and the success of the results was a good deal more difficult to measure. There was the question of how long you needed to "inactivate" the virus for it to be safe without being ineffective, and at what temperature, and in what concentration. After you were quite sure the virus was dead, you then had to explore different ways to increase its potency, to avoid having to inject people with a quart of vaccine. Then you had to decide the best sites for injections, the best spacing for the multiple shots that would be required, and the best intervals for testing blood samples to see if antibody levels had risen and stayed elevated. There were usually about sixty variables being tested at once in the Virus Research Lab.

Still, work moved fast. In January 1950, the laboratory started tissue-culture production of poliovirus. That June, Salk wrote to [National Foundation Research Director] Harry Weaver outlining the steps by which he planned to extend his research. After five single-spaced pages discussing the efficiency of applying tissue-culture techniques to the virus-typing program and the possibility of using "discard" monkeys to search for virus strains of low infectivity, Salk moved on to the interesting subject of "further studies on vaccination of animals and of man."

Ready to Test

Salk's tests had shown that monkeys injected with killed-tissue-culture virus combined with adjuvant produced more antibodies than monkeys subjected to natural infection. To him the next step was obvious. "Without much further thought," he wrote, "I think we could consider inactivation of this material with ultraviolet light for [the] immunization of children. I have investigated the local possibility for such an experiment and find that not too far from here there are institutions for Hydrocephalics and other similar unfortunates. I think that we may be able to obtain permission for a study of immunization using tissue culture material . . . I think we might be able to transfer patients to the Municipal Hospital, keeping them under isolation and under very close supervision."

Salk acknowledged that his suggestion was unlikely to be approved anytime soon. "This is more of a dream than a reality," he conceded, "but something that might be considered. Some of the earliest experiments that might be tried, both in chimpanzees and in the institutionalized children, and, perhaps, inmates of prisons who might volunteer for such studies, would be vaccination followed by the administration of [attenuated] virus after the titre of antibody is increased and becomes stabilized."

Salk's dream was Weaver's nightmare—taking helpless children, wards of the state, isolating them in Municipal Hospital, injecting them with an unproved vaccine, and exposing them to live poliovirus, even in an attenuated form. Although Salk's proposal was not far from standard experimental procedures in 1950, Weaver knew better than to think the public would regard the test of any polio vaccine as a routine experiment. Far more work was needed before Salk would have a vaccine ready for testing. The last thing he needed was a reputation for premature experiments conducted without sufficient regard for the interests of his volunteers. If anyone was harmed during tests, the press would be accusing Salk and the National Foundation of medical atrocities.

Secure in his conviction of his careful work, his good intentions, and the infallibility of his laboratory results, Salk never even imagined such a response. He did anticipate objections to a killed-virus vaccine on immunological grounds from the conservative element of the profession, and he suggested a degree of "flexibility" by which his funding proposal might bypass the skeptical review of the Committee on Standards, but he was eager to push forward to the goal of ending polio, and impatient with any doubts or delays. He ended his letter with a stirring call to action: "I think that the time has come for initiating the critical experiments for immunologic prevention and more than that, the time has come for these experiments to be carried out in man.". . .

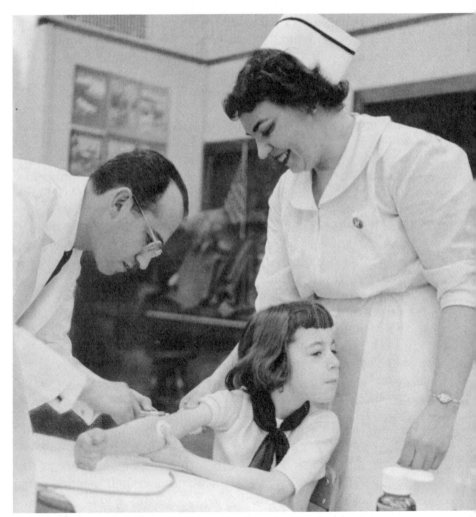

In the 1950s Dr. Jonas Salk developed a vaccine for polio. Here, he inoculates a young girl against the disease.

First in Line

Although he first denied it, Jonas Salk has since acknowledged that he tested his polio vaccine on himself and other members of his laboratory before trying it out on the population at large. Asked to comment on his actions thirty years later, Salk said, "I look upon it as ritual and symbolic. You wouldn't do unto others that which you wouldn't do unto yourself."

And so it is, ritual and symbolic. What we are dealing with here is as much magic as method; the ancient need to prove your bravery before you can claim any power or authority; the primal conviction that the experiment will fail if you don't mix a drop of your own life's blood into the final potion. Scientists who conduct experiments upon themselves are considered slightly mad but also quite heroic. When they take their experiments to others, a larger, stricter set of ethical questions enters.

The history of man's inhumanity to man is full of examples of unwilling volunteers, from the victims of the Spanish Inquisition to the "research subjects" of the Nazi Reich. Less barbaric, but equally common, are the neurotic martyrs who are eager to sacrifice their time, their health, and even their lives for the furtherance of science. These unsought guinea pigs are the last people any reasonable scientist would want to use, however. Whether or not they are otherwise suited to the project, they are disqualified by their very eagerness to help; the same mentality that makes them volunteer makes it highly likely that they will fake their responses in whatever way they think will please the doctor most.

The most reliable choices for human trials are people who are acting from self-interest. In low-risk studies, money is a popular motivational tool, especially since a cash payment for showing up carries no incentive to influence the results. High-risk studies are often carried out in prisons, where inmates are often sadly accustomed to weighing different kinds of dangers and see their participation in medical experiments as a way to shorten their sentences. Scientists always like to use what they call captive populations, which includes not just prison inmates but any group whose whereabouts and behavior can be monitored by others. Schoolchildren, who spend most of their time in large institutions that routinely keep track of their attendance and their health, are another favorite captive population.

By the end of 1954, hundreds of thousands of schoolchildren had served as willing guinea pigs for the Salk polio vaccine, but the first tests were done on small, isolated groups that were sometimes unaware of the other studies taking place elsewhere. If you talk to people who were living in Pittsburgh in the early 1950s, dozens of them will tell you, in considerable detail, how it came to pass that they, or their children, or their neighbor's best friend's cousin, were the first to receive the Salk vaccine. "I worked in the lab," they explain. "I was a family friend." "We were neighbors." "I was sick that day and had to come in early." *Nobody knows that,* they'll add, *except now I've told you. I was the first. Really. Me.*

In fact, there were many stages of trial and development, and many people in the vanguard. The very first group to try one of the killed-virus preparations was the staff of the Virus Research Lab. This made practical as well as symbolic sense, since they were constantly exposed to live poliovirus and had no doubts about their preparation's safety. No one knew yet how well the vaccine worked, but it couldn't hurt to try it. A high-school student who had a part-time job in the laboratory recalls the low level of ceremony attached to the process: after she had worked there for a few days, Dr. Salk came through the lab, told her to roll up her sleeve, and vaccinated her as though he were stamping a crate of fruit.

Children as Test Subjects

From there the chronology of tests depended on medical and ethical considerations, and also on the mechanics of getting approval and producing vaccine. Following his penchant for doing several things at once, Salk approached the directors of two nearby institutions for permission to conduct vaccine trials. The first to answer was the Polk State School, a residence for retarded males, children and adults, maintained by the Pennsylvania Department of Welfare in nearby Venango County.

Dr. Gale Walker, the director of the school, was all in favor of the program. Paralytic poliomyelitis had never been a serious problem at Polk, but there had been enough cases for Walker to argue with a clear conscience that the vaccinations would benefit the inmates. He also saw the great merits that Polk had for Salk: a place where patients stayed for an average of twelve years, living in isolation from the general community and its diseases, where very accurate records were kept on residents and strict controls of diet and activity could be maintained during the study. Although Walker was a physician, he had no prior theories or policies about polio that kept him from accepting Salk's assurances of safety, and while he was very aware of his own responsibility, legally and ethically, as the director of a state institution for people who were not capable of taking care of themselves, he saw the experiment as a valuable opportunity to raise the status of the Polk School while assisting in a worthwhile project. He was also a pleasant fellow, fun to relax with over drinks and dinner, able to hold his own in the war stories about fights for money and power, ready to give good advice in designing the kind of official forms and letters that get the answers you want.

Looser Terms of Consent

As Jonas Salk has often remarked, it would be impossible to repeat his polio work today, when such ventures need to be passed by human-subject review boards and peer review boards and various other qualifying agencies. In 1952 you got the permission of the people involved and went out and did it, and then wrote up your results in a scientific journal. If something terrible happened, the blame would be on your head and the blood on your hands, and of course your career would be over—but in the planning stages, at least, life was a great deal easier for the medical experimenter than it has since become. Still, the consent forms were no small issue. Unlike prisoners, that other, favorite "captive population" in the temporary custody of the state, the inmates at Polk could hardly be expected to give anything like informed consent to the experiments. Because many of them had no family to sign for them, the request had to go all the way to the state Department of Welfare in Harrisburg. . . .

The negotiations had lasted five months, but on May 23, 1952, Salk drove the eighty miles from his home to the Polk School to take blood samples from the people who would be receiving vaccine. It was important to know what their blood antibody level was to start with, before they received any vaccinations, so he could measure how much the levels later rose. Salk packed syringes and vials for the blood samples, index cards for the records, and lollipops for the one hundred inmates who took part. Even the simplest children like lollipops, and they would look forward to the doctor's return.

Despite its convenience, the Polk School was a difficult assignment. Lorraine Friedman accompanied Salk on his visits there, to keep the records of which blood sample went with which subject, and she doubted she would stay in the job much longer if they had to make many such trips. It was a long ride, a couple of hours in the car each way, and when you got there the scene wasn't pretty. Children and adults were housed at Polk according to their mental age, and it was hard to go into a building with men older than she was who had the mental age of children or even infants. It smelled bad, too, because the men didn't exactly take good care of themselves, any more than any other toddler does.

Second Test Site

It was much more pleasant to work at the second institution Salk used for his early tests, the D.T. Watson Home for Crippled Children. The object here was to prove Salk's contention that his killed-virus vaccine created higher levels of immunity to polio than a natural infection, which could be shown by measuring the before and after antibody levels of children recovering from the disease. The unstated reality was that the children at Watson would not be harmed if the vaccine wasn't quite as good as Dr. Salk thought. . . .

Salk's Vaccine Works

Salk was already negotiating with the director of the Watson Home, Dr. Jessie Wright, before he began the work at Polk. Wright was a leading authority on the rehabilitation of polio victims and well known to the National Foundation for Infantile Paralysis, which had given her many grants for programs to teach physical therapy and had appointed her to its advisory committees on post-polio care. She was a terrifying woman, well over two hundred pounds of iron determination, demanding of her staff and sometimes hard on patients who weren't putting forth enough effort to get their muscles moving, but she had no trouble accommodating Salk's experiments. Neither did Lucile Cochran, the small, soft-spoken superintendent of nursing at Watson since 1927, who really ran the home. When Jonas Salk brought his vaccine to the Watson Home, Cochran was the first to volunteer to take it, and it was she who convinced reluctant, heartbroken, guilt-ridden parents that they should be proud to let their children participate in his experiments, not fearful of bringing greater harm to these already burdened lives.

On June 12, 1952, two-and-a-half weeks after his first trip to the Polk School, Salk drove to Sewickley Heights to take prevaccination blood samples from forty-five children and twenty-seven members of the Watson staff. On July 2, having typed the blood samples to see who had antibodies to which strain of polio, Salk returned to give his first injections. Thirty children were injected with an inactivated vaccine prepared from Type I poliovirus, two with a vaccine of Type II and eleven with a vaccine of Type III. That night a very nervous Dr. Salk drove back to Watson from his home in Wexford to see for himself that nobody had gotten sick. Nobody had. Over the summer, he would return several times to take further blood samples. Antibody levels had risen, and were staying up. The killed-virus vaccine produced stronger antibody response than the original infection. The vaccine formula was far from perfect and it was still too soon to tell how long its effects would last, but, indisputably, it worked. . . .

A Landmark Development

When people describe Salk's polio vaccine and the one later developed by Albert Sabin, they most often mark the difference as between an injected vaccine and one taken orally, in a sugar cube or as part of a sweet syrup. Since inoculation is the most ancient form of vaccination, most people assume that the Salk vaccine, which after all came first, is in some way more traditional.

In fact, the opposite is true. Salk's innovation was his claim that it was indeed possible to achieve lasting immunity to a disease without ever having an actual infection, and that the immunity gained from a killed-virus vaccine might even be more powerful than that achieved through infection. The Sabin vaccine, by contrast, follows classic principles of immunology by provoking an infection with a harmless strain of virus, thus protecting the patient from later exposure to more dangerous infections. As Edward Jenner had used cowpox to conquer smallpox and Pasteur had used dried and weakened rabies virus to halt the progress of hydrophobia, so Sabin intended to use a weakened form of poliovirus to conquer the paralytic strains of the disease.

These were not empty distinctions. The choice to support the Salk vaccine or wait for a more traditional live-virus product raised very real questions in medicine, immunological theory, and public health administration.

Finding a Vaccine for Hepatitis B

By Baruch S. Blumberg

The hepatitis B virus may not make headlines, but according to Dr. Baruch S. Blumberg, author of the following selection, it has killed more people than the notorious AIDS epidemic. Worldwide, hepatitis B strikes hundreds of millions of people, inducing deadly liver cancer in many of its victims. Now, however, the rate of infection is declining, thanks to the vaccine Blumberg invented. In the following extract from his book about the hunt for the deadly virus, Blumberg illuminates what the Nobel Prize committee has recognized as one of the great triumphs of twentieth-century medicine. He describes the unusual process by which he and his research colleagues created the vaccine for hepatitis B in 1969 and the struggle to get it tested and marketed in the 1970s and early 1980s. Once those hurdles had been cleared, the hepatitis vaccine soon became one of the most widely administered in the world. Blumberg holds an MD from Columbia University and a PhD in biochemistry from Oxford University. He is Distinguished Senior Scientist at the Fox Chase Cancer Center and the director of the NASA Astrobiology Institute. He was awarded the 1976 Nobel Prize in Physiology or Medicine for his work on hepatitis B.

The most significant outcome of our research has, probably, been the invention and the introduction of the hepatitis B vaccine, one of the most widely used vaccines in the world and the first "cancer vaccine." By "cancer vaccine," I mean an agent that can *prevent* cancer—in this case, one of the most common cancers in the world, primary cancer of the liver. . . . The apparent success of the HBV vaccine in the prevention of primary cancer of the liver has encouraged the search for other vaccines

Baruch S. Blumberg, *Hepatitis B: The Hunt for a Killer Virus*. Princeton, NJ: Princeton University Press, 2002. Copyright © 2002 by Princeton University Press. All rights reserved. Reproduced by permission.

for cancer prevention, a very hopeful step in the control of this widespread and feared group of diseases.

In early 1969, at one of the staff council meetings of the Institute for Cancer Research, Tim Talbot, then director, told us a piece of unwelcome news. He had been informed by the National Cancer Institute that in the future, support would be diminished and applicant institutions would be expected to seek additional sources of money elsewhere. The implication was that we should try to patent and commercialize the products of our research. (I remind the reader that this was years before the advent of molecular biology and the entrepreneurial biotechnology industry that it engendered, which has turned many scientists into businesspersons.) As it turned out, I do not think that this threat was actualized, and the generous funding from the federal government continued for several more years. At the time, though, we could only assume that our funding was in jeopardy. The notion that a principal source of research support might be constrained, like the prospect of hanging, can sharply focus the mind. Action was needed.

Deciding on Hepatitis B

I spoke to [microbiologist] Irv Millmar and told him that we had to file a patent for a hepatitis B vaccine. We had been thinking about this matter ever since our first population studies; even though the virus had been discovered barely two years earlier, and we had only just started the testing of donor blood in the hospitals, we started on the invention of the vaccine. I was unburdened by any preconceived ideas as to how a vaccine should be made, although I had a general knowledge from medical school of the theory of their production and use. Irv, on the other hand, had considerable experience. He had worked at the vaccine facility of the Merck Institute for Therapeutic Research in West Point, a suburb of Philadelphia. He had had no experience of hepatitis there but did invent and patent a purified pertussis vaccine superior to any others then available. Unfortunately, Merck decided not to produce it, and that, in part, was the reason that Irv came to work with us. He thought, when we first recruited him, that he would be working on serum protein polymorphisms, but by the time he arrived we were well into the hepatitis caper, and Irv was drawn back into infectious disease research.

Regardless of my inexperience with the invention of vaccines, I had a keen perception of the value of public health and preventive medicine. In Suriname, in Africa, in the central Pacific, and indeed in Alaska—the venues of much of my early research—I had witnessed the paramount importance of public health measures, including vaccination. Much of the disease in developing parts of the world could be prevented if the water and food supply were safeguarded from contamination by human waste, if insect vectors for viruses, parasites, and other infectious agents were controlled, and if childhood vaccination were routinely implemented.

What was the evidence that we could make a vaccine? It was thin, but compelling. One of the big problems in making a vaccine is identifying the protective antibody—that is, a gamma globulin protein present in the blood of an immunized person, or a specific reaction of the immune cells that would protect against infection with a specific infectious agent. Much of the concern about developing a vaccine for HIV, the causative agent for AIDS, is centered on this issue. The molecular biology of HIV is well understood, probably better than any other virus that has ever been identified, but the protective antigens and mechanisms are not known. This makes it very difficult for scientists to decide which antigen to use for the vaccine. However, from the very beginning of the research on HBV [hepatitis B virus], there were very good indications about what must be the protective antibody. The data were pretty simple: in our early tests on thousands of individual sera [blood serums], we had rarely seen a person who had [the antigen] HBsAg in the blood—that is, was a carrier of HBV—and, at the same time, had the antibody against the surface antigen (anti-HBs). This is consistent with the hypothesis that anti-HBs is protective against infection. The problem was further simplified by the stark reality that anti-HBs was the only known antibody. Providentially, the first antibody we knew was the one that protects. . . .

Obtaining a Patent

In the patent application we described a method for separating the HBsAg particles using centrifugation in various media, such as sugar solution or cesium chloride, and applying enzymes to remove any serum protein remaining and also to impair or destroy any viable virus that might remain, followed by column separation and treatment by several methods to kill residual virus of any kind. Substances to increase the antigenicity of the HBsAg—that is, to increase the ability of the vaccine to elicit a protective response from the vaccinated person—and preservatives to increase shelf life could be added—and *voilà*, the vaccine. Under the electron microscope we could see the small particles . . . in large numbers and densely packed. We filed with the U.S. Patent Office on 8 October 1969, and the patent was issued, without much hassle, on 18 January 1972.

Ours was a unique method for making a vaccine. None had been prepared in this manner before, and none have been since. There are several processes for making vaccines. The first vaccine, against smallpox, consisted of the human virus contained in the fluid extruded from the pustules of a person who had been mildly infected. The notion was that a person would be more likely to survive a controlled infection than a natural one, and that this induced infection would provide protection against subsequent natural infections that might be more serious. That may have been true, but the mortality rate from vaccination with the human virus was unacceptably high, of the order of 10 percent. Edward Jenner's (1749–1823) original contribution came when he noted that milkmaids had better complexions than other women: they did not bear the facial scarring that follows recovery from human smallpox. Milkmaids were prone to infection with cowpox virus, an infectious agent in cattle similar to human smallpox. Why didn't the milkmaids succumb to smallpox? Cowpox does not cause serious or fatal illness in humans, and the scarring is much less severe than with human smallpox. Jenner theorized that infection with cowpox somehow prevented infection with the human virus. He administered the cowpox virus as a preventive vaccine, and it achieved great success, although its use was by no means unmarred by controversy. For example, there were objections on what were considered by some to be religious grounds. It was argued that using the preventive measures would thwart God's will. The word "vaccine," derived from the Latin root *vacca* (as in the French *vache*), is a reminder of the bovine origins of the first vaccine.

Types of Vaccines

Scientists have created other vaccines through a process of "attenuating" natural infectious agents—that is, decreasing their ability to cause disease—by transmitting them serially through experimental animals or through tissue cultures. The Sabin polio vaccine is of this nature. Such vaccines can be administered easily, by mouth. Further, because they are infectious, they can spread to members of the community who have not been vaccinated—each individual vaccination thus has an amplified effect. The disadvantage is that some people become ill from the attenuated vaccine, and deaths occasionally occur. These are very infrequent; when polio was a terrible scourge, the risk from the use of the vaccine to a few members of the population warranted its use in the population as a whole. But when polio became rare, as it is now, there were in some communities more cases of illness due to the vaccine than to natural infection.

Killed vaccines are another option. Scientists create these by taking the offending virus or other microorganism, killing it by heating or by some chemical process, and then using the resulting denatured, but antigenic, protein as the vaccine. (The Salk polio vaccine was made this way.) Sometimes the whole organism is used and sometimes only a portion of it. With the advent of molecular biology it has become possible to be precisely selective, and to clone a gene from the virus for a particular antigen and produce only that as a vaccine. Even fancier vaccines are now being designed—for example, DNA vaccines in which the DNA that produces the desired protein is injected into the host and the vaccine antigen is produced by the host.

A Unique Approach

Our vaccine wasn't made by any of these processes. Rather, we took antigen from individuals who had a great deal of it and used it to inoculate others who didn't have any: a "people's vaccine," as we sometimes jokingly called it. Our ability to do this was based on the fact that the virus produced very large quantities of the small, noninfectious particles containing only the surface antigen. This was probably an immunologic strategy of the virus, producing excess amounts of the antigen in the blood to divert the antibodies produced by the host's immune system to the small particles and thereby to spare the whole virus, which could get on with its mischief of replication and damage to the liver cells. In the war parlance of the infectious disease field, this is sometimes referred to as a "smoke screen."

The vaccine was invented. What were we to do next? To transform the vaccine from a theory to an actuality, we had to interest a pharmaceutical manufacturer in the project. For Chase Cancer Center (FCCC) was not set up to produce and test a vaccine. The equipment needed to maintain production standards required for a vaccine to be used in humans was not available in a research laboratory, nor did we wish to redirect the basic science activities of the institution. In 1969, when we first invented the vaccine, there was little faith in the hepatitis community or among the pharmaceutical companies that we had identified the virus—much less produced, by a totally unconventional method, a vaccine that would be practical and economically profitable. There was another issue that probably diminished interest in the vaccine. Hepatitis was not considered to be a serious disease in the developed world. In most people's experience, it was a very unpleasant acute disease that lasted for a few days or weeks, and from which recovery was nearly always complete. Also, it was regarded as primarily a disease of other places, one that you might encounter on a holiday visit to the tropics, or that was contracted overseas by people in the military. The long-term consequences of infection, chronic liver disease and cancer of the liver, were not known until the Au test and its improvements were available to show the connection.

Indications of Potential Use

There were several developments that moved matters forward. In April 1970 Dr. Saul Krugman, professor of pediatrics at New York University, and his colleagues reported a series of experiments that drew attention to the possibilities of the vaccine. They boiled serum containing Australia antigen for one minute and used it as a vaccine to inoculate Down's syndrome children, who were then given unboiled serum containing Australia antigen. The boiled serum appeared to confer some, but not complete, protection against subsequent exposure. Although these experiments were criticized on ethical grounds, and were faulted to some extent scientifically as well (in the initial experiments there were no controls), they did have the effect of impressing scientists and vaccine manufacturers as to the possibility of a vaccine.

There was also additional evidence that anti-HBs was effective. Beginning in November 1970 Tom London had been monitoring and attempting, with a great deal of success, to prevent the development of hepatitis in renal dialysis units in Philadelphia. Ed Lustbader executed a fascinating analysis of the mass of data Tom had collected over several years. It was originally presented at a meeting in Paris and published in French; it was later published in more complete form in English. He compared the probability of *not* developing hepatitis in initially uninfected renal dialysis patients who entered with anti-HBs in their blood to that of patients who lacked the substance. The differnces were impressive after nine months of treatment on the dialysis unit (usually about three visits a week), only 50 percent of the patients who did not have anti-HBs on entry remained uninfected, while of those who entered with anti-HBs, more than 90 percent remained uninfected. This was a dramatic illustration of the protective property of the antibody that could be produced by the vaccine. Additionally, by the mid-1970s a series of experimental studies done on primates in several laboratories appeared to show that the vaccine was protective, confirming the preliminary findings on animal inoculation that had been presented in the vaccine patent application.

A Strange Twist

By 1971 we were in discussion with the scientists at Merck & Co., whose facility for vaccine research was located in West Point, Pennsylvania, not far from Philadelphia, and they expressed an interest in licensing the vaccine. Nothing much happened immediately. The scientific community was still testing the hypothesis that our research was really valid, and that we had identified the virus that causes hepatitis B. We had spoken and written about our concept for the vaccine and discussed it with colleagues in the hepatitis field, but it still required more research and confirmation by others. Research on hepatitis B has never been very well funded, and there were not many investigators in the field to do the necessary studies. It took time for the subsequent steps to unfold.

The federal government had decided, strangely, to grant us ownership of the foreign, but not the domestic, rights to the patent. This compelled Irv Millman and me to seriously dedicate ourselves to identifying a company we could license. . . .

In 1975 FCCC licensed Merck to develop the vaccine. Dr. Maurice Hilleman, who had considerable experience in the development and manufacture of vaccines and in hepatitis research, was the executive in charge of the program. Merck was very effective, and soon they had sufficient knowledge of the vaccine, and a sufficient quantity of it, to undertake field trials.

Dr. Wolf Szmuness and his colleagues in New York City conducted the first formal trial published. It was a very well designed
and well executed study, and we and all the beneficiaries of the
vaccine owe a great deal to Wolf for producing a study so convincing that it probably speeded up the acceptance of the vaccine
by more than a year. Wolf was an interesting man who had surmounted many difficulties in his career and life. He and his family were caught up in the turmoil of the German invasion of
Poland at the start of World War II, and they fled to the east. He
was educated in the Soviet Union and returned to Poland after the
war. After his medical training, he became a public health physician and had experience administering and testing vaccines in his
homeland. In the 1960s, there was a series of pogroms directed
against the remnant of the Jewish population in Poland that had
survived the war, and Wolf and his family fled again, this time to
the United States. He visited our laboratory, and we discussed the
possibility of an appointment for him. However—probably wisely,
as it turned out—he decided to work at the New York Blood Center, from where he organized the field trial for our HBV vaccine.

Formal Trials

First, Wolf wanted to identify a population at high risk for hepatitis. The early clinical and epidemiological studies had given us
some idea of the methods of transmission. These included mother-
to-child, sexual, transfusion, and use of contaminated injection
needles. Individuals with impaired immune responses were particularly susceptible. The subsequent work on HIV, which is transmitted by the same methods as HBV (but is less infectious), has
made the public very aware of the mechanisms by which blood-
borne viruses are spread. Populations that had a high probability
of becoming infected with HBV were pretty well known and have
already been discussed. These included the Down's syndrome patients, Hansen's disease patients, renal dialysis patients, and others. Some of the first carriers we encountered were members of
the homosexual community in Philadelphia, and, at a clinical
level, it was known that hepatitis was common in this population.
Wolf and his colleagues did a systematic study in the New York
City gay male community and found that the rate of infection was
very high. In a sample of about ten thousand people, he found the
prevalence of serological markers of HBV infection to be 68 per-

cent, very much higher than in other segments of the population. He also estimated the annual incidence rate—that is, the percentage of people who became infected within a year—and found that it was nearly 20 percent. Wolf told me that in subsequent studies it was even higher; as many as a third of those previously uninfected would become so within a year. It also became apparent that the members of this community were well educated, intelligent, and willing to volunteer for a research project that could benefit themselves and others. He decided to enlist their cooperation to test the vaccine.

Hundreds of Randomized Tests

To obtain the necessary statistical power, he required about 400 individuals who would receive the vaccine and an additional 400 who would receive a placebo. In the event, between November 1978 and October 1979, 1,083 individuals (549 vaccine, 534 placebo) were enrolled in the trial. On the basis of random selection individuals were designated to receive either the vaccine or the placebo, and each was assigned an identifying code. The recipients did not know whether they received vaccine or placebo, and the physicians who were to do the evaluation also did not know. The code was retained, to be connected with a name only after the studies were complete. The vaccine was administered in three doses, the first two one month apart and the third six months after the first. Ninety-three percent of the subjects received all three inoculations, an indication of the excellent compliance and the loyalty of the subjects. They were evaluated for the occurrence of a hepatitis event for at least six months; most were followed for a year. What happened?

Excellent Results

When the code was broken, the results were impressive. First, there was no difference in deleterious side effects between those who had been given the placebo and those who had received the vaccine. As far as I can tell, in the many years since this first trial and after a billion doses of vaccine have been administered, although concerns have been raised, there is still no convincing evidence of detrimental side effects due to the vaccine. Second, the response to the vaccine was excellent. Ninety-six percent of those vaccinated developed antibody after completing the three-dose regimen. Third, there was a striking difference between the vaccinated and the controls with respect to the development of hepatitis B. A total of fifty-two individuals developed hepatitis B as scored by chemical abnormalities and the appearance of HBsAg in the blood. Only seven of these were in the vaccinated group, and of these only one had completed the full course of vaccination. It is likely that some of these vaccinated people had actually been infected shortly before the vaccinations began. There was an additional finding of great clinical importance. The vaccinated people who did not develop anti-HBs did not become carriers of HBV more frequently than those who received placebo. Had this not been the case, then our findings would have raised the possibility that persons who were destined to become carriers, possibly because of an inherited propensity to do so, would not respond to vaccination. If this were true, then a major value of the vaccine would have been lost. But the results reported by Wolf and the others taught that this was not the case, and that it would be possible to vaccinate even those who were at greater risk of becoming carriers. This conclusion was supported in a study in South Africa that showed, for the first time, that vaccinated infants who were born of carrier mothers, and were known to be at great risk of becoming carriers, did develop anti-HBs and were protected against infection and the carrier state.

There were subsequent field trials that also supported the efficacy of the vaccine. Within two years of the publication of Wolf's paper, in the early 1980s, the FDA approved the blood-derived vaccine, and within a few years, millions of children and adults were being vaccinated yearly. (In 2000 it was estimated that a billion doses of the vaccine had been administered.) It is now one of the most commonly used vaccines in the world.

Key Benefit

The most important practical outcome of research on hepatitis B has been the campaign to prevent primary cancer of the liver, one of the most common and deadly cancers in the world. The early reports on the outcome of this campaign are very promising. If they are supported in the future, the world is well on its way to a new and effective method for the prevention of cancer. Primary cancer of the liver is not the only cancer linked to a virus, and the research on HBV and liver cancer may provide a guide to the prevention of other cancers in the future.

Smallpox Eradicated Through Global Use of Vaccine

By Frank Fenner

Smallpox was the first infectious disease to be eradicated in the world. The victory was achieved through a globally coordinated effort at vaccinating those most at risk of infection. In the selection that follows, Australian medical researcher Frank Fenner, who played a leading role in the campaign to eliminate smallpox, recounts the upbringing and career that led him to that pivotal achievement. Notably, Fenner credits the Soviet Union with providing the detailed plan for eradication through targeted vaccinations. The United Nations General Assembly was by no means united in its 1966 vote to go ahead with the eradication plan. However, Fenner shows, the actual push to eliminate smallpox from the thirty-one countries where it remained widespread got broad international cooperation. Thanks to that sustained effort, one of the worst scourges endured by humankind vanished within about ten years. On May 8, 1980, Fenner had the honor of presenting the Global Commission's report on its success to the World Health Organization. He then retired to write a book about this remarkable milestone in medicine. Although a danger of smallpox outbreak persists (through accidental or deliberate release of remaining laboratory stocks of the virus), no case of smallpox has been recorded since that date.

Frank Fenner, "Nature, Nurture, and My Experience with Smallpox Eradication," *Medical Journal of Australia*, vol. 171, 1999, pp. 638–41. Copyright © 1999 by the *Medical Journal of Australia*. Reproduced by permission.

I believe that nature (one's genes) and nurture (one's upbringing and education) play equal roles in the life of every person, and that chance plays a critical part in the course of that life. I will try to analyse how these three elements contributed to my role in the global eradication of smallpox.

Family and Education

My parents were both talented people, born in Victoria of migrant (predominantly German) parents, and educated at the Melbourne Teachers College and the University of Melbourne. I was the second of five children. When I was two years old my father was appointed Superintendent of Technical Education in South Australia. He had been educated in geology and biology and pursued research in physiography that gained him the DSc [Doctor of Science] from the University of Melbourne. He continued scientific work in his spare time, producing both university-level and school books on the geography of South Australia and scientific papers on physiography and australites, writing science notes each fortnight for a Melbourne magazine, *The Australasian*, and producing three books of essays on scientific topics.

Influenced by my father, I accumulated a good collection of fossils, and wished to study geology. However, he persuaded me that career prospects for geologists were very poor and that medicine offered a great variety of possible careers, including research, which I even then contemplated. As well as being active in university life and sport (hockey and tennis), I became involved with the University of Adelaide—South Australian Museum anthropological expeditions from my second year in university onwards. My MD degree was based on this work and studies on Aboriginal skulls.

After graduating in December 1938, I became a resident medical officer at the Royal Adelaide Hospital, where I heard Prime Minister Robert Menzies announce, on 3 September 1939, that Australia was at war with Germany. Most of my fellow residents enlisted. However, for reasons that I cannot recall, I decided to study for a Diploma of Tropical Medicine at the University of Sydney before I enlisted. If this is viewed as a chance event, it certainly had a major effect on my career. The skills that I acquired led to my appointment, in 1942, as pathologist to the 2/2 Australian General Hospital, a 1200-bed hospital near Hughenden in central north Queensland, and in 1943 as a malariologist in Papua New Guinea.

A chance consequence of my transfer to this hospital was meeting my future wife. She was a nursing sister who worked as a transfusion expert and was awarded an Associate Royal Red Cross (a military award given to nurses in the armed forces for outstanding services) for her work. Because at Hughenden there was not a great call for transfusions, she worked part-time in my laboratory, helping with malaria diagnosis. She was subsequently a tower of strength in the social aspects of my role as a departmental head and director of the John Curtin School, as well as raising our family and being involved in community work.

Infectious Diseases

My experience with malaria, scrub typhus and dengue in Papua New Guinea awakened an interest in infectious diseases, and led directly to my first post-war job, at the Walter and Eliza Hall Institute. Its Director, Macfarlane Burnet, asked me to work on the experimental epidemiology of infectious ectromelia of mice, the viral cause of which he had just shown was related to vaccinia, and thus to smallpox virus. Scientifically, the most important aspect of this work was the observation, by chance, that non-fatal cases usually had a rash (thereafter we called the disease mousepox). This led to experiments on what happened during the incubation period of this disease, and, by analogy, during the long incubation periods of human diseases such as smallpox and chickenpox. Burnet also launched me on my career as a writer of books on scientific matters, a field exploited by very few experimental scientists, but in which Burnet was a master. We coauthored the second edition of *The Production of Antibodies*, which was later to become famous for the prediction of immunological tolerance, cited as the grounds for the award of the 1960 Nobel Prize to Burnet.

After two and a half years at the Hall Institute, Burnet arranged for me to work with the renowned bacteriologist René Dubos at the Rockefeller Institute for Medical Research in New York. There, I worked on *Mycobacterium tuberculosis*. In February 1949, Sir Howard Florey offered me the foundation Chair of Microbiology in the John Curtin School of Medical Research (JCSMR), in the newly established Australian National University.

In 1950 Canberra was a very small town and, as there were no suitable laboratories there, the university had arranged with Burnet to allow me to work for a few years in the Hall Institute, where I continued with work on mycobacteria, principally on *M. ulcerans*, which had been discovered in Melbourne a few years earlier. Although I was anxious to work again on viruses, I had decided that I had skimmed the cream off mousepox.

Studying Rabbitpox

Early in 1951, myxomatosis spread throughout south-eastern Australia. As the CSIRO (the Commonwealth Scientific and Industrial Research Organisation), which was responsible for introducing the disease for rabbit control, had no virologists on its staff, I decided to make myxomatosis the main activity of my embryonic department. The virus concerned was also a poxvirus. Studies on myxomatosis, especially on changes in its virulence and the resistance of rabbits to it, were the focus of my research for the next 14 years, and provided the best natural experiment on the coevolution of viral virulence and host resistance available for a disease of vertebrates.

Initially, myxoma virus was extraordinarily virulent, killing over 99% of naturally infected rabbits. I was anxious to study the genetics of virulence of this poxvirus. However, myxoma virus was difficult to work with in the laboratory, so I screened strains of *Orthopoxvirus*, the genus to which smallpox virus belongs, and selected a variant of vaccinia virus called rabbitpox virus. Rabbitpox virus yielded many white-pock mutants, which I used to demonstrate molecular recombination. By 1962 sufficient data on myxomatosis had accumulated for me to collaborate with CSIRO zoologist Francis Ratcliffe on the book *Myxomatosis*.

Another chance event associated with books occurred about this time, again with Burnet. In 1955 he had written *The Principles of Animal Virology*, a second edition of which was published in 1960. In 1964 the publishers approached him for a third edition; he suggested that they approach me. Looking over *The Principles of Animal Virology*, I decided that I could not write a third edition of Burnet's book, and offered instead to write another book on much the same topic, entitled *The Biology of Animal Viruses*.

Publication of this book (in 1968) influenced my subsequent career. To produce it required giving up full-time laboratory work. The year I finished writing this tome (1967), the then Dean of

JCSMR resigned. I was faced with a choice of essentially starting benchwork again, to all intents and purposes as a "PhD student", or seeking the directorship of JCSMR. I chose the latter, and was appointed in September 1967.

Campaign to End Smallpox

The same year was notable for the launch of the Intensified Smallpox Eradication Programme. In 1968 the Chief of the Smallpox Eradication Unit of the World Health Organization (WHO), D.A. Henderson, invited me to join an international group of virologists with expertise in poxviruses, to discuss the possibility that monkeys with monkeypox virus (discovered a few years earlier in a monkey colony in Copenhagen) might constitute an animal reservoir of smallpox virus. We met in Moscow in March 1969, commencing an association with the Intensified Smallpox Eradication Programme that has continued to this day. I attended meetings of this committee every second year, initially as rapporteur and then as chairman. My main scientific contribution was to use my experience with white-pock mutants of rabbitpox virus to dispose of the hypothesis that smallpox virus was a white-pock mutant of monkeypox virus.

During this period my term as Director of the JCSMR came to an end and I became Director of the Centre for Resource and Environmental Studies. I resigned from most committees concerned with medicine and took on new responsibilities in the environment field, but maintained contact with the Intensified Smallpox Eradication Programme.

Apart from a visionary suggestion by Edward Jenner in 1801, the first proposal to eradicate smallpox had been made in 1953 by the first Director-General of WHO, Dr Brock Chisholm, but the World Health Assembly dismissed his proposal as unrealistic. Smallpox was again considered by the Assembly in 1958, when the Soviet Union put forward a carefully planned proposal for eradication, which was endorsed by the Assembly. The Russian suggestion was that global eradication could be achieved in 4 to 5 years by vaccinating and revaccinating up to 80% of the population of every endemic country, to produce a level of herd immunity sufficient to break the chains of transmission.

By 1966 it was clear that progress along these lines, while successful in several small countries, would never achieve global eradication, and the Assembly adopted, by a narrow margin, a resolution which included acceptance of the need for central coordination of national programs and WHO finance from its regular budget. The Intensified Smallpox Eradication Programme was launched in 1967, to be coordinated by a Smallpox Eradication Unit at WHO Headquarters in Geneva and with the goal of global eradication within 10 years. This effort was led by D.A. Henderson and Isao Arita (Assistant Chief and, from 1976 to 1982, Chief of the Smallpox Eradication Unit). Success was achieved in October 1977, just a few months after the target date.

In 1967 smallpox was endemic in 31 countries and imported cases had been reported in another 11 countries; there were probably 15 to 20 million cases of smallpox annually, with some two million deaths. The first problem facing the Smallpox Eradication Unit was to ensure that all vaccine used in the field was of acceptable potency. WHO Reference Centres for Smallpox Vaccine were established in Toronto, Canada, and Bilthoven, The Netherlands, an international meeting of vaccine producers was held, and training courses established. Regular quality control testing by the centres was applied to vaccine donated through WHO, donated under bilateral aid programs, and produced in the endemic countries themselves. By 1970 these measures had ensured that most of the vaccine used in the program reached WHO standards for potency, heat stability and bacterial content.

Aggressive Vaccination Effort

The other major change in strategy was the elevation of surveillance and containment to a pre-eminent place. Discovery of a case was followed by containment by vaccination of all contacts, and then for all persons, in ever-increasing distances from the affected household. Associated with containment, an attempt was made to discover the source of the index case and follow this up with vaccination in that village.

By systematically applying these strategies, and by dint of a great deal of hard work and some good luck, smallpox was progressively eliminated from each of the countries in which it had been endemic in 1967. Concurrently with the elimination of smallpox from countries, groups of countries or continents, a system of "certification" of eradication by teams of independent international experts was developed. I served as a member of some of these teams and in 1977 was asked to chair a Global Commission for the Certification of Smallpox Eradication. I became more fully involved with the certification program, and, as well as serving on the International Commissions for India and Malawi, carried out inspections in China, South Africa and Namibia, countries then not members of WHO.

On the afternoon of Sunday, 9 December 1979, after four days of intensive discussion and argument, all members of the Global Commission accepted its final report. This proclaimed that the world had been freed of smallpox. The report also made 19 recommendations on vaccination, vaccine stocks, stocks of smallpox virus, monkeypox, publications and the like. On 8 May 1980, I presented this report to the World Health Assembly; it was accepted with acclamation.

My association with the smallpox eradication program did not end there, for I was appointed chairman of the Committee on Orthopoxvirus Infections, which monitored the implementation of the recommendations and has continued to meet periodically as an *ad hoc* committee until this year.

More demanding was my involvement with fulfilling the recommendation that a book about the program should be produced. Influenced by my father's example and my parents' genes, I had by this time published several scientific books, so I looked forward to this prospect. I had now (1980) formally retired and applied myself full-time to this task, assisted by the three former heads of the Smallpox Eradication Unit. Eight years later, in January 1988, a massive book of almost 1500 pages, *Smallpox and Its Eradication*, was launched at a meeting of the Executive Board of WHO. Later that year three of the authors, Henderson, Arita and I, shared the Japan Prize, given that year for preventive medicine.

Beating Back Measles

By C.A. de Quadros, B.S. Hersh, A.C. Nogueira,
P.A. Carrasco, and C.M. da Silveira

Measles is a highly contagious viral disease that used to be quite common in the United States until the development of an effective vaccine. However, it continues to afflict millions of children in the world's poorer countries. Although commonly regarded as a mild disease, measles can have serious consequences, including pneumonia, brain damage, and even death. The World Health Organization (WHO) estimates that more than half of the 1.6 million children who die from preventable diseases each year are killed by measles. With no cure in sight, physicians regard the measles vaccine as the most important tool in dealing with the disease. In the following selection, immunization specialists from the Pan American Health Organization (PAHO) describe the successes and challenges of a campaign to eradicate measles from the Americas through coordinated vaccination efforts. Their experiences are being studied by experts involved in the WHO's strategy to greatly reduce the incidence of measles in other parts of the world where it continues to afflict children. Lead author C.A. de Quadros is a staff physician with the Pan American Health Organization. In addition to his medical degree, he holds a master's of public health. His coauthors are on the staff of PAHO's Special Program for Vaccines and Immunization.

I n 1994, the countries of the Region of the Americas established the goal of eliminating measles from the Western Hemisphere by the year 2000. Measles is one of the most highly infectious diseases, and in the prevaccine era, essentially everyone eventually acquired measles infection, usually as a very young child. Humans are the only reservoir for measles infection, although some

C.A. de Quadros, B.S. Hersh, A.C. Nogueira, P.A. Carrasco, and C.M. da Silveira, "Measles Eradication: Experience in the Americas," *CDC Morbidity and Mortality Weekly Report*, December 31, 1999, pp. 57–64.

other primates, such as monkeys, can be infected. The patient is most infectious during the prodromal [early] phase of the disease before the onset of symptoms such as fever and rash. Communicability decreases rapidly after the appearance of rash.

Live attenuated measles vaccine, first licensed for use in the USA in 1963, was in widespread use by the late 1970s. Immunization with this vaccine has been demonstrated to be protective for over 20 years, but immunity following vaccination is thought to be life-long. Vaccine efficacy has been shown to be 90–95%. Because of interference of maternal antibodies, vaccine efficacy increases steadily after 6 months of age, reaching its maximum plateau of 95–98% at 12–15 months of age.

By 1982, virtually all countries in the world had incorporated measles vaccine into their routine vaccination schedules and, since then, coverage has increased substantially. By 1990, the estimated overall global coverage for children by 2 years of age was approximately 70%. Before the introduction of measles vaccine, epidemics characteristically tended to recur every 2–3 years in most densely populous areas, but with the widespread use of measles vaccine, the interval between outbreaks has lengthened and an increase in the average age of infection is observed. In the developing countries which recently introduced the vaccine and have not yet achieved high immunization coverage, measles remains endemic with most cases occurring in young children and infants. WHO has estimated that 40 million measles cases, with 1 million deaths, are still occurring annually in the world.

Eradication Strategy

The Pan American Health Organization (PAHO) recommends a strategy that aims to interrupt rapidly measles transmission by initially conducting a one-time-only mass campaign targeting all children aged 9 months to 14 years and to maintain interruption of transmission by sustaining high population immunity through vaccination of infants at routine health services facilities, supplemented by periodic mass campaigns conducted approximately every 4 years, targeting all 1-4-year-olds, regardless of previous vaccination status. "Fever and rash" surveillance and measles virus surveillance are other key elements of the strategy.

The initial "catch-up" measles vaccination campaign is conducted during periods of low measles transmission. All children aged 9 months to 14 years, irrespective of vaccination history or reported history of measles infection, are immunized with measles vaccine within a very short period of time, usually one week to one month. These campaigns result in a rapid increase in population immunity and, if high enough coverage is achieved, measles transmission is interrupted. After a catch-up campaign has been conducted, there may still remain pockets of susceptible children. To detect these, a post-catch-up campaign evaluation is conducted and special vaccination (mop-up) activities are carried out in such areas to increase their level of coverage.

After the initial catch-up campaign and mop-up operations, routine immunization services (keep-up) should ensure that all new birth cohorts of children are vaccinated with a dose of measles vaccine at 12–15 months of age. However, there will inevitably be an accumulation of susceptible preschool-aged children over time. Two major factors contribute to the accumulation of susceptibles. First, measles vaccine is not 100% effective, thus leaving some children unprotected despite vaccination. Second, measles vaccination coverage for each birth cohort will fall short of 100%, however effective the programme.

Thus, the PAHO strategy calls for periodic vaccination campaigns to be conducted among preschool-aged children (children less than 5 years of age). This is recommended whenever the estimated number of susceptible preschool-aged children approaches the size of an average birth cohort. In the Americas it is recommended that such follow-up campaigns be conducted every 4 years.

A sensitive surveillance system is essential for a measles elimination programme. This includes the notification and timely investigation of infants and children with suspected measles. Serological testing for anti-measles antibodies in blood specimens obtained from suspected cases is used to confirm or rule out measles virus infection. A confirmed measles case must either have serological confirmation or an epidemiological link to another laboratory-confirmed measles case. Laboratory sequencing of the measles virus genome from isolates can help to determine geographical sources of outbreaks and identify pathways of transmission.

Since 1991, all PAHO member countries, with the exception of the USA, have conducted catch-up measles vaccination campaigns, and most countries have already conducted at least one follow-up campaign.

Major Reductions Achieved

In the Region of the Americas, reported cases have decreased markedly and the majority of countries have reported a 99% reduction in measles incidence compared to the prevaccine era. Several countries have already interrupted transmission. In Cuba, after the catch-up campaign conducted in 1987 and a follow-up campaign conducted in 1991, fewer than 20 confirmed measles cases were reported annually between 1989 and 1992, with the last serologically confirmed case occurring in June 1993.

Other countries in the Region of the Americas in which transmission apparently has been interrupted include the English-speaking Caribbean, which conducted its catch-up measles vaccination campaign during May 1991. Between September 1991 and March 1997, only two confirmed measles cases were reported in the English-speaking Caribbean—in Barbados (one acquired the infection in New York City, and no source of infection could be found for the other). No secondary spread of infection occurred. After Chile conducted its catch-up campaign during 1992, only one case was discovered in 1992 (imported from Peru) and one in 1993 (imported from Venezuela). No further spread occurred until a recent importation from Brazil, in 1997. Transmission in this outbreak has now been interrupted.

During 1996 the Region of the Americas recorded an all-time low of only 2109 confirmed measles cases. In 1997, however, there was a relative resurgence of the disease in Brazil. Up to 31 January 1998, a total of 78,033 suspected measles cases was reported from the countries of the Americas. One third of these (26,722 (34.2%)) have been confirmed; and 25,559 of these were reported from Brazil alone which, with Canada (580 confirmed cases), accounted for 97.8% of the total confirmed cases in the region. Other countries reporting measles cases in 1997 included Guadeloupe (128 cases), USA (127 cases), Paraguay (124 cases), Argentina (58 cases), Chile (47 cases), and Costa Rica (14 cases). The outbreaks in Argentina, Chile, Costa Rica, . . . and Paraguay originated from importations from Brazil, and the Guadeloupe epidemic was due to an importation from metropolitan France in late 1996. This island had not implemented PAHO's recommended measles eradication strategy.

In the USA, over half of the cases originated from importations from Europe and Asia. Spread from importations has been limited and the largest outbreak in 1997 was only 8 cases. In 1995 and 1996, there were no measles importations from Latin America or the Caribbean into the USA. In 1997, however, there were 5 confirmed imported cases from Brazil.

The majority of cases from Brazil have been reported from Sao Paulo State, the only state in the country which did not conduct a follow-up vaccination campaign in 1995. To date, over 20,000 cases have been confirmed in this outbreak, with most cases in the city of Sao Paulo. Over 50% of cases occurred in young adults aged 20–29 years. The highest age-specific incidences are in infants, young adults aged 20–29 years, and children aged 1–4 years, respectively. To date, 20 measles-related deaths have been reported, most in infants aged less than 1 year. An investigation of measles cases in adults found that the majority were occurring among young adults who were members of certain risk-groups, including men who recently migrated to cities from rural areas in the north-east of the country to work in construction projects, other manual labourers, students, health care workers, persons working in the tourist industry, and military recruits.

Measles virus has been isolated from several patients from this outbreak and the genomic sequencing of these isolates revealed that the virus circulating in Sao Paulo is virtually identical to that currently circulating in Western Europe, which strongly suggests importation from the latter area. The Sao Paulo outbreak is waning after implementation of an aggressive outbreak response, which included a follow-up campaign targeting all children aged 1–4 years, selective mop-up vaccination in schools, and vaccination of young adult members of groups at high-risk for measles.

Until 1997, the English-speaking Caribbean had not reported a single confirmed case of measles in a period of over 5 years. However, in 1997 two laboratory-confirmed measles cases were detected. The first was reported from the Bahamas. The patient, a young adult, had rash onset in March 1997. The direct source of transmission was not identified, but it is strongly suspected that the patient contracted measles from a tourist. A search, involving a review of over 80,000 diagnoses from health facilities in the country, was made to identify any additional cases of measles. The second case was reported from Trinidad and Tobago. It occurred in a young adult Italian sailor who had rash onset in April. The patient had acquired measles in Italy. A specimen was collected and found to be positive for measles at the measles laboratory of the

Caribbean Epidemiology Centre (CAREC). No spread of cases was identified despite careful investigation.

Lessons Learned

While the resurgence of measles in the Americas during 1997 represents a major increase compared to cases reported in 1996, these cases represent only about 10% of those reported in 1990. Nevertheless, important lessons can be learned from this experience. First, the lack of a timely follow-up vaccination campaign in Sao Paulo, in 1995, for children aged 1–4 years, combined with low routine measles vaccination coverage (keep-up) among infants using a 2-dose schedule, allowed for a rapid and dangerous accumulation of susceptible children. Second, the presence of large numbers of young adults who escaped both natural measles infection and measles vaccination increased the risk of a measles outbreak. Third, measles virus was imported into Sao Paulo, probably from Europe. Finally, the high population density in Sao Paulo facilitated contact between persons infected with measles and susceptible persons.

Measles case surveillance combined with molecular epidemiological data suggest that the countries of the Region of the Americas are constantly being challenged by imported measles virus from other regions of the world where measles remains endemic. During 1997, 27 separate importations of measles virus were detected from Europe, 18 from Asia, and 2 from Africa which resulted in measles transmission. These data, however, probably severely underestimate the true number of measles importations since many imported cases may not seek medical care and do not result in further transmission.

The outbreaks in Brazil, Canada and other countries of the region suggest that there may be a significant number of young adults who remain susceptible to the disease. For practical purposes, persons born before 1960 in most countries of the Region of the Americas can be assumed to have been exposed to naturally circulating measles virus, and thus be immune to the disease. Therefore, the overwhelming majority of adults are already immune, and most susceptible young adults are at very low risk of being exposed to measles virus.

Mass campaigns among young adults are not recommended. However, experience has shown that certain institutional settings (e.g., colleges and universities, military barracks, health care facilities, large factories, and prisons) can facilitate measles transmission, if measles virus is introduced to such populations. In addition to persons living or working in these settings, adolescents and young adults who travel to countries with endemic measles transmission are at increased risk of being exposed to and contracting measles. To prevent the occurrence of measles outbreaks among adolescents and young adults, efforts are needed to ensure measles immunity in these potentially high-risk groups and persons travelling to measles-endemic countries.

The measles experience of 1997 clearly demonstrates that there are two major challenges to the region's measles eradication goal by the year 2000. First, the countries of the Region of the Americas need to maintain the highest population immunity possible in infants and children, and to target vaccination to adolescents and young adults who are at highest risk for being exposed to measles virus. Second, increased efforts are needed in other regions of the world to improve measles control and to decrease the number of exported measles cases to the Region of the Americas. As long as measles virus circulates anywhere in the world, the Region of the Americas will remain at risk for measles. The successful achievement of the measles elimination goal in the Region of the Americas will require full implementation of PAHO's recommended immunization strategy in all countries of the region and improved measles control/elimination in other regions of the world, especially Europe and Asia, with the ultimate goal of global eradication of the measles virus.

A Vaccine for Chicken Pox

By the World Health Organization

Of all the childhood diseases, one of the most common and least-feared is chicken pox. The sight of a victim struggling to resist scratching the itchy pustules that come with the disease has long been a source of mirth. However, chicken pox is no joke. The World Health Organization (WHO), author of the selection that follows, reports that until a vaccine for varicella (the proper name for chicken pox) was introduced, about one hundred people a year died from the disease. Additionally, more than ten thousand people a year were hospitalized because of complications from varicella. Since 1995, the varicella vaccine has saved Americans an estimated five times its cost, according to WHO. However, it is not without some risks, and its ability to protect against recurrences of the varicella virus in later life is not yet known. Nevertheless, WHO recommends it be extensively used in hopes of eradicating the disease. At the same time, it acknowledges that, given the relatively low rate of complications from chicken pox, there are other disease threats that command a higher priority in worldwide vaccination campaigns. The World Health Organization is a UN agency specializing in global health issues. It was established on April 7, 1948. WHO is governed by 192 member states through the World Health Assembly.

Varicella [or chickenpox] is a highly communicable viral disease with worldwide distribution. In temperate climates of the Northern Hemisphere, varicella occurs mainly in the period from late winter to early spring. Secondary attack rates reach close to 90% in susceptible household contacts. Varicella-zoster virus (VZV) is the causative agent and is transmitted by droplets,

World Health Organization, "Immunizations, Vaccines and Biologicals: Varicella Vaccine," www.who.int, May 2003. Copyright © 2003 by the World Health Organization. Reproduced by permission.

aerosol or direct contact, and patients are usually contagious from a few days before rash onset until the rash has crusted over. Once a case has occurred in a susceptible population, it is very hard to prevent an outbreak. As subclinical [unnoticeable] infection is rare, the disease is experienced by almost every human being. . . .

Symptoms and Effects

Varicella is characterized by an itchy, vesicular rash, usually starting on the scalp and face, and initially accompanied by fever and malaise. As the rash gradually spreads to the trunk and extremities, the first vesicles dry out. It normally takes about 7–10 days for all crusts to disappear. . . .

Although varicella is usually a benign childhood disease, and rarely rated as an important public health problem, the course may occasionally be complicated by VZV-induced pneumonia or encephalitis. . . . In patients suffering from immunodeficiencies, including HIV infection, varicella tends to be severe and zoster may be recurrent. Severe and fatal varicella may also occur occasionally in children taking systemic steroids for treatment of asthma. In general, complications as well as fatalities from varicella are more commonly observed in adults than in children. Case-fatality ratios (deaths per 100 000 cases) in healthy adults are 30–40 times higher than among children five to nine years of age. Hence, if a vaccination programme is undertaken, it is important to ensure high vaccination coverage in order that prevention programmes do not cause changes in the epidemiology of varicella resulting in higher incidence rates in adults.

In about 10%–20% of the cases, varicella is followed later in life by herpes zoster, or shingles, a painful vesicular rash with dermatomal distribution. Most cases of zoster occur after the age of 50 or in immunocompromised persons. It is a relatively common complication in HIV-positive persons. . . .

The Pathogen

VZV is a double-stranded DNA virus belonging to the herpesvirus family. Only one serotype is known, and humans are the only reservoir. VZV enters the host through the nasopharyngeal mucosa [nasal tissues], and almost invariably produces clinical disease in susceptible individuals. The incubation period is usually

14–16 . . . days. Following varicella, the virus persists in sensory nerve ganglia, from where it may later be reactivated to cause zoster. Serum antibodies against viral membrane proteins and glycoproteins are utilized in diagnostic tests, but are less reliable as correlates of immunity, particularly to zoster. . . .

Immune Response

Natural infection induces lifelong immunity to clinical varicella in almost all immunocompetent persons. Newborn babies of immune mothers are protected by passively acquired antibodies during their first months of life. Temporary protection of non-immune individuals can be obtained by injection of varicella-zoster immune globulin within three days of exposure. The immunity acquired in the course of varicella prevents neither the establishment of a latent VZV infection, nor the possibility of subsequent reactivation as zoster. Although antibody assays are conveniently used as an indication of previous infection or response to vaccination, failure to detect antibodies against VZV does not necessarily imply susceptibility, as the corresponding cell-mediated immunity may still be intact. On the other hand, about 20% of persons aged 55–65 show no measurable cell-mediated immunity to VZV in spite of persisting antibodies, and a history of previous varicella. Zoster is closely correlated to a fall in the level of VZV-specific T-cells [a kind of antibody] and an episode of zoster will reactivate the specific T-cell response.

Benefit of Vaccine Control

Except for vaccination, no countermeasures are likely to control the dissemination of varicella or the frequency of zoster in a susceptible community. Varicella-zoster immune globulin and anti-herpesviral drugs are very costly, and mainly applied for post-exposure prophylaxis or the treatment of varicella in persons at high risk of severe disease. Due to its extremely contagious nature, varicella is experienced by almost every child or young adult in the world. Each year from 1990 to 1994, prior to availability of varicella vaccine, about 4 million cases of varicella occurred in the United States. Of these cases approximately 10 000 required hospitalization and 100 died. Although varicella is not commonly perceived as an important public health problem, the socioeconomic consequences in industrialized countries of a disease that affects practically every child and causes the carer to be absent from work should not be underestimated.

The recently marketed varicella vaccines have been shown to be safe and effective. From a societal perspective, a recent cost-benefit analysis in the United States showed that routine chickenpox vaccination is likely to save five times the investment. Even when only direct costs were considered, benefits almost balanced the costs. Similar studies from developing countries are not available. However, the socioeconomic aspect of varicella is likely to be of less importance in countries with a different social organization. On the other hand, the public health impact of varicella and zoster may be increasing in regions with high rates of HIV.

It is not yet sufficiently documented that the varicella vaccine, administered either in childhood or in adult populations, will protect against zoster. However, several indications, including the results of vaccination studies in certain immunodeficient groups, are encouraging in this regard. The public health as well as the socioeconomic impact of this vaccine would increase drastically if it was proved to protect against zoster in the general population. In industrialized countries considerable amounts are spent on medical care in complicated cases of zoster in immunocompromised or elderly persons, and the increasing incidence of zoster in HIV-affected areas is well documented.

Vaccination Methods

The currently marketed varicella vaccines are based on the so-called Oka strain of VZV, which has been modified through sequential propagation in different cell cultures. Various formulations of such live, attenuated vaccines have been tested extensively and are approved for use in Japan, the Republic of Korea, the United States and several countries in Europe. Some formulations are approved for use at nine months of age and older.

Following a single dose of the above-mentioned vaccines, seroconversion [an immune response] is seen in about 95% of healthy children. From a logistic as well as an epidemiological point of view, the optimal age for varicella vaccination is 12–24 months. In Japan and several other countries one dose of the vaccine is considered sufficient, regardless of age. In the United States, two doses, four to eight weeks apart, are recommended for adolescents and adults, in whom 78% were found to have sero-converted [antibodies in their blood] after the first, and 99% after the second dose of the vaccine. Children below 13 years of age receive only one dose.

Small studies, using formulations different to that currently licensed in the United States, show that when the vaccine is administered within three days after exposure to VZV, a post-exposure protective efficacy of at least 90% may be expected. Varicella in persons who have received the vaccine ("break-through varicella") is substantially less severe than the disease in unvaccinated individuals. Further studies are needed to clarify the post-exposure efficacy of the currently-licensed product, especially in outbreak situations. . . .

As judged from the Japanese experience, immunity to varicella following vaccination lasts for at least 10–20 years. In the United States, childhood vaccination against varicella provides 70%–90% protection against infection, and more than 95% protection against severe disease 7–10 years after immunization. From investigation of a varicella outbreak in a day-care centre, post-licensure efficacy was found to be 100% in preventing severe disease and 86% in preventing all disease. The attack rate in unvaccinated susceptible children was 88%. It is likely, but as yet not proved, that some protection is also achieved against zoster. However, in Japan as well as in the United States, the vaccine coverage in the population is quite limited, and the continued circulation of wild type VZV is likely to cause post-vaccination boosting. Hence, the long-term protection induced by the vaccine alone is difficult to assess at this time.

In immunocompromised persons, including patients with advanced HIV infection, varicella vaccination is currently contraindicated for fear of disseminated vaccine-induced disease. Vaccine safety is however being evaluated in asymptomatic HIV-infected children with CD4 counts [a measure of T-cells indicating immune strength] of more than 1000, and a killed varicella vaccine has been studied in VZV-positive bone marrow transplant patients where a multiple-dose schedule has been shown to reduce the severity of zoster. Furthermore, in carefully supervised trials, patients with leukaemia in remission or solid tumours before chemotherapy, and uraemic patients waiting for transplantation, have received the vaccine. In most cases, one to two doses resulted in high rates of protection, with only moderate side-effects. A significant reduction in the rate of zoster has also been recorded in these patients.

Vaccine Risks

In healthy children the adverse effects of the vaccination are limited to some local swelling and redness at the site of injection during the first hours following vaccination (27%), and in a few cases (fewer than 5%) the vaccinees experience a mild varicella-like disease with rash within four weeks. In a placebo-controlled study involving 900 healthy children and adolescents, pain and redness at the site of vaccination were the only documented adverse events following vaccination. The vaccine was similarly well tolerated by already-immune persons who were inadvertently immunized. Rare occasions of mild zoster following vaccination show that the currently used vaccine strains may induce latency, with the subsequent risk of reactivation. . . .

Global Perspective

The likelihood that every child will contract varicella, combined with a socioeconomic structure that implies high indirect costs for each case, make varicella relatively important in industrialized countries with temperate climates. Routine childhood vaccination against this disease is estimated to be cost-effective in such areas. Limited seroprevalence studies have suggested that susceptibility to varicella is more common among adults in tropical than in temperate climates. Thus, from the public health point of view, varicella could prove to be more important in tropical regions than previously assumed, in particular in areas where HIV is highly endemic. The impact of varicella in the global context requires further investigation. On the other hand, in most developing countries, other new vaccines, including hepatitis B, rotavirus, as well as conjugated Hib and pneumococcal vaccines, have the potential for a much greater public health impact, and should therefore be given priority over varicella vaccines. Hence, at the present time WHO does not recommend the inclusion of varicella vaccination into the routine immunization programmes of developing countries.

Varicella vaccine may be used either at an individual level to protect susceptible adolescents and adults, or at a population level, to cover all children as part of a national immunization programme. Vaccination of adolescents and adults will protect at-risk individuals, but will not have a significant impact on the epidemiology of the disease on a population basis. On the other hand, extensive use as a routine vaccine in children will have a significant impact on the epidemiology of the disease. If sustained high coverage can be achieved, the disease may virtually disappear. If only partial coverage can be obtained, the epidemiology may shift, leading to an increase in the number of cases in older children and adults. Hence, routine childhood varicella immunization programmes should emphasize high, sustained coverage.

CHAPTER 3

Setbacks and Controversies

An Overview of Safety Issues

By the National Immunization Program

All medical treatments carry some risk, and vaccines are certainly no exception. Indeed, few procedures have more detailed projections of terrible consequences for a minority of recipients than vaccines. In the following selection, the National Immunization Program (NIP) offers an overview of vaccine safety, including details of how people who suffer bad reactions are compensated. As the selection makes clear, this compensation system came about because lawsuits by parents who believed their children had been injured or killed by vaccines drove the cost of the national program beyond public endurance. Congress passed an act in 1986 creating a national no-fault system for collecting reports of adverse reactions and paying out set sums to the victims. Although vaccine injuries are rare, the system collects more than ten thousand reports on adverse incidents each year, the NIP reports. Meantime, it says, vaccines continue to become safer. The National Immunization Program is a unit of the federal government's Centers for Disease Control and Prevention. As part of its activities, NIP provides the documents required to file a complaint or safety report on vaccines.

Perhaps the greatest success story in public health is the reduction of infectious diseases resulting from the use of vaccines. Routine immunization has eradicated smallpox from the globe and led to the near elimination of wild polio virus. Vaccines have reduced preventable infectious diseases to an all-time low and now few people experience the devastating effects of measles, pertussis and other illnesses. Prior to approval by the Food and Drug Administration (FDA), vaccines are extensively tested by scientists to ensure that they are effective and safe. Vac-

National Immunization Program, "Overview of Vaccine Safety," www.cdc.gov, 2000.

cines are the best defense we have against infectious diseases. However, no vaccine is 100% safe or effective. Differences in the way individual immune systems react to a vaccine account for rare occasions when people are not protected following immunization or when they experience side effects.

As infectious diseases continue to decline, some people have become less interested in the consequences of preventable illnesses like diphtheria and tetanus. Instead, they have become increasingly concerned about the risks associated with vaccines. After all, vaccines are given to healthy individuals, many of whom are children, and therefore a high standard of safety is required. Since vaccination is such a common and memorable event, any illness following immunization may be attributed to the vaccine. While some of these reactions may be caused by the vaccine, many of them are unrelated events that occur after vaccination by coincidence. Therefore, the scientific research that attempts to distinguish true vaccine side effects from unrelated, chance occurrences is crucial. This knowledge is necessary in order to maintain public confidence in immunization programs. As science continues to advance, we are constantly striving to develop safer vaccines and improve delivery in order to better protect ourselves against disease. This overview will focus on vaccine research, how vaccines are licensed, how safety is monitored, and how risks are communicated to the public.

Lawsuits over Vaccines

The topic of vaccine safety became prominent during the mid 1970's with increases in lawsuits filed on behalf of those presumably injured by the diphtheria, pertussis, tetanus (DPT) vaccine. Legal decisions were made and damages awarded despite the lack of scientific evidence to support vaccine injury claims. As a result of the liability, prices soared and several manufacturers halted production. A vaccine shortage resulted and public health officials became concerned about the return of epidemic disease. In order to reduce liability and respond to public health concerns, Congress passed the National Childhood Vaccine Injury Act (NCVIA) in 1986. This act was influential in many ways.

As a result of the NCVIA, the National Vaccine Program Office (NVPO) was established within the Department of Health and Human Services (DHHS). The responsibility of NVPO is to coordinate immunization-related activities between all DHHS agencies including the Centers for Disease Control and Prevention (CDC), Food and Drug Administration (FDA), National Institutes of Health (NIH) and the Health Resources and Services Administration (HRSA).

The NCVIA requires that all health care providers who administer vaccines containing diphtheria, tetanus, pertussis, polio, measles, mumps, rubella, hepatitis B, *Haemophilus influenzae* type b and varicella must provide a Vaccine Information Statement (VIS) to the vaccine recipient, their parent or legal guardian prior to each dose. A VIS must be given with every vaccination including each dose in a multi-dose series. Each VIS contains a brief description of the disease as well as the risks and benefits of the vaccine. VISs are developed by the CDC and distributed to state and local health departments as well as individual providers.

The NCVIA also mandates that all health care providers must report certain adverse events following vaccination to the Vaccine Adverse Event Reporting System (VAERS). This system will be described in detail later in the overview.

No-Fault Compensation System

Under the NCVIA, the National Vaccine Injury Compensation Program (NVICP) was created to compensate those injured by vaccines on a "no fault" basis. This program will be described in detail later in the overview.

The NCVIA established a committee from the Institute of Medicine (IOM) to review the existing literature on vaccine adverse events (health effects occurring after immunization that may or may not be related to the vaccine). This group concluded that there are limitations in our knowledge of the risks associated with vaccines. Of the 76 adverse events they reviewed for a causal relationship, 50 (66%) had no or inadequate research. Specifically, IOM identified the following problems:

1. limited understanding of biological processes that underlie adverse events

2. incomplete and inconsistent information from individual reports

3. poorly constructed research studies (not enough people enrolled for a long enough period of time)

4. inadequate systems to track vaccine adverse events

5. few experimental studies published in the medical literature.

Significant progress has been made over the past few years to better monitor adverse events and conduct research relevant to vaccine safety. Before vaccines are licensed by the FDA, they are extensively tested in the laboratory and in human beings to ensure their safety. First, computers are used to predict how the vaccine will interact with the immune system. Then researchers test the vaccine on animals including mice, guinea pigs, rabbits and monkeys. Once the vaccine successfully completes these laboratory tests, it is approved for use in clinical studies by the FDA. During clinical trials, the vaccine is tested on human beings. Participation in these studies is completely voluntary. Many individuals choose to contribute their time and energy for the advancement of science. Informed consent must be obtained from all participants before they become involved in research. This ensures that they understand the purpose of the study, potential risks and are willing to participate. Volunteers agree to receive the vaccine and undergo any medical testing necessary to assess its safety and efficacy.

Tough Requirements

Vaccine licensure is a lengthy process that may take ten years or longer. The FDA requires that vaccines undergo three phases of clinical trials in human beings before they can be licensed for use in the general public. Phase one trials are small, involving only 20–100 volunteers, and last only a few months. The purpose of phase one trials is to evaluate basic safety and identify very common adverse events. Phase two trials are larger and involve several hundred participants. These studies last anywhere from several months to two years and collect additional information on safety and efficacy. Data gained from phase two trials can be used to determine the composition of the vaccine, how many doses are necessary and a profile of common adverse events. Unless the vaccine is completely ineffective or causes serious side effects, the trials are expanded to phase three which involve several hundred to several thousand volunteers. Typically these trials last several years. Because the vaccinated group can be compared to those who have not received the vaccine, researchers are able to identify true side effects.

If the clinical trials demonstrate that the vaccine is safe and effective, the manufacturer applies to the FDA for two licenses, one for the vaccine (product license) and one for the production plant (establishment license). During the application process, the FDA reviews the clinical trial data and proposed product labeling. In addition, the FDA inspects the plant and goes over manufacturing protocols to ensure that vaccines are produced in a safe and consistent manner. Only after the FDA is satisfied that the vaccine is safe is it licensed for use in the general population.

After a vaccine is licensed for public use, its safety is continually monitored. The FDA requires all manufacturers to submit samples from each vaccine lot prior to its release. In addition, the manufacturers must provide the FDA with their test results for vaccine safety, potency and purity. Each lot must be tested because vaccines are sensitive to environmental factors (like temperature) and can be contaminated during production. During the last ten years, only three vaccine lots have been recalled by the FDA. One lot was mislabeled and another was contaminated with particles during production. A third lot was recalled after the FDA discovered potential problems with the manufacturing process at a production plant.

While clinical trials provide important information on vaccine safety, the data are somewhat limited because of the small number (hundreds to thousands) of study participants. Rare side effects and delayed reactions may not be evident until the vaccine is administered to millions of people. Therefore, the Federal Government has established a surveillance system to monitor adverse events that occur following vaccination. This project is known as the Vaccine Adverse Events Reporting System (VAERS). More recently, large-linked databases (LLDBs) containing information on millions of individuals have been created in order to study rare vaccine side effects.

Bad Effects Reported

The National Childhood Vaccine Injury Act of 1986 mandated that all health care providers report certain adverse events that occur following vaccination. As a result, the Vaccine Adverse Events Reporting System (VAERS) was established by the FDA and the Centers for Disease Control and Prevention (CDC) in 1990. VAERS provides a mechanism for the collection and analysis of adverse events associated with vaccines currently licensed in the United States. Adverse events are defined as health effects that occur after immunization that may or may not be related to the vaccine. VAERS data are continually monitored in order to detect previously unknown adverse events or increases in known adverse events.

Approximately 10,000–12,000 VAERS reports are filed annually, with 20% classified as serious (causing disability, hospitalization, life threatening illness or death). Anyone can file a VAERS report including health care providers, manufacturers, vaccine recipients or, when appropriate, parents/guardians. Those who have experienced an adverse reaction following immunization are encouraged to seek help from a health care professional when filling out the form. VAERS forms can be obtained in several ways. Each year the form is mailed to more than 200,000 physicians specializing in pediatrics, family practice, internal medicine, infectious diseases, emergency medicine, obstetrics and gynecology. In addition, copies are sent to health departments and clinics that administer vaccines. The VAERS form requests the following information: the type of vaccine received, the timing of vaccination, the onset of the adverse event, current illnesses or medication, past history of adverse events following vaccination and demographic information about the recipient (age, gender, etc.). The form is pre-addressed and stamped so it can be mailed directly to VAERS. . . .

A contractor, under the supervision of FDA and CDC, collects the information and enters it into a database. Those reporting an adverse event to VAERS receive a confirmation letter by mail indicating that the form was received. This letter will contain a VAERS identification number. Additional information may be submitted to VAERS using the assigned identification number. Selected cases of serious adverse reactions are followed up at 60 days and one year post-vaccination to check the recovery status of the patient. The FDA and CDC have access to VAERS data and use this information to monitor vaccine safety and conduct appropriate research studies. VAERS data (minus any personal information) is also available to the public.

Investigating Safety

While VAERS provides useful information on vaccine safety, the data are somewhat limited. Specifically, judgments about causality (whether the vaccine was truly responsible for an adverse event) cannot be made from VAERS reports because of incomplete information. VAERS reports often lack important information such as laboratory results. As a result, researchers have turned more recently to large-linked databases (LLDBs) in order to study vaccine safety. LLDBs provide scientists with access to the complete medical records of millions of individuals receiving vaccines (all identifying information is deleted to protect the confidentiality of the patient). One example of a LLDB is the Vaccine Safety Datalink (VSD) project described below, which is coordinated by the CDC. Studies conducted using LLDBs, like the VSD, are also known as post-marketing research or phase four clinical trials.

The gaps that exist in the scientific knowledge of rare vaccine side effects prompted the CDC to develop the Vaccine Safety Datalink (VSD) project in 1990. This project involves partnerships with seven large health maintenance organizations (HMOs) to continually monitor vaccine safety. VSD is an example of a large-linked database (LLDB) and includes information on more than six million people. All vaccines administered within the study population are recorded. Available data include vaccine type, date of vaccination, concurrent vaccinations (those given during the same visit), the manufacturer, lot number and injection site. Medical records are then monitored for potential adverse events resulting from immunization. The VSD project allows for planned vaccine safety studies as well as timely investigations of hypotheses. At present, the VSD project is examining potential associations between vaccines and a number of serious conditions. The database is also being used to test new vaccine safety hypotheses that result from the medical literature, VAERS, changes in the immunization schedule or from the introduction of new vaccines. This project is a powerful and cost-effective tool for the ongoing evaluation of vaccine safety.

A Table of Vaccine Injuries

In order to reduce the liability of manufacturers and health care providers, the National Childhood Vaccine Injury Act of 1986 established the National Vaccine Injury Compensation Program (NVICP). This program is intended to compensate those individuals who have been injured by vaccines on a "no-fault" basis. No fault means that people filing claims are not required to prove negligence on the part of either the health care provider or manufacturer to receive compensation. The program covers all routinely recommended childhood vaccinations. Settlements are based on the Vaccine Injury Table which summarizes the adverse events caused by vaccines. This table was developed by a panel of experts who reviewed the medical literature and identified the serious adverse events that are reasonably certain to be caused by vaccines. Examples of table injuries include anaphylaxis (severe allergic reaction), paralytic polio, and encephalopathy (general brain disorder). The Vaccine Injury Table was created to justly compensate those injured by vaccines while separating out unrelated claims. As more information becomes available from research on vaccine side effects, the Vaccine Injury Table is updated. . . .

Progress in Safety

In the last decade, numerous changes in vaccine production and administration have reduced the number of adverse events and resulted in safer vaccines. A more purified acellular pertussis vaccine has been licensed for use and has replaced the whole-cell pertussis vaccine used in DTP (diphtheria, tetanus, pertussis vaccine). Several studies have evaluated the safety and efficacy of DTaP as compared to DTP and have concluded that DTaP is effective in preventing disease and that mild side effects and serious adverse events occurred less frequently when the DTaP vaccine was given. Recent changes in the schedule of polio vaccines have also resulted in fewer reports of serious side effects. In 1997, the Advisory Committee on Immunization Practice recommended a change in the vaccination schedule to include sequential administration of inactivated polio vaccine (IPV) and oral polio vaccine (OPV). This sequential schedule was expected to produce a high level of individual protection against the disease caused by wild polio virus, while reducing by 50 to 70% vaccine-associated paralytic polio (VAPP) that occurs in 8–10 people a year who receive OPV. Today, only IPV is on the recommended childhood immunization schedule.

Informing the Public

At some point, almost every person in the United States is vaccinated. Therefore, many individuals question how vaccines are made, if they are effective and whether they are safe. People seek answers to these questions from a wide variety of sources including family, friends, health care providers, the Internet, television and medical literature. The information they receive is complex and, at times, inaccurate or misleading. Therefore, health professionals have a responsibility to provide accurate, understandable information and to handle vaccine safety concerns appropriately. As mentioned previously, the NCVIA requires all health care providers who administer vaccines to discuss the potential risks and benefits of immunization. In these situations, risk communication is a necessary skill.

Risk communication involves a dynamic exchange of information between individuals, groups and institutions. This information must acknowledge and define the risks associated with vaccination in a way the public can understand. This is difficult given the current environment where few people experience the devastation of vaccine-preventable diseases. It is further complicated by the fact that immunization is associated with some degree of personal discomfort when needles are used to administer vaccines. . . .

The importance of vaccine safety will continue to grow throughout the twenty-first century. The development and licensure of new vaccines will add to the already complicated immunization schedule. Scientists may also perfect new ways of administering immunizations including edible vaccines and needleless injections. However they are formulated or delivered, vaccines will remain the most effective tool we possess for preventing disease and improving public health in the future.

Barriers to the Development of New Vaccines

By Shannon Brownlee

The great success of vaccines in reducing childhood mortality during the twentieth century created expectations of continued success. In some fields, such as cancer or AIDS research, nature has resisted easy solutions. However, as the following selection shows, even apart from medical complexities the obstacles to development of new vaccines can be formidable. Author Shannon Brownlee says that since the 1970s, few new vaccines or antibiotics have been developed. The reason, she asserts, is largely economic. The long odds against winning approval of a new vaccine weighed against the hundreds of billions of dollars needed to develop one discourage drug companies from investing in them. However, new threats are mounting, both from old enemies like tuberculosis, which is gaining resistance, and from new exotic pathogens such as the deadly Ebola virus. She suggests that greater government incentives will be required to improve the situation. Science journalist Shannon Brownlee is a senior fellow at the New American Foundation. She previously served as a staff writer at *Discover* magazine and as a senior writer at *U.S. News & World Report.*

To anybody who has followed the course of biomedical science over the last two decades, the progress being made in understanding severe acute respiratory syndrome (SARS) appears nothing short of miraculous. SARS emerged as a global health threat in March [2003], and now, just two months later, scientists have isolated the virus causing the disease and published a complete map of the pathogen's genes. By comparison, the se-

Shannon Brownlee, "Shot in the Arm," *The New Republic*, vol. 228, May 12, 2002, p. 17. Copyright © 2002 by The New Republic, Inc. Reproduced by permission.

quencing of the human genome, an admittedly larger task, has taken more than a decade. Meanwhile, a diagnostic test for SARS, which will be produced by F. Hoffmann-La Roche, Ltd., of Basel, Switzerland, could be ready in as little as six weeks, a vastly shorter amount of time than it took to develop tests for older diseases like AIDS.

Limited Response

The fact that the medical and biotech communities are moving so quickly on the SARS front must mean that companies are similarly hard at work on a vaccine and antiviral drugs to treat it, and we can all expect to be protected from the disease within a couple of years, right? Not exactly. While SARS is rapidly turning into a health emergency in China and could have a serious impact in a virulent form in North America, biotech and pharmaceutical companies aren't exactly elbowing each other out of the way to come up with anti-SARS products. And both the government and the marketplace itself are to blame.

Even after Tommy G. Thompson, secretary of Health and Human Services, called a meeting of 60 industry executives two weeks ago [in April 2003] to personally ask for their help battling SARS, companies have been willing to appoint only small teams to look at the problem or to scour their shelves for possible antiviral compounds, which would be tried in federal laboratories. Few, if any, companies have been willing to launch a full-scale search for drugs to fight SARS.

New Vaccines Not in Pipeline

In large part, the reason for their reticence is economic. In recent decades, the pharmaceutical industry has virtually abandoned the market for drugs designed to combat microbes such as the virus that causes SARS. Convinced that infectious disease had all but been eradicated, pharmaceutical companies stopped looking for the next penicillin in the 1970s and instead turned their attention to drugs for such chronic—and extremely profitable—conditions as hypertension, high cholesterol, depression, impotence, allergies, and baldness. As a result, by the late '80s, even as many bacterial infections were becoming resistant to existing antibiotics, there weren't many new drugs in pharmaceutical-company pipelines. Indeed, in the past 30 years, the Food and Drug Administration (FDA) has approved only one new class of antibiotic.

Emerging Threats

Yet, in recent years, the world has seen a succession of emerging infections, many coming from developing Asia and Africa, ranging from AIDS and the hantavirus to Ebola, Legionnaires' disease, and now SARS. Even ancient scourges like tuberculosis are developing resistance to existing antibiotics. Yet only in response to the AIDS epidemic have we seen new treatments come out of the drug and biotech industries. And that required a massive investment in publicly funded basic research, supported by the government, as well as private research into antivirals and vaccines, conducted by industry executives with the understanding that the market for AIDS drugs and vaccines in the developed world—where consumers can pay high prices—is enormous.

High Cost, High Risk

Drug companies are now scrambling to play catch-up and produce new antibiotics and antivirals, but they are not about to pursue cures for diseases like SARS on their own. Going after an emerging infectious disease demands that companies rearrange priorities, shift research funds, and even move personnel and laboratory equipment away from drugs they are currently developing. That's not a decision executives are going to make lightly without a clear sense of what the market for an ultimate product might be. When only one in 100 promising new biological or chemical entities makes it all the way to FDA approval, and companies spend between $500 and $800 million on average to get a single product to market, it should come as no surprise that investors are wary of letting drug and biotech companies waste time and money on pursuing products that might not have a market. "No company like mine can take a risk on a drug or vaccine when we have no idea what the market will be," says Una Ryan, president and chief executive of AVANT Immunotherapeutics, Inc., a vaccine company based in Needham, Massachusetts. After all, even with a crash program, a SARS vaccine might be available in one year, but antiviral drugs will take considerably longer and cost a considerable amount to develop, test for safe human use, and market.

Government's Role

Given the pharmaceutical industry's unwillingness to focus on infectious diseases, the government may have to step in and support research on viruses like SARS. But, though the National Institutes of Health announced this week it was stepping up research on a SARS vaccine, the [George W.] Bush administration has not encouraged private-sector research. In fact, it has scared industry away by expropriating drugs from manufacturers. Two years ago, for example, companies watched aghast during the anthrax scare as Secretary Thompson obtained a rock-bottom price from German pharmaceutical giant Bayer for its antibiotic Cipro, which combats anthrax, by threatening to yank the company's patent on the drug and allowing generic manufacturers to sell it. Most bigger pharmaceutical and biotech companies have little stomach for a situation in which the government lowers profit margins in such a manner. As Sidney Taurel, the chairman and chief executive of drug giant Eli Lilly, put it in a speech on Capitol Hill last year, "Government is not going to get new miracle drugs for cost plus ten percent."

SARS is only an indicator of a wider trend. Just as the government has done little to encourage companies to research emerging viruses, so too has it failed to recognize the reality of what it will take to get drugs and vaccines to combat terrorism. In its proposed anti-bioterrorism program, Project BioShield—a plan for purchasing drugs, vaccines, and diagnostic tests for a national bioterrorism stockpile—the Bush administration would allow a company to spend several million dollars of its own money on developing a new drug or vaccine, only to see the government possibly award the contract for producing it to another company. "There is not a pharmaceutical company in the solar system that will agree to some of the terms in BioShield," says George Painter, CEO of Chimerix, Inc., a start-up that is developing a drug to treat smallpox. In addition to possibly giving away discoveries made by one company to another firm, Project BioShield excludes products that might have a commercial market outside the government bioterror stockpile. So let's say a small, struggling biotech company comes up with a new, broad-spectrum antibiotic that can fight both tularemia, a potential bioterror threat, and bacterial infections caused by a nasty bug known as staphylococcus—a product that is desperately needed by hospitals. The government specifically refuses to help the company through the research and development process, and it won't contract the company to manufacture the drug if and when it wins FDA approval. To top it off, BioShield offers companies no protection from liability should products developed with government funding cause side effects.

Public Concern About Drug Prices

Why are Project BioShield and the government's response to SARS and other infectious diseases so ignorant of market factors? Blame consumer outrage over the rising cost of drugs and profits in the pharmaceutical industry. As one government official put it, "The last thing the administration wants to do is look like they're giving a windfall to the pharmaceutical industry at a time when we're talking about drug prices."

To be sure, there are plenty of reasons to criticize the pharmaceutical industry, including its accounting and pricing practices, its army of lobbyists, and its willingness to devote a huge percentage of its budget to marketing. But, for all their faults, the biotech and pharmaceutical industries are still the nation's best—and only—hope for producing drugs and vaccines needed to battle emerging diseases and bioterror threats. If we are serious about being prepared, we will have to play by the market's rules.

Vaccinating the Armed Forces Against Anthrax Is Risky

By Garth L. Nicolson, Meryl Nass, and Nancy L. Nicolson

In 1999, the United States Department of Defense, fearing an attack on its personnel by an enemy using bioweaponry, ordered all active members of the military to be vaccinated against anthrax. According to Garth L. Nicolson, Meryl Nass, and Nancy L. Nicolson, the safety of the vaccine has not been sufficiently established. These medical professionals dispute the military's claims that the vaccine has a low incidence of negative reactions and no long-term problems at all. However, the authors admit that all they have to go on are anecdotal reports of illnesses that have arisen among military personnel since the vaccination program began. The difficulty they face is that no safety data have been released. However, they claim that a suspiciously high incidence of maladies has occurred in the wake of the anthrax immunizations among personnel at Dover Air Force Base in Delaware. Unlike vaccines for the public, which are approved and regulated by the federal Food and Drug Administration, the military obtains its anthrax vaccine from a single, unregulated provider. The authors charge that the supplier did not fully comply with FDA's guidelines, and that vaccine quality might have been substandard. In light of the uncertain risks and level of protection, the authors argue that alternatives to vaccination as a defense against bioterror should be considered. Meryl Nass is a Maine-based physician who has testified before Congress on the causes of Gulf War Syndrome. Nancy and Garth Nicolson are biomedical research scientists with the In-

Garth L. Nicolson, Meryl Nass, and Nancy L. Nicolson, "Anthrax Vaccine: Controversy over Safety and Efficacy," *Antimicrobics and Infectious Disease Newsletter*, vol. 18, 2000, pp. 1–6. Copyright © 2000 by Garth L. Nicolson, Meryl Nass, and Nancy L. Nicolson. Reproduced by permission.

stitute for Molecular Medicine in California. All three have long been publicly challenging the safety of vaccines administered to military personnel.

I n 1999 2.4 million U.S. Armed Forces personnel, including more than one million reserve and National Guard members, were ordered to receive anthrax vaccine over a period of several years. This was justified to counter an increasing threat from hostile countries and possibly terrorist groups that now or in the future will likely possess the capability of fielding weaponized anthrax spores as a Biological Weapon (BW). This decision has resulted in courts-martial and disciplinary hearings among U.S. Armed Forces personnel who have refused the anthrax vaccine on safety grounds. Are these individuals overreacting to misperceived risks from the anthrax vaccine that the military considers safe, or are there real safety concerns that should be considered?

Bacillus anthracis (anthrax) is a relatively common spore-forming soil bacterium found rarely in the U.S. but more commonly in some areas of the world as an endogenous infectious agent. *Bacillus anthracis* infection can cause death within six days of exposure to a lethal dose usually by inhalation of spores. To be effective as a BW agent a microorganism must be highly infectious, very pathogenic and stable in the air and environment for the period of time needed for dissemination and infection of large numbers of people. Spore-forming bacteria like *Bacillus anthracis* are ideal for this purpose. Spores are relatively inactive metabolically and are much more resistant to sunlight, heat, dryness and chemicals than the replicating microorganism. 'Weaponized' versions of anthrax spores are more pathogenic and survive better than spores from native strains of *Bacillus anthracis*. It is estimated that as few as 50,000 weaponized anthrax spores can kill a human after inhalation and fewer can kill small primates.

Easy to Make and Deploy

Although weaponized anthrax spores are probably the most easily manufactured BW weapon they are only one of dozens of lethal and incapacitating (causing nonlethal sicknesses) BW agents that have been produced in large quantities suitable for BW deployment and tactical use. *Bacillus anthracis* is also one of the few BW agents for which a vaccine exists that is capable of preventing some (but not all) lethal infections. Although dozens of additional microbial candidates for BW have been produced in various quantities by several countries such as bacteria (*Clostridium botulinum, Brucella melitensis, Yersinia pestis, Clostridium perfringens, Bacillus cereus, Francisella tularensis, Coxiella burnetii*, among others), toxins (ricin, aflatoxin, *Clostridium botulinum* toxin, *Staphylococcal enterotoxin* B toxin tricothecene mycotoxins, etc.), viruses (Ebola, West Nile fever, Marburg, small pox, etc.) and miscellaneous BW (rickettsias, mycoplasmas, fungi, etc.), weaponized *Bacillus anthracis* is considered one of the greatest threats because of the ease of its production, storage and dissemination (spores) as a lethal BW agent.

There are basically three methods to counter anthrax BW: active immunization, passive immunization and prophylactic antibiotics. Antibiotics have to be administered shortly before or after exposure, otherwise they won't be effective, and they cannot prevent a lethal infection once the *Bacillus anthracis* has produced signs of illness. Passive immunoprophylaxis requires quantities of immune sera or monoclonal antibodies not currently available, and their administration in a monitored hospital setting. Active immunity using vaccines on the other hand can be administered years before exposure as long as immunity is maintained. Thus vaccines can be effective as long as there is enough immunity to neutralize the *Bacillus anthracis* before it starts rapidly replicating *en masse* from its inactive spore form and producing lethal toxins. From a practical standpoint, only antibiotics and vaccines can protect the large numbers of people who could be exposed in a BW attack, and antibiotics are more effective when the BW agent(s) and its(their) antibiotic sensitivity are identified so the appropriate antibiotic(s) can be used.

Are anthrax vaccines then a reliable method of protecting against *Bacillus anthracis* BW? Not necessarily. Although vaccines can protect against accidental exposure of relatively small doses of anthrax spores that infect skin wounds, such as encountered occasionally in meat processing, it remains unproven whether anthrax vaccines will actually protect against a lethal aerosol dose of inhaled anthrax spores of the weaponized variety that are used as BW agents. This is especially true if mixtures of BW agents are used instead of single BW agents.

The anthrax vaccine in use remains unproven in its ability to stop a lethal dose of weaponized *Bacillus anthracis* spores, and there are questions about its safety. According to the U.S. Army Medical Research Institute for Infectious Disease (USAMRIID) at Fort Detrict, MD, the anthrax vaccine used by the military was determined to be safe, and adverse reactions were found to occur only at the rate of one per 50,000 doses (less than 0.002%). This has now been revised to a rate of 0.02–0.2% or higher. Moreover, in recent testimony by one of us [M.N.] to the National Academy of Sciences the safety of the anthrax vaccine and the rates of adverse reactions were questioned. Using Dover AFB as an example, the rate of chronic health problems after receiving the anthrax vaccine may be as high as 7%. The difference is that the official rates are for acute reactions only. The Department of Defense (DoD) claims that the rate for vaccine chronic reactions is zero.

A major part of the problem in assessing vaccine safety is in how vaccine adverse effects are reported. Many people who suffer from adverse anthrax vaccine effects are reluctant to step forward to seek medical care, because they have seen their colleagues' concerns dismissed as due to depression or stress. They also fear that they could lose their ability to perform their duties, as a number of the pilots and airmen at Dover AFB are now on DNIF (duties not including flying) status because of undiagnosed illnesses that began after they received their anthrax vaccinations. Lt. Colonel Randy Randolf, director of the U.S. Army's vaccination program, counters that all vaccines, the anthrax vaccine included, can produce adverse effects, such as soreness, redness, itching, swelling, and lumps at the injection site. He has stated that about 30% of men and 60% of women report these local reactions, but they usually last only a short time. Lt. Col. Randolf further describes that beyond the injection site, from 5% up to 35% of people have noticed muscle aches, joint aches, headaches, rash, chills, fever, nausea, loss of appetite, malaise, or related symptoms. It is commonly thought that these symptoms go away after a few days, and apparently there have been no completed studies of the long-term side effects of anthrax vaccine using active surveillance. Although the DoD began such a study at Tripler Army Medical Center, Honolulu in September, 1998, they have yet to release any preliminary data on long-term problems that developed after anthrax vaccination.

The difference between what military and civilian physicians conclude about adverse reactions and the anthrax vaccine seems to be based on whether you accept that vaccines can cause chronic illnesses beyond the initial reporting period of vaccine adverse effects. The high incidence of unusual chronic health problems at Dover AFB include systemic signs and symptoms, such as vomiting, diarrhea, polyarthralgias, fever, splenic tenderness, cognitive problems, polymyalgias, weakness and numbness, and these problems can occur well after the usual reporting period for vaccine adverse effects. Patients with preexisting autoimmune illnesses such as rheumatoid arthritis, lupus, multiple sclerosis, among others, are probably more likely to suffer a serious adverse reaction, as are those with neurologic disease, such as those who had polio in childhood. Stevens Johnson Syndrome, a severe allergic reaction in which there is loss of epidermis (skin) and the lining of the GI tract, was found in some patients as well as more classic allergic signs and symptoms. Even more serious, many anthrax vaccine recipients report seizures with complete loss of consciousness. Respiratory distress and a variety of pulmonary illnesses have also been reported. Because these types of reactions have rarely been identified with other vaccines and because few of those reporting illness have been subjected to an exhaustive medical evaluation, including sophisticated immunological testing, the mechanisms by which anthrax vaccine may be causing illnesses have not been elucidated. Furthermore, the entire stockpile of anthrax vaccine is owned by the DoD, and none has yet been made available for thorough, independent testing.

A Sole and Secretive Supplier

One of the most difficult problems in dealing with anthrax vaccine safety is obtaining specific information on the anthrax vaccine and how it was determined to be safe. Most military vaccines in the U.S. are from 'sole-source' manufacturers. In the case of FDA-approved vaccines, a number of strict production and safety requirements must be fulfilled, and evidence for effectiveness in humans must be presented to the FDA before approval for production and sale is granted. However, in the case of the anthrax vaccine there seem to be missing elements in this safety net.

The sole producer of the anthrax vaccine was originally Michigan Biologic Products, Inc., a state-owned corporation that obtained U.S. Government approval for the anthrax vaccine at a time when FDA approval was not required. The anthrax vaccine was approved by the Bureau of Biologics at NIH in 1970, two years before efficacy data and approval were required by the FDA. In the case of the anthrax vaccine, long-term, safety data were not supplied with the license application, and none has yet been supplied to the FDA. As it turns out, the *Bacillus anthracis* vaccine now being produced may be different or the procedure for vaccine preparation modified from the original vaccine approved by NIH. The usual requirement is that any new product or modification in preparation must be examined and approved by the FDA, but the FDA has apparently not examined or approved every modification made to the current vaccine for anthrax.

The original license and the facility producing the anthrax vaccine was owned by Michigan Biologic Products, Inc. of the Michigan State Department of Health. The new owner of both is a company called Bioport, Inc., owned by a group of investors led by Admiral William Crowe, Jr., former head of the Joint Chiefs of Staff, DoD, and Faud El-Hibri, a German citizen of Lebanese descent who has since obtained American citizenship. The facility was sold to Admiral Crowe's investor group after the DoD decided to vaccinate all of its servicemen and servicewomen against anthrax. Recently Bioport ran into financial problems and negotiated a series of changes in its DoD contract that increases by three-fold the per dose price of the anthrax vaccine supplied to the military. This and other problems have resulted in a congressional investigation into the financial relationship between DoD and the new owners of Bioport, which may constitute a conflict of interest.

Safety Issues

Problems with the anthrax vaccine have raised questions about previous vaccine programs. The former commander of the US-AMRIID, Dr. Phillip Russell, admitted in an infectious disease journal (*Infectious Disease Clinics of North America*, 1990) that unlicensed anthrax vaccines were used on Armed Forces personnel before the Gulf War. There is, of course, no record of safety available for unlicensed vaccines. In fact, there were no published studies of safety or efficacy for the current anthrax vaccine until very recently, well after the decision was made to vaccinate. A recent brief publication from the USAMRIID in *JAMA* provides some safety information about the anthrax vaccine, but it refers to previously unpublished data that are not available for evaluation.

The normal procedure for post-marketing vaccine evaluation requires that the FDA must review adverse vaccine reactions collected through the Vaccine Adverse Event Reporting System (VAERS). Adverse events are usually recorded independently by a FDA-approved contractor. The contractor then sends its data to the FDA, and the FDA assembles a committee that then evaluates adverse events for the likelihood that the vaccine might have caused them, and it can recommend further study. However, in the case of the anthrax vaccine, military physicians were instructed that only certain adverse effects could be vaccine reactions, such as classic immediate allergic reactions, and others, such as joint pain, cognitive disturbances, etc. could not be due to the vaccine. Physicians treating these patients had no access to published data on anthrax vaccine side effects, and there is no entry for anthrax vaccine in the Physicians Desk Reference (PDR). The package insert for the vaccine is based on data collected from an earlier anthrax vaccine, and it does not list the range of possible reactions that could occur. Thus until recently none of the long-term chronic effects of the vaccine were even reported by medical providers. In the case of the anthrax vaccine, only reactions that resulted in hospitalization or immediate loss of 24 hours of duty time were reported to a military clearing-house for vaccine reactions. This has changed recently, and it appears now that other adverse vaccine effects will be entered in the medical records of patients, but whether they are always reported to the FDA remains questionable. We feel strongly that traditional and accepted means of FDA vaccine evaluation must be implemented for military vaccines, just as they are required for commercial vaccines. Only then can the safety of the anthrax vaccine be evaluated. The anthrax vaccine should be treated just like any other commercial vaccine and not given special waivers or treatment in the evaluation process. Only then will the public be satisfied that the current anthrax vaccine is safe.

For years Michigan Biologic Products, Inc. had been warned by the FDA of intent to revoke their license to produce vaccines because of violations in the production and testing of their vaccines. As recently as 1997, MBPI received format written notification from the FDA that they had not complied with FDA-mandated requirements. However, since MBPI was the only manufacturer of anthrax vaccine, they were given a waiver and allowed to remain open, pending FDA compliance. During this time vaccine lots were distributed to the military. In 1998 some of these vaccine lots were retested, and only 6 out of 31 lots passed initial supplemental testing. Most of the retested vaccine lots had expired or had been redated for an additional 3-year period once or even twice. This is obviously unacceptable.

The question has been raised whether expired or failed vaccine lots were used for vaccinating military personnel during the Gulf War. Since supplemental testing on anthrax vaccines used in the Gulf War was not undertaken, and some of these lots apparently also had previously expired and had been redated, some personnel could have received out-of-date vaccines, or worse, contaminated vaccines. Information is not available on whether U.S. Forces received contaminated vaccines (no such testing has been made public), but the British Gulf War veterans report that several vaccine lots from the Gulf War were reported to be contaminated with "unknown microorganisms." Thus some of the health problems associated with the anthrax vaccine could be related to possible vaccine contamination. . . .

Facing Multiple Threats

If BW agents are ever deployed in war or terrorist attacks, many times the lethal (human) dose could be encountered in an aerosolized BW and chemical mixture that is designed to inhibit and overwhelm the body's defensive abilities. These mixtures, called 'Russian Doll Cocktails,' contain microorganisms plus immune inhibitors and other chemicals to impede the immune system's ability to contain the infection by blocking pulmonary defenses. The pulmonary immune system, particularly the pulmonary macrophage, is the first level of defense against inhaled foreign microorganisms and its suppression could result in systemic infection. BW use on the battlefield of the future will likely involve *multiple* BW agents, not just one or even a few agents. Countries like Iraq operate under 'Soviet War Doctrine,' a battle strategy that stresses combinations of conventional and unconventional weapons. Thus combinations of multiple BW, CW (Chemical Warfare) or even NW (Nuclear Warfare) agents may be used together to heighten BW virulence and confuse the diagnosis and treatment of casualties. The rationale is to overwhelm a medical corps' ability to effectively manage large numbers of casualties with unknown or incomplete diagnoses. Iraqi Field Manuals found during the Gulf War described this strategy in detail.

Unfortunately, BW can be developed and produced at a fraction of the cost of other weapons of mass destruction making it likely that future terrorists will choose BW agents over other weapons for terrorist attacks.

The U.S. military's strategy of defense against BW agents is prior immunization using multiple vaccines. Unfortunately, this can only be successful if the exact BW agents likely to be encountered are known in great detail and for some time in advance of exposure. For example, the vaccine against *Bacillus anthracis* requires a rather lengthy immunization protocol, administering multiple vaccine and booster doses over more than a year. If multiple vaccines were to be administered, then they would have to be administered at different times to prevent immune suppression or excessive stimulation. Obviously, this strategy requires advance knowledge of the threat and careful long-term preparation against the threat. To prepare for any new threat that arises will require some time, possibly years or over a decade. Recent reports have appeared indicating that the Russians have developed anthrax strains for which it is claimed protective vaccines do not exist. What is the evidence that our 'multivalent' *Bacillus anthracis* vaccine will protect against all known anthrax strains?

Alternative Protection

Other strategies besides the vaccine approach to BW defense are available. During the Gulf War the French forces elected not to use vaccines as a primary defense against Iraqi BW and not to use anti-nerve agents as a defense against Iraqi Chemical Warfare agents. Instead, they used prophylactic antibiotics to counter Iraqi BW agents, and they depended on protective suits to counter Iraqi chemicals. Interestingly, the French Armed Forces were the *only* nation in the Coalition Forces that did not report any cases of Gulf War Illness (GWI), nor were there any illnesses reported in the immediate families of French Gulf War veterans.

What assurances do we have that future vaccines will be free of microbial contamination that could cause disease? Obviously, the purity and safety of vaccines depend on their ability to remain free of contamination by microorganisms. FDA-mandated vaccine preparation methods are generally considered adequate to prevent this possibility, but unless each 'batch' or lot of vaccine is routinely tested for possible contamination, including animal testing, this remains a possibility that must be carefully examined, not un-critically dismissed by untrained bureaucrats as a remote hypo-thetical possibility.

If prophylactic antibiotic or antiviral agents are used for BW defense, can these be defeated? Yes, BW agents can be modified or 'constructed' that have integrated into their genomes antibiotic- or antiviral-resistance genes. Similar to the 'engineering' of more lethal BW agents to circumvent known vaccines, such microor-ganisms can be 'engineered' to resist specific antibiotic or antivi-ral agents. Interestingly, certain U.S. units were issued antibiotics like ciprofloxacin and doxycycline just before the ground offen-sive in the Gulf War. These antibiotics would be expected to be ef-fective in preventing infections of at least two of the agents iden-tified in veterans with Gulf War Illness *(Mycoplasma fermentas and Brucella spp.)*. Examination of the numbers, deployments and types of casualties and their diagnoses in the units administered antibiotics before and during the Gulf War could tell us if the French approach to BW defense was more or less effective than our approach of administering multiple vaccines to prevent BW casualties.

Vaccinating the Armed Forces Against Anthrax Is Safe

By the U.S. Food and Drug Administration

Questions raised before Congress and the courts about the reliability of the military's anthrax vaccination program came to a dramatic head near the end of 2003. On December 22, a U.S. District Court, responding to a lawsuit by disgruntled members of the armed forces, issued a preliminary injunction against the program. The next day, the Department of Defense announced it would halt anthrax vaccinations until the legal situation was resolved. Just a few weeks later, on January 7, 2004, the court suspended its injunction. With the legal barrier removed, the Department of Defense announced it would immediately resume its anthrax vaccination program. The court's about-face may have been prompted by the release, two days before, of a U.S. Food and Drug Administration (FDA) ruling that the military's "anthrax vaccine adsorbed" (AVA) is both safe and effective. In the following selection from that ruling the FDA notes that its panel (a group of experts commissioned to evaluate the safety and effectiveness of vaccines) felt that there were too few cases of inhalation anthrax on record to judge the effectiveness of the armed forces vaccine. If used as a bioweapon, inhalation (or airborne) anthrax is the type the military expects to encounter. However, the FDA goes beyond its own panel's conclusions on that point and finds the vaccine effective against all types of anthrax. The Food and Drug Administration is a federal agency responsible for protecting the public health by assuring the safety, efficacy, and security of medical drugs devices, along with the nation's food supply. It also aims to

U.S. Food and Drug Administration, "Anthrax Vaccine Final Rule & Final Order, Biological Products; Bacterial Vaccines and Toxoids; Implementation of Efficacy Review," *Federal Register*, vol. 69, January 5, 2004.

provide the public with accurate, science-based information about
foods and medicines needed for health.

I n its report, the Panel found that Anthrax Vaccine Adsorbed
(AVA), manufactured by Michigan Department of Public Health
(MDPH now BioPort) was safe and effective for its intended
use and recommended that the vaccine be placed in Category I
[safe, effective, and not misbranded]. In the December 1985 proposal, FDA agreed with the Panel's recommendation. During the
comment period for the December 1985 proposal, FDA received
no comments opposing the placement of AVA into Category I.

Basis of Evaluation

The Panel based its evaluation of the safety and efficacy of AVA on
two studies: A well controlled field study conducted in the 1950s,
"the Brachman study," and an open-label [noncontrolled] safety
study conducted by the National Center for Disease Control (CDC,
now the Centers for Disease Control and Prevention). The Panel
also considered surveillance data on the occurrence of anthrax disease in the United States in at-risk industrial settings as supportive
of the effectiveness of the vaccine. In its determination that the data
support the safety and efficacy of AVA, FDA has identified points
of disagreement with statements in the Panel report. However, FDA
has determined that the data do support the safety and efficacy of
the vaccine and, thus, the agency continues to accept the Panel's
recommendation and places AVA in Category I.

The Definitive Study

The Brachman study included 1,249 workers in four textile mills
in the northeastern United States that processed imported goat hair.
Of these 1,249 workers, 379 received anthrax vaccine, 414 received
placebo, 116 received incomplete inoculations of either vaccine or
placebo, and 340 received no treatment but were monitored for the
occurrence of anthrax disease as an observational group. The
Brachman study used an earlier version of the protective antigen-
based anthrax vaccine administered subcutaneously [by injection]
at 0, 2, and 4 weeks and 6, 12, and 18 months. During the trial, 26
cases of anthrax were reported across the four mills: 5 inhalation

and 21 cutaneous [skin] anthrax cases. Prior to vaccination, the yearly average number of human anthrax cases was 1.2 cases per 100 employees in these mills. Of the five inhalation anthrax cases (four of which were fatal), two received placebo and three were in the observational group. Of the 21 cutaneous anthrax cases, 15 received placebo, 3 were in the observational group, and 3 received anthrax vaccine. Of the three cases in the vaccine group, one case occurred just prior to administration of the third dose, one case occurred 13 months after the individual received the third of the six doses (but no subsequent doses), and one case occurred prior to receiving the fourth dose of vaccine.

Doubts Overruled

In its report, the Panel stated that the Brachman study results demonstrate "a 93 percent protection against cutaneous anthrax" and that "inhalation anthrax occurred too infrequently to assess the protective effect of vaccine against this form of the disease". On the latter point, FDA does not agree with the Panel report. Because the Brachman comparison of anthrax cases between the placebo and vaccine groups included both inhalation and cutaneous cases, FDA has determined that the calculated efficacy of the vaccine to prevent all types of anthrax disease combined was, in fact, 92.5 percent. The efficacy analysis in the Brachman study includes all cases of anthrax disease regardless of the route of exposure or manifestation of disease. FDA agrees that the five cases of inhalation anthrax reported in the course of the Brachman study are too few to support an independent statistical analysis. However, of these cases, two occurred in the placebo group, three occurred in the observational group, and no cases occurred in the vaccine group. Therefore, the indication section of the labeling for AVA does not specify the route of exposure, and the vaccine is indicated for active immunization against *Bacillus anthracis* [the anthrax bacterium], independent of the route of exposure.

Anthrax Records Supportive

As stated previously in this document, the Panel also considered epidemiological data—sometimes called surveillance data—on the occurrence of anthrax disease in at-risk industrial settings collected by the CDC and summarized for the years 1962–1974 as supportive of the effectiveness of AVA. In that time period, individuals received either vaccine produced by MDPH, now BioPort, or an earlier version of anthrax vaccine. Twenty-seven cases of anthrax disease were identified. Three cases were not mill employees but people who worked in or near mills; none of these cases were vaccinated. Twenty-four cases were mill employees; three were partially immunized (one with one dose, two with two doses); the remainder (89 percent) were unvaccinated. These data provide confirmation that the risk of disease still existed for those persons who were not vaccinated and that those persons who had not received the full vaccination series (six doses) were susceptible to anthrax infection, while no cases occurred in those who had received the full vaccination series. In 1998, the Department of Defense (DoD) initiated the Anthrax Vaccination Program, calling for mandatory vaccination of service members. Thereafter, concerns about the vaccine caused the U.S. Congress to direct DoD to support an independent examination of AVA by the IOM. The IOM committee reviewed all available data, both published and unpublished, heard from Federal agencies, the manufacturer, and researchers. The committee in its published report concluded that AVA, as licensed, is an effective vaccine to protect humans against anthrax including inhalation anthrax. FDA agrees with the report's finding that studies in humans and animal models support the conclusion that AVA is effective against *B. anthracis* strains that are dependent upon the anthrax toxin as a mechanism of virulence, regardless of the route of exposure.

Generally Safe

CDC conducted an open-label study under an investigational new drug application (IND) between 1967 and 1971 in which approximately 7,000 persons, including textile employees, laboratory workers, and other at-risk individuals, were vaccinated with anthrax vaccine and monitored for adverse reactions to vaccination. The vaccine was administered in 0.5 ml doses according to a 0, 2, and 4 week initial dose schedule followed by additional doses at 6, 12, and 18 months with annual boosters thereafter. Several lots, approximately 15,000 doses, of AVA manufactured by MDPH were used in this study period. In its report, the Panel found that the CDC data "suggests that this product is fairly well tolerated with the majority of reactions consisting of local erythema and edema.

Severe local reactions and systemic reactions are relatively rare".

Subsequent to the publication of the Panel's recommendations, DoD conducted a small, randomized clinical study of the safety and immunogenicity of AVA. These more recent DoD data as well as post licensure adverse event surveillance data available from the Vaccine Adverse Event Reporting System (VAERS) further support the safety of AVA. These data were reviewed by FDA and provided the basis for a description of the types and severities of adverse events associated with administration of AVA included in labeling revisions approved by FDA in January 2002. . . .

Same Vaccine Throughout

The Panel report states:

3. *Analysis*—a. *Efficacy*—(2) *Human.* The vaccine manufactured by the Michigan Department of Public Health has not been employed in a controlled field trial. A similar vaccine prepared by Merck Sharp & Dohme for Fort Detrick was employed by Brachman . . . in a placebo-controlled field trial in mills processing imported goat hair. . . . The Michigan Department of Public Health vaccine is patterned after that of Merck Sharp & Dohme with various minor production changes.

FDA has found that contrary to the Panel's statement, the vaccine used in the Brachman study was not manufactured by Merck Sharp & Dohme, but instead this initial version was provided to Dr. Brachman by Dr. G. Wright of Fort Detrick, U.S. Army, DoD. The DoD version of the anthrax vaccine used in the Brachman study was manufactured using an aerobic culture method. Subsequent to the Brachman trial, DoD modified the vaccine's manufacturing process to, among other things, optimize production of a stable and immunogenic formulation of vaccine antigen and to increase the scale of manufacture. In the early 1960s, DoD entered into a contract with Merck Sharp & Dohme to standardize the manufacturing process for large-scale production of the anthrax vaccine and to produce anthrax vaccine using an anaerobic [no-oxygen] method. Thereafter, in the 1960s, DoD entered into a similar contract with MDPH to further standardize the manufacturing process and to scale up production for further clinical testing and immunization of persons at risk of exposure to anthrax spores. This DoD-MDPH contract resulted in the production of the anthrax vaccine that CDC used in the open-label safety study and that was licensed in 1970.

Different Versions, Same Response

While the Panel attributes the manufacture of the vaccine used in the Brachman study to Merck Sharp & Dohme, FDA has reviewed the historical development of AVA and concluded that DoD's continuous involvement with, and intimate knowledge of, the formulation and manufacturing processes of all of these versions of the anthrax vaccine provide a foundation for a determination that the MDPH anthrax vaccine is comparable to the original DoD vaccine. The comparability of the MDPH anthrax vaccine to the DoD vaccine has been verified through potency data that demonstrate the ability of all three versions of the vaccine to protect guinea pigs and rabbits against challenge with virulent *B. anthracis*. In addition, there are data comparing the safety and immunogenicity of the MDPH vaccine with the DoD vaccine. These data, while limited in the number of vaccines and samples evaluated, reveal that the serological responses to the MDPH vaccine and the DoD vaccine were similar with respect to peak antibody response and seroconversion [transformation in the body of antigen (the vaccine) into antibodies (germ-killers)].

Concerns Within the Catholic Church

By Edward J. Furton

Given the Catholic Church's stand against the practice of abortion, this selection questions the morality of accepting vaccines derived from cell lines with their origins in tissue from aborted fetuses. The author, Edward J. Furton, claims that many popular vaccines fall into this category. However, while allowing that the moral objections are valid in a Catholic frame of reference, Furton says that these objections can be overcome. It is possible, he argues, to separate one's disapproval of abortion from the acceptance of a vaccine that may have originated in aborted fetal tissue. Moreover, Furton states that it is impossible to avoid benefiting from past immorality in the world; if one is not intent on abetting abortion then there is no complicity by utilizing a vaccine created from fetal cell lines. To refuse a vaccine, then, is to go beyond what Catholic morality requires and to risk contracting a serious and preventable disease. Since many contagious diseases are especially prone to afflict the young, the author says that there is an even stronger moral imperative than condemning abortion: to protect children by administering vaccinations, whatever their origin. Edward J. Furton, PhD, is the editor of *Ethics and Medics*, a journal published by the National Catholic Bioethics Center.

Many commonly used vaccines have their origin in cell lines that were originally developed from an aborted fetus. This poses a serious moral dilemma for those who oppose abortion. Two questions need to be examined; first, may a Catholic, in good conscience, use vaccines derived from aborted

Edward J. Furton, "Vaccines Originating in Abortion," *Ethics and Medics*, vol. 24, March 1999. Copyright © 1999 by The National Catholic Bioethics Center. Reproduced by permission.

materials, or is one obliged to refuse them? And second, may a Catholic parent refuse to vaccinate a child?

Human Cell Lines

The production of vaccines begins with the growth of a weakened strain of a known virus in culture. When this weakened strain is processed and later injected into the body, it provokes an immune response that leads to the production of antibodies. Should a person who has been immunized encounter the virus at full strength, his body is ready to fend off the infection.

Two human cell lines (MRC-5 and WI-38) that are used to grow these weakened virus strains have their origins in cells derived from the lung tissue of aborted fetuses (Dan Maher, "On the Use of Certain Vaccines," unpublished manuscript [1998, NCBC]). Although these human cell lines could have been produced using cells taken from other sources (thus avoiding the moral problem entirely), the fact is that they were not. In many cases, there is no other choice than either to make use of a tainted vaccine or to forgo vaccination altogether.

Thus "Meruvax," a widely used vaccine for rubella (German measles) sold by Merck & Co., Inc., uses the WI-38 cell line. The chicken pox vaccine "Varivax" produced by the same company, uses both MRC-5 and WI-38. SmithKline Beecham offers a vaccine called "Havrix" that has its origins in MRC-5. "Havrix" guards against hepatitis A infections.

Whether immunization with these vaccines is permissible depends upon whether their use involves the Catholic in cooperation with evil. Briefly, *formal* cooperation arises when an individual shares in the intention or the action of another who does what is wrong. Immoral material cooperation occurs when one who cooperates makes an essential contribution to the circumstances of a wrongdoer's act. Thus the question about vaccines derived from aborted fetuses concerns whether or not their use involves the Catholic in immoral cooperation with the evil of abortion.

The answer, in short, would appear to be "no." For it seems impossible for an individual to cooperate with an action that is now completed and exists in the past. Clearly, use of a vaccine in the present does not cause the one who is immunized to share in the immoral intention or action of those who carried out the abortion in the past. Neither does such use provide some circumstance essential to the commission of that past act. Thus use of these vaccines would seem permissible.

Objections and Responses

One might object, however, that if we consent to the use of these vaccines, then we also consent to their origins in aborted fetal material. Such consent would represent a type of material cooperation with abortion. Yet another objection would be that use involves receiving a benefit from the immoral actions of others. What difference does it make, one might wonder, if the original immorality is now a part of the past? Most troubling, however, is the possibility that the present use of these vaccines might encourage future abortions. If that were true, then one might expect vaccination to constitute immoral cooperation with abortion.

These are good and important objections, but they can be met. First, if consent is defined as an act of agreement or approval, then consent of itself cannot involve the one who uses a tainted vaccine in cooperation. For approval of the immoral act of another is only an assent of the mind, not an actual intention to perform the immoral act. Moreover, approval for an act of abortion is exactly what the faithful Catholic refuses to grant. In light of this refusal, it would be unfair to suggest that by using the vaccine he has a state of mind that directly contradicts his own interior state of disapproval. Even if one were somehow to think that the original abortion was a good act, this would only mean that this person possessed a false opinion about an abortion. A false opinion about an abortion, however, is not the same as formal or material cooperation with an abortion.

As for receiving benefits from past immoralities, that is a common feature of our fallen world. Human history is filled with injustice. Acts of wrongdoing in the past regularly redound to the benefit of descendants who had no hand in the original crimes. It would be a high standard indeed if we were to require all benefits that we receive in the present to be completely free of every immorality of the past.

Neither does it seem that use of these vaccines will encourage future abortions. Regrettably, the cell lines that gave rise to MRC-5 and WI-38 began with tissue taken from aborted human beings, but these immoral actions were one-time events. Since their first beginnings, the cells used for these lines have continued to duplicate and grow in culture. There is little incentive to begin new human cell lines when these are well established and their various scientific properties well understood.

Appearance of Hypocrisy

Yet another objection concerns the problem of scandal. When a Catholic allows himself to be immunized with these vaccines it may appear to others that he acts hypocritically. Catholics, it will be said, talk a lot about moral principles, but when it comes to their own health or that of their children, they appear willing to abandon all previous moral conviction.

There would appear to be no objective basis for the charge that one who uses these vaccines cooperates in moral wrongdoing; therefore, any scandal caused by their use must be purely subjective in character. Appearances, however, can be important. For this reason, some Catholics decide to refuse vaccination in order to express their strong opposition to the practice of abortion. Still others are convinced, contrary to the arguments offered here, that vaccination does involve some form of cooperation with abortion. They believe that refusal is the only way to avoid complicity.

Nonetheless, refusal appears to represent a course of action that goes beyond what is morally required. When carried out in the light of a fully formed conscience, heroic acts based on sound moral principle can be highly praiseworthy. That would seem to be the case here. Those in the medical profession who refuse to be immunized with tainted vaccines often suffer harm to their careers. Health care facilities require that all employees be properly immunized against infectious diseases. When health care employees refuse to do so, they can expect to be dismissed from their posts.

Vaccination of Children

Refusal also involves some risk that one will contract a serious and perhaps even fatal disease, though the danger is lessened when most others in a given society are properly immunized. This gives rise to a hope. If there were a sufficient number of people who were prepared to refuse these vaccines, would the manufacturers feel compelled to begin new cell lines that did not have their origins in abortion? The development of widespread public opposition to tainted vaccines might lead to the eradication of the present dilemma for future generations.

Although initially appealing, there is one consideration that makes this scenario highly unlikely: parents have a moral obligation to provide vaccinations to their children. An adult may choose a heroic course of action that risks his own life and limb, but generally speaking, a child may not. The child is not capable of fully forming his conscience or of appreciating the risks that attend refusal of vaccination. Nor does it seem appropriate for a parent to refuse on behalf of a child and thereby risk the child's well-being.

Children are vaccinated at a very early age. The rubella vaccine, for example, is given between the ages of 12 and 15 months, with later boosters. When not provided, a child may develop a variety of serious complications, such as encephalitis, which infects 1 in 1,000 to 2,000 rubella victims. A significant percentage of these will also suffer permanent brain damage or death. Clearly a parent takes a significant risk when he refuses to have a child immunized.

Rubella is but one of many diseases, and encephalitis but one of many complications. Any widespread effort to force the hand of vaccine manufacturers would require considerable human suffering. Heroic refusals by adults are laudable, but parents have a moral obligation to secure the life and health of their children. As with so many issues of this type, it appears that the only proper recourse is to make appeals for redress to our legislatures and our courts. The true scandal here is not that Catholics use these vaccines, but that the researchers and scientists who bring us these products do not take into sufficient account the moral convictions of millions of their fellow citizens.

The Risks of Letting People Opt Out

By Carolyn Poirot

Responding to the fears of some parents, legislators in Texas passed a law in 2003 allowing for exemptions from the requirements of childhood immunizations. In the selection that follows, Carolyn Poirot explains that the law creates a procedure for parents to file an affidavit expressing a conscientious objection to vaccines. Health care experts are concerned that the law may add to an already rising number of contagious diseases spreading among children in Texas. Another state that allows exemptions, Colorado, has experienced a rise in outbreaks of infectious diseases in schools that have a higher than average number of vaccine-refusers, according to Poirot. In states where exemption is especially easy to obtain, Poirot says, some parents will choose that path simply to avoid the effort required to get their children's vaccination records up to date. The consequences could spread beyond the unvaccinated because a vaccination does not always create complete immunity. Carolyn Poirot writes on health and medical issues for the *Fort Worth Star-Telegram*.

U nder a new law that went into effect Sept. 1, [2003] parents can get a child exempted from immunizations required by the state for "reasons of conscience." But obtaining and completing the affidavit needed for an exemption to the immunizations required for attending child-care facilities, elementary and secondary schools and colleges will take some effort.

It might not be enough effort, though, to prevent a resurgence of vaccine-preventable diseases, such as measles and pertussis,

Carolyn Poirot, "Saying No to Vaccinations," *Fort Worth Star-Telegram*, September 9, 2003. Copyright © 2003 by Star Telegram and wire service sources, www.dfw.com. All rights reserved. Reproduced by permission.

public health experts say. Disease rates go up as exemption rates go up, and no one knows yet how many additional exemptions will be granted under the new state law.

[In the first week of September] the Texas Department of Health began mailing out about 600 copies of the official affidavit, which must be completed by parents who want to claim conscientious objection to vaccinations. The 600 affidavits are in response to 350 written requests for one or more forms received through the end of August. More are expected from parents, who have 30 days from the start of school to get their children's immunizations up to date or file an official exemption form.

"We don't know how many to expect," said Doug McBride, press officer for the state health department. "From the public health protection perspective, we hope it's not very many, but it is a legal option. We ask parents to base their requests for exemptions on accurate information."

Childhood Diseases on the Rise

Even without the new exemptions, Texas has experienced a resurgence in pertussis (whooping cough), with 1,240 cases in 2002— mostly in infants and young children not yet caught up in the school safety net. This year 297 cases of pertussis have been reported through the end of August.

Before the new law, parents could cite only medical or religious reasons to request an exemption for their child. Statewide, about 1 percent of public school students have claimed exemptions in the past for medical or religious reasons.

In the Fort Worth school district last year, the numbers were even lower, with a total of 33 students opting out of required immunizations for medical reasons and 28 for religious reasons, from among the district's 81,000 students, says Jackie Thompson, the district's health director.

No one knows how many more there will be under the new law, which maintains medical exemptions and rolls religious exemptions into the broader "conscientious objector" category.

"On average, exemptors are 22.2 times more likely to acquire measles and 5.9 times more likely to acquire pertussis than vaccinated children," says Daniel Salmon, associate director for policy and behavioral research at Johns Hopkins Bloomberg School of Public Health.

He is co-author of a Colorado study that looked at all reported cases of measles and pertussis in that state between 1987 and 1998.

The study, published in the Dec. 27, 2000, issue of the *Journal of the American Medical Association*, also found that schools with pertussis outbreaks had more exemptions (average of 4.7 percent of students) than schools without outbreaks (1.3 percent of students), and that at least 11 percent of vaccinated children in measles outbreaks acquired infection through contact with an exempted child despite their own vaccination.

Salmon says the complexity of the exemption process in terms of paperwork or effort required is adversely associated with the number of exemptions filed.

"The harder you make it to get an exemption, the less exemptions," Salmon said in a telephone interview.

In many states, the process of claiming a nonmedical exemption requires less effort than fulfilling immunization requirements, and some parents take the path of least resistance, Salmon said.

In California, for example, it is easier to claim an exemption than to verify your child's shot record.

"In California, they hand me a form that I take to my healthcare provider to fill out what shots my child has gotten when—or I turn the form over and sign a note that immunizations are contrary to my philosophical beliefs and hand it back to them. That's all there is to it," Salmon said.

He helped write a stricter new Arkansas law that requires demonstration of a strong conviction against vaccinations, counseling on the risks of not vaccinating, a notarized letter and annual reviews for nonmedical exemptions.

Easy to Opt Out

In Texas, the law is not nearly as difficult administratively, Salmon says.

"Texas' new law is actually pretty easy, and that's a little disturbing. I don't know how many more exemptions you will see. Only time will tell, but I do know that with harder criteria, you have fewer exemptions. I am concerned that the new law will mean more."

Dr. Mark Shelton, director of the department of infectious diseases at Cook Children's Medical Center in Fort Worth, says physicians are very concerned because when you look at other states with more liberal exemptions you find population pockets with no protection.

"We don't know what's going to happen in Texas, but we are worried it will mean more exemptions and more disease. We already have a pertussis problem in North Texas, and in some places—Ireland, for example—they are having big outbreaks of measles.

"I would just remind parents that vaccines protect their children and other children, and the risks of not taking a particular vaccine are far greater than the risks of vaccinating," Shelton says. "Most parents believe strongly in the value of vaccination, so we don't foresee large numbers, but if you have five in a school, and you get an outbreak, you have a big problem."

Vaccines Are Not Foolproof

Outbreaks are complicated by the fact that some children will not develop complete immunity from the vaccines (vaccine failures) and there is no way to identify those children. Also, there will always be some who do not get vaccinated because of individual health circumstances.

Medical exemptions are allowed for individuals who are immunocompromised, have allergic reactions to vaccine constituents, or have a moderate-to-severe illness that could be aggravated by a particular vaccination. Medical exemptions require a statement from a physician.

"Public health personnel should recognize the potential effect of exemptors in outbreaks in their communities, and parents should be made aware of the risks involved in not vaccinating their children," Salmon says. "The increase in community risk is due to pockets of unprotected or susceptible people who create a weakness in our armor against infectious disease. State laws provide a safety net ensuring that all or nearly all children over 5 years of age are fully vaccinated."

Online Campaigns Against Vaccines

By Laeth Nasir

From the early days of modern vaccination, there has always been some organized resistance to the whole idea of mass immunization. With the advent of the Internet, however, the opposition has grown more influential. In the selection that follows, Laeth Nasir shares the results of a survey of Web sites concerned with childhood vaccination. He finds that up to half of those that appear on any of the search engines he surveyed were antivaccination. According to Nasir, many of the sites are associated with alternative medicine. For example, many chiropractic organizations are involved in antivaccination activities. Nasir also cites homeopathy as a hotbed of antivaccination resistance. The arguments presented on antivaccination sites often involve emotional and sometimes bizarre arguments, Nasir reports, along with claims about the infringement of civil liberties. The opposition to vaccines, though representing a minority of the population, extends at least throughout the English-speaking world. Canada has a substantial antivaccine community, associated largely with chiropractors. Australia, according to Nasir, has the highest rate both of immunization refusers and of alternative-medicine users. Dr. Laeth Nasir is a family physician with the Department of Family Medicine at the University of Nebraska Medical Center in Omaha. He also practices at least one form of alternative medicine, acupuncture.

The first reported antivaccination groups formed in response to the vaccination acts that introduced compulsory immunization in 19th century England. At the time, a significant segment of public opinion opposed compulsory vaccination as an infringement on individual liberties and as interference with the will of God.

Laeth Nasir, "Reconnoitering the Antivaccination Web Sites: News from the Front," *The Journal of Family Practice,* Department of Family Medicine, University of Nebraska Medical Center, April 16, 2000. Copyright © 2000 by Dowden Health Media, Inc. Reproduced by permission.

Among the most vocal groups in the movement to repeal the vaccination acts were practitioners and followers of natural and homeopathic therapies. Although the antivaccination groups were unsuccessful in repealing the acts, important concessions were achieved, including the right of exemption for individuals with philosophical objections to the procedure.

More recently, with major reductions in vaccine-preventable diseases and a decline in public knowledge about these illnesses, politically active antivaccination groups are gaining support, particularly in the United States and Western Europe. Beginning in the 1970s, antivaccination groups were successful in temporarily curtailing the use of pertussis vaccines in several industrialized countries, including Sweden, Japan, the United Kingdom, Italy, and Australia, resulting in significant public health consequences.

One of the factors cited as contributing to the higher profile of antivaccination groups has been the increasing popularity of the Internet. For some parents, the Internet may be more accessible than specific literature or a health care professional. It has been estimated that 21% of the adults in the United States regularly access the Internet, and 42% of these individuals use the Internet to obtain medical information for themselves or their children. Some have called the problem of misleading or inaccurate information on the Internet a modern Pandora's box.

Sampling Web Sites

For this study, conducted from March 1999 through January 2000, Web sites were classified as being antivaccination if they expressed opposition to routine universal childhood vaccination for any reason. Web sites were found using standard search engines (Infoseek, Netscape, Lycos, and Excite) and the search terms "vaccination" and "immunization." Links between Web pages were used to search for additional sites. Using this strategy, 51 antivaccination sites focusing primarily on routine childhood immunizations were identified. Four of the sites were excluded from the analysis because they were in a language other than English. Twenty-six of the remaining sites were chosen for closer study using a random number table. The sites were analyzed for content, common themes, philosophy, links, and strategies offered for avoiding routine immunization.

From 2 to 5 of the first 10 "hits" from each search on each

search engine were antivaccination sites. The majority of the sites reviewed (16) were identified as belonging to groups in the United States. The others were in Australia (3), New Zealand (2), the United Kingdom (4), and Canada (1).

Fifteen of the 26 sites evaluated appear to be associated with groups or individuals practicing or promoting alternative medicine, as indicated by direct statements on the sites, promotion of alternative practices or products, or direct links to alternative medicine sites. Homeopathy and naturopathy were the alternative therapies most commonly cited, but others such as chiropractic and herbal medicine were also represented. At least 1 site is apparently operated by physicians.

Claims of Harm

All of the sites reviewed listed adverse effects due to immunization. The majority provided documented vaccine effects, and many claim chronic immunologic, psychiatric, or behavioral problems ranging from conditions such as Crohn's disease to impulsive violence and attention deficit disorder. Several of the articles offer case histories of children who have died or been severely injured, presumably as a result of vaccination.

Several of the Web sites reviewed include speculation on reasons for the promotion of immunization by physicians and other health authorities. Theories include ignorance on the part of well-meaning physicians or the fear of exposure to legal or peer sanction for holding unconventional views. Some authors suggest that physicians purposely exaggerate the dangers of childhood illnesses to frighten parents into compliance. For example: "Doctors are known for using fear or pressure to get parents/guardians to vaccinate instead of giving them the chance to decide on their own after weighing the pros and cons." Some sites suggest that pharmaceutical companies benefit from the illnesses brought about by their vaccines, and emphasis is placed on conflicts of interest that are said to exist between pharmaceutical companies, physicians, and the medical establishment. It is claimed that these conflicts result in physicians turning a blind eye to adverse reactions due to immunizations, nonreporting of adverse reactions to the Vaccine Adverse Effects Reporting System, and deliberate suppression of information regarding safe and effective alternatives to vaccination.

Other articles offer more unusual theories. One warns of the imminent development of a "Supervaccine" containing "raw DNA from 40 different kinds of bacteria and viruses that will be given to all newborn infants and timed [sic] released into the body throughout life."

Concerns about civil liberties were mentioned on 5 of the sites reviewed. One site claims that "the system will monitor, intimidate, harass and punish conscientious parents, their children and health care providers if they do not conform with every government recommended vaccination health care policy." This site offers instructions on how to remove children from a state vaccine registry.

Hidden Bias

Nearly all of the Web sites reviewed make an effort to appear unbiased about vaccination. This is often reflected in the names chosen for the organizations and Web sites and also in many of their mission statements. For example: "Our mission: to help the public make informed and intelligent decisions about childhood and adult vaccines." Several Web sites are very skillful in maintaining ambiguity on their home page: for example, "Vaccination. Does it work? Is it safe? Investigate so that you can make an informed choice." Typically, moving to the next page exposes the reader to an alarming list of adverse effects.

Many of these Web sites list contraindications to vaccination. In addition to those that are generally accepted, several sites list conditions that are not normally recognized as contraindications. Some of the advice offered to parents is directly at odds with accepted medical practice.

Several pages provide advice and resources for parents wishing to avoid childhood vaccination. "How to Legally Avoid School Immunizations" reviews religious and philosophical exemptions to immunization and strategies for obtaining them. Instructions are provided to help parents write letters to exempt their children from vaccination.

Link to Alternative Medicine

Antivaccination Web sites are not difficult to find. Parents surfing the Web for information on vaccination are very likely to encounter one or more of these sites.

Most of the sites reviewed in this study use several arguments to make a case against vaccination. Fifteen of the 26 sites reviewed appear to be associated with groups or individuals advocating the use of alternative medicine to treat or prevent infectious disease. The association between anti-immunization attitudes and promoters of unconventional therapies has been noted previously. One study from the United Kingdom reported that the use of homeopathy by the family was the most common reason for parental refusal of childhood immunizations. A study carried out in the United States reported that one third of a national sample of chiropractors opposed immunization.

With the rise in popularity of alternative and complementary medicine among the general public, more individuals may be advised to avoid immunizations by providers of alternative care. Although there is no direct evidence that increased use of complementary medicine results in a decline in immunization rates, Australia, which has the lowest childhood immunization rate in the developed world, also has the highest reported use of complementary medicine in the general population.

Other organizations appear to be contributing to the antivaccination debate as well, each focusing on its own agenda, such as civil liberties or conspiracy theories. In this respect, the modern antivaccination movement appears to share many characteristics with these types of movements in the past. What is new is the availability of this information to many individuals who may not be able to assess its reliability. Another difference is the ease with which the new medium allows small geographically isolated groups to network.

Although the actual number of proponents of the antivaccination movement is unknown, the efforts of a dedicated minority coupled with declining public awareness of the seriousness of vaccine preventable diseases may set the stage for the erosion of an important cornerstone of public health. Physicians should be aware of this growing movement and consider offering anticipatory guidance to parents about questionable material on the Internet. Research clarifying the relationship between alternative health care beliefs and immunization practices is urgently needed.

CHAPTER 4

Future Prospects and Challenges

The Plight of Poor Countries in the Vaccine Marketplace

By Henry Wilde

Most preventable childhood deaths occur in the poor countries of the world. According to the United Nations Children's Fund, better known as UNICEF, 3 million children die each year from diseases that are preventable with currently available vaccines, and 30 million infants each year still do not have access to basic immunization services. However, in the selection that follows, the picture becomes even darker. Physician Henry Wilde, who lives and practices in Southeast Asia, discusses the need for many new vaccines for diseases that are spreading throughout the developing world. Acknowledging the financial difficulties that drug companies face in creating products for people who cannot afford to buy them, Wilde argues that international organizations must step up their involvement. The global distribution of hepatitis B vaccine offers a good model for overcoming the barriers, he says. Henry Wilde lives in Thailand, where he serves on the medical staff of Queen Saovabha Memorial Institute and holds a post at Chulalongkorn University in Bangkok.

Have you ever wondered why we do not have a modern tissue-culture vaccine against Japanese encephalitis, a disease that has now spread across most of Asia? Many of us know that the Japanese encephalitis virus grows in Barbour-

Henry Wilde, "What Are Today's Orphaned Vaccines?" *Clinical Infectious Diseases*, July 30, 2001. Copyright © 2001 by The Infectious Diseases Society of America. All rights reserved. Reproduced by permission of the University of Chicago Press and the author.

Stoenner-Kelly, Vero, neuroblastoma, and probably other common tissue-culture cell lines. We also know that several international manufacturers and research laboratories have carried out projects that have revealed that making a tissue-culture Japanese encephalitis vaccine is possible. Is this vaccine really needed, or are we happy with the present-day "dinosaur products" that are made from thousands of suckling mouse brains, which are not entirely free of adverse reactions?

A recent article by Gray et al., followed by an editorial, discussed orphaned vaccines and, specifically, the adult adenovirus vaccine made for the military in the United States. This group of viruses usually does not cause life-threatening disease, as does Japanese encephalitis, but the vaccine was made for a select population that is at increased risk of morbidity. Its production was discontinued because it was not profitable to make it for such a small (albeit insured) market. The editorial discusses the lack of interest of the vaccine industry in products that are not profitable and not likely to return investments before patents expire. The editorial neglected to note that this state of affairs is likely to worsen as the development costs become ever higher. Furthermore, this will affect mostly vaccines (and drugs) that are of primary importance for poor tropical countries, which are unable to pay high prices for new developed vaccines, particularly ones that will be used mostly in the public sector.

Firms in a Bind

One must also sympathize, however, with the international manufacturers that are producing new and innovative vaccines and drugs at ever-higher costs. All of them are responsible to their stockholders, and all are in business to make a profit. Today, development of a vaccine requires anywhere from $300 million to $1 billion in research and development costs. New good clinical practices standards and local regulatory rules are not always rational; they are often made by persons who do not live in the areas that would benefit most from the new vaccines. Many new rules are driven by the litigious environment of North America and Europe and not necessarily by a genuine wish to create a super-safe product. All of these factors add significantly to costs and cause further delays in the introduction of life-saving products. It now takes from 14 to 18 years to bring a new product from the research bench to the market. The money for all this has to come from somewhere, and usually it is not from governments. Further barriers that need to be overcome before a new product becomes widely available are detailed below.

Many countries demand additional local immunogenicity, efficacy, and safety studies for products that have been extensively tested in their country of origin and have been accepted and used there. Such additional tests are often poorly done, and they can add costs and result in long delays before the product becomes available.

Corruption and favoritism in the approval process by local government agencies is a common problem in developing countries. It represents an important venue for extra income for officials who have the final decision in the approval process. They are also subject to pressures from potential competitors, who have a vested interest in keeping out new (and perhaps better) products.

Thus, it is not surprising that a large international company is reluctant to manufacture a new vaccine (or drug) that is to be used mostly in poor developing countries and that is not likely to have a large market in Europe or North America. Such companies much prefer to make a product that can first be widely sold in America and Europe at a price that allows the company to recover research and development costs within a reasonable time, before the patent expires and copies are made by generic-drug firms.

Market Barriers

Consider a modern Japanese encephalitis vaccine. In America, Europe, and Australia, it would sell only to a few tourists, missionaries, and expatriates, at a price that would bring in a return for investment costs in a reasonable time span. The main need for this vaccine, however, is in the Expanded Programs of Immunization (EPI) in Asia, where it would have to be sold at $1 per dose to be affordable to the public sector. It would take [a] decade to recover research and development costs in this manner. Stockholders of large firms do not like this type of product, and this may well be a reason why a modern Japanese encephalitis vaccine does not yet exist on the international market. To what extent this problem will also have an impact on more complex dengue and malaria vaccines is difficult to determine, but surely economics have also had an impact there.

I recently asked a friend in the research division of a large international pharmaceutical firm what will happen with an HIV vaccine, once one is developed. The reply was chilling: "I will give it to my young son and will have to pay several hundred dollars for it." No HIV vaccine would become available for the poor in Africa, Asia, and South America for decades after it appeared in the West, and then it would be available only if the manufacturers were willing to create a two-tier price system and if a major "Marshall Plan" were mounted by rich countries to pay for it.

Grounds for Hope

Do we despair that there will be no remedy for all of this, or is there some hope that we might be able to obtain a viable modern vaccine for Japanese encephalitis, dengue, malaria, and HIV infection? Perhaps there is some hope. We might learn from the experience with the hepatitis B vaccine from the late 1980s and early 1990s. This vaccine had been marketed for several years in rich countries, with a sales emphasis on health care workers, persons with certain high-risk lifestyles, and (later) American Indians and Eskimos. The manufacturers and the World Health Organization showed little initial interest in an international effort to include this vaccine in the EPI for developing countries, where chronic hepatitis B is endemic. The picture changed only after the nongovernment-organization-funded International Task Force for Hepatitis B Control was organized and was able to obtain an inexpensive, safe, effective vaccine, manufactured in Asia, for a pilot project in Thailand and Indonesia. The international manufacturers of hepatitis B vaccine then managed to reduce prices for the public sector, which created a two-tier price system, and the vaccine became part of the EPI in many countries.

The newly founded International Vaccine Institute, at the National University Campus (Seoul, Korea), which is supported by the World Health Organization, several nongovernmental organizations, and a large American foundation, is now endeavoring to catalyze technology transfer from industry and academic researchers to developing countries that need the products and can manufacture them locally. If successful, this might become a conduit for technology transfer for orphaned vaccines. One can thus conclude that there may be some hope, but only if one or more of the following happen:

1. A way should be found to curtail, streamline, and rationalize mounting "red tape" that regulatory officials create, which hinders and delays development of life-saving biological agents worldwide.

2. There is already a two-tier price system in place for many drugs and vaccines, but they are usually devised only after manufacturers have recovered development costs from sales in Europe and America. The interval between introduction of a new product and its appearance in the poor world at a lower price must be shortened.

3. Technology transfer and sustainable funding for local production of important vaccines in suitable developing countries must be made available.

4. Finally, bureaucratic barriers and corrupt practices by regulatory and customs services in many countries need to be curtailed.

Vaccines Stage a Comeback

By Michael D. Lemonick and Alice Park

The kind of public fervor over disease prevention that accompanied Jonas Salk's 1955 announcement of a polio vaccine ebbed considerably in the decades that followed. For some members of the public, enthusiasm for vaccines turned into suspicion, and by the 1970s numerous lawsuits threatened to undermine the nation's immunization program. Congress stepped in to solve that problem, but as the selection that follows indicates, public enthusiasm for vaccines would not resurface until 2001. *Time* magazine journalists Michael D. Lemonick and Alice Park write that it took the anthrax mailings in the wake of the September 11 terrorist attacks to restore the American public's view of the importance of vaccines. The anonymous and sometimes deadly attacks brought a controversial vaccine for anthrax back into the spotlight. At the same time, however, many other lines of prevention research have drawn renewed attention, raising hopes, they say, that vaccine innovation will get going once again. Michael D. Lemonick is an associate editor at *Time*, specializing in science. He has also served as executive editor of *Discover* magazine. Alice Park frequently joins Lemonick in writing about science. She has published numerous science and medical articles in other magazines as well.

They defeated some of the deadliest diseases known to man. Now they are helping defend us against bioterrorism. And soon, inoculations may protect us from killers like AIDS, Ebola, heart disease and even cancer.

You seldom see them on the cover of *Prevention Magazine*, but vaccines are the great prevention success story of modern medicine. They are not perceived as new or sexy; they have been around

Michael D. Lemonick and Alice Park, "Vaccines Stage a Comeback," *Time*, January 21, 2003. Copyright © 2003 by Time, Inc. Reproduced by permission.

since the days of George Washington, when Edward Jenner first scraped the scabs from milkmaids infected with cowpox to inoculate people against smallpox. By the end of the 20th century, vaccines had conquered many of man's most dreaded plagues, eliminating smallpox and all but wiping out mumps, measles, rubella, whooping cough, diphtheria and polio, at least in the developed world. Vaccines had done their work so well, in fact, that in the context of 21st century medicine, with its smart drugs and high-tech interventions, they seemed almost quaint and out of date, a kind of biomedical backwater.

Back in the News

That perception changed dramatically after Sept. 11 and the anthrax attacks. Suddenly, vaccines were back in the headlines. The U.S. government was scrambling to build up its supplies of smallpox inoculations, and an anthrax vaccine that had been stuck in a legal and scientific morass for years was thrust back on the fast tract.

Yet defense against bioterrorism is only part of the vaccine renaissance. Over the past few years, dramatic advances in the fields of immunology, virology and genetics have jump-started this long-stalled field of medicine. All the easy things that vaccines can do had been done, and researchers were ready to move on to far tougher challenges—using vaccines to fight off cancer, for example, or attack the protein deposits that clog the brains of Alzheimer's patients or even as a potential treatment for heart disease. "We are in a new era of vaccine research," says Dr. Gary Nabel, director of the Vaccine Research Center at the National Institute of Allergy and Infectious Diseases (NIAID). "It's an amazingly exciting time to be in this field."

An important trigger for this turnaround, surprisingly enough, was vaccine research's most notable failure. In the 1980s, as the AIDS epidemic began to spread, scientists tried to fight it as they had polio and chickenpox—by crippling the virus and using it to train a patient's immune system to ward off the real infection. Nobody really understood how the process worked at the molecular level, but until AIDS came along, that didn't matter much.

HIV, however, proved too sophisticated for such crude tactics. The virus managed to take advantage of loopholes that even experts hadn't expected, such as hiding within immune-system cells to avoid detection and mutating so rapidly that the body's defenses couldn't keep up. Immunologists' only hope of closing those loopholes was to delve more deeply into the exquisite complexity of the immune system in an effort to understand its secrets.

Better Understanding

That effort has paid off. After more than a decade of research, scientists now know that the immune system doesn't simply flick on and off like a light switch. Instead, it responds to a bacterial, viral or parasitic invasion with a combination of defensive weapons matched precisely to the severity of the threat.

That kind of fine-tuning necessarily makes the immune system complicated—but to understand the vaccination revolution, you first have to understand the complications. The simplest immune reaction—triggered by a mosquito bite, for example, or an allergen—is inflammation. When the insect bites, the immune system uses cellular troops that have had no special training. Cells called leukocytes, neutrophils and mast cells routinely cruise the bloodstream sniffing for an unfamiliar chemical signature. If they find it, they signal for reinforcements that swarm to kill the invader—the equivalent of an infantry attack.

If the invading bugs are too powerful for this first line of defense, the immune system sends in a second wave of cells. These represent what is known as the innate immune system. Unlike the first wave of defenders, which are crude killing machines, these cells are preprogrammed with biochemical weapons that can target specific types of invaders, including common viruses like influenza and rhinovirus (which causes the common cold).

Even this two-stage counterattack isn't always sufficient, however. When that's the case, it's time for the heavy artillery—the even more specialized cells of the acquired immune response. These cells learn from experience. Once they have been exposed to a virus or bacterium, they will recognize it if it shows up a second time. That's why, for example, you can get chickenpox once but rarely twice.

That much was known decades ago; what drives vaccine researchers today is the effort to understand and manipulate this highly tuned system. The acquired immune response, for example, actually comes in two parts. The first involves antibodies, the molecules produced to match, like a key fitting into a lock, the multiple proteins that coat the surfaces of viruses and bacteria. The more keys on the immune cell's ring, the more likely that the cell can lock onto and destroy pathogen.

Back and Forth Tactics

Sometimes, though, the bugs use biochemical trickery to disguise themselves and evade antibodies. The acquired immune system's counterstrategy: so-called antigen-presenting cells, including dendritic cells that latch onto invading bugs and strip them of their chemical camouflage. Thus exposed, the pathogens are prepped for destruction by killer T cells, whose job is to engulf and destroy them. The killer Ts are meanwhile lured to the site of infection in the greatest possible numbers by signaling chemicals known as cytokines, released by the dendritic cells.

The whole process resembles a highly trained military force or, in Nabel's happier analogy, a musical collaboration. And while it works beautifully most of the time, the immune system needs extra help against some diseases. "You literally have an immunologic orchestra," Nabel says, "and if the different sections don't come in in the proper sequence or are not harmonized in the proper way, you may end up with a piece that you're not very happy with."

One way that can happen is if a bacterial or viral illness gets out of control before the immune system can respond. That's where vaccines come in. "What a vaccine does," says Nabel, "is alert these specialized cells that an incoming agent could be a problem, and allow the immune system to respond more quickly and effectively than if it had never seen the bug before." In effect, he says, "you move up the immunologic-response chain of events so the final, acquired response kicks in faster."

That hasn't worked so far for deadly diseases like tuberculosis, malaria or AIDS, in part because no model for natural immunity exists for any of them. Thus scientists cannot crib from nature for vaccines, as Jenner did for smallpox. But that is changing as researchers get a sense of how many instruments in the immune-system orchestra they have at their disposal, and how to get the best performance from them. With HIV, for example, the virus mutates too rapidly. No sooner has the acquired immune system learned to identify and lock in on it than HIV develops new antigens on its surface and turns invisible again.

But a recent strategy, shown effective for the first time at

NIAID, may be able to thwart this evasive action. Known as "prime-boost," it gives the immune system a whiff of the virus' scent before hitting it with the actual vaccine. In Nabel's lab, that whiff consists of a snippet of DNA from HIV's outer coating—not enough to trigger a full immune response but, as his work was the first to show in animals, enough to put the system on alert. In the past this strategy hasn't worked in humans because our immune system, unlike those of other mammals, doesn't respond robustly enough to DNA alone. To amplify DNA's poor signal strength, Nabel's group sends in the "boost"—a crippled common-cold virus packed with a payload of viral antigens—a few days after priming, and the immune system goes into high gear. That's the theory, anyway.

Defense Against Ebola

It's too early to know whether this strategy will work against HIV, but it is already working against another deadly virus. Ebola, though it has claimed far fewer victims than HIV, has enormous potential for devastation. There is no cure or vaccine for it—but in a recent trial, Nabel's group has shown that DNA priming can protect monkeys from Ebola.

A patient-ready AIDS vaccine may not be available for human trials for another decade, but once it is, Nabel and others plan to use every trick they have learned to boost its effectiveness. They may, for example, mix cytokines with the vaccine, counting on these chemicals to rally extra killer T cells against the virus. They may give a small jolt of electricity along with the priming dose of viral DNA; that shock seems to enhance the DNA's ability to trigger a response. And they are even experimenting with firing the DNA directly into immune-system cells at high pressure with so-called gene guns to make sure the nucleic acids have maximum impact.

One of the inventors of the gene gun thinks that shooting viral DNA could someday replace traditional vaccines. Dr. Stephen Johnston, director of the Center for Biomedical Inventions at the University of Texas Southwestern Medical Center in Dallas, is using medicine's newfound skill at sequencing genomes to figure out precisely what genes express, or turn on, when a bug first enters a host's cells. Using microarrays, also known as "DNA chips," Johnston is working to identify those genes, then snip them from a pathogen's genome and use them, or the proteins they make, as vaccines to trigger an immune response.

Looking Ahead to Heart Disease

A similar strategy could lead to vaccines against malaria and TB. But while conquering such hitherto vaccine-resistant diseases would be dramatic, it would be positively revolutionary to extend vaccines to illnesses that have seemed beyond their reach. One such candidate is heart disease—which may involve the immune system in ways nobody ever imagined just a few years ago. The buildup of fatty cholesterol deposits on artery walls may begin, it turns out, with an inflammation perhaps caused by bacteria. This immune response alters the arteries in ways that make them prone to cholesterol damage. A vaccine that could prevent the initial infection or tamp down the inflammatory response might, doctors believe, prevent the chain of events that leads to heart attacks from getting started in the first place.

Cancer would seem to be the last disease you could prevent or treat with a vaccine. After all, infection plays no role in cancer, except in a few rare types of malignancy. And a cancer cell, unlike an invading pathogen, isn't wholly foreign to the body. Nevertheless, researchers are learning that the immune system can even be trained to go after tumors. CanVaxin, for example, a vaccine for the deadly skin cancer melanoma, is made from cancer-cell lines taken from three different patients; among them, they express more than 20 disabled tumor antigens that the immune system can learn to recognize.

"What we've been able to show," says Dr. Guy Gammon, vice president of clinical development for CancerVax, the biotech company that makes the vaccine, "is that not only do a majority of patients make an immune response, but that those making a strong response survive longer."

Promising Indicators

Indeed, in early clinical trials on people whose tumors had been surgically removed, those receiving the vaccine lived on average twice as long as controls. To make the vaccine even more potent, company scientists are testing a version of CanVaxin enhanced with cytokines to help boost the response of patients with immune systems damaged by chemotherapy. In Canada a vaccine called Melacine, made by Corixa, is also fighting melanoma, shrinking tumors as effectively as chemotherapy but with fewer side effects. It is currently in trials in the U.S.

Researchers are heartened by their preliminary success with a more complicated regimen, in which inoculations are custom-made from—and for—each patient. Early in 2001, scientists from Stanford University reported some shrinkage of advanced colon or lung tumors in half of a dozen patients. The vaccines they used were made of dendritic cells harvested from the patients themselves and mixed with a protein found on colon and lung tumors. These were then put back into the patients. "Our hope is to make these vaccines more potent and to try them in earlier-stage disease, possibly even using them to prevent disease," says the lead researcher, Dr. Lawrence Fong.

And that's undoubtedly only the beginning. Just a decade ago, medical science despaired of ever finding vaccines that would be able to ward off illnesses like malaria and tuberculosis, which have plagued humanity for thousands of years, and AIDS, which looked as though it might turn out to be even deadlier than these ancient killers. The notion that this venerable disease-prevention strategy would prove effective against these and others seemed farfetched.

Now it's clear that the age of vaccines was proclaimed over much too soon. Some of the new inoculations now under development won't pan out, of course. But doctors have learned their lesson, and if history is any guide, it's a happy one: any statement about the limits of vaccinations has a good chance of being proved wrong—and sooner than anyone expects.

Meeting the Challenge of Bioterrorism

By Philip K. Russell

In the aftermath of the suicidal airliner attacks on the World Trade Center and the Pentagon in 2001, Americans became vividly aware of another kind of threat: terrorism by deliberate release of infectious disease. Beginning in October 2001, a series of deadly anthrax attacks by mail killed a man in Florida, and then took the lives of several others while threatening the health of elected officials and their staffs in Washington, D.C. The Senate's work was severely disrupted by the forced closure of the Hart Senate Office building after anthrax-tainted packages were delivered there. Since that time, at least twenty cases of suspected or confirmed bioterrorism have been reported in the United States alone. British astrophysicist Martin Rees, in his book *Our Final Hour*, predicts that bioterrorism will claim a million victims by the year 2020. However, the U.S. government has long been preparing for the threat. In 1999, the Centers for Disease Control and Prevention (CDC) asked Philip K. Russell of the Johns Hopkins Center for Civilian Biodefense Studies to write a special paper for its publication *Emerging Infectious Diseases*. In the following selection from that paper, Russell outlines from a pre–September 11, 2001, perspective what the leading bioterror threats and possible vaccine defenses are. Russell is a professor at the Center for Immunization Research at the Johns Hopkins School of Public Health and a former commander at the U.S. Army Medical Research and Development Command.

Philip K. Russell, "Vaccines in Civilian Defense Against Bioterrorism," *Emerging Infectious Diseases*, vol. 5, July/August 1999, pp. 531–33. Copyright © 1999 by the National Center for Infectious Diseases. Reproduced by permission.

I n the United States, over the past half century, we have lived under the protective umbrella of vaccination programs that shield our population from a dozen serious and sometimes fatal naturally transmitted illnesses. Vaccination has been the single most cost-effective public health intervention. However, the value of vaccines in protecting the population against the deliberate release of infectious organisms is not so clear-cut.

The U.S. armed forces have recognized the military value of vaccines against biological threats and have a long-standing research and development program for a series of vaccines to protect service members from hostile use of a biological agent. Vaccination against anthrax is under way in all three armed services. The Department of Defense has a large program to develop and license additional vaccines for biological defense. For the military, vaccination is an effective means of countering a known threat because the population at risk is easily defined and a high level of vaccine coverage can be achieved.

Difficulty of Mass Vaccination

In evaluating the role of vaccines for protecting the civilian population, quite different answers are reached. Despite the protective efficacy of vaccines against individual organisms, the very high costs and the great difficulties involved in vaccinating large populations, along with the broad spectrum of potential agents, make it impossible to use vaccines to protect the general population against bioterrorism. Thus, vaccines cannot be considered a first line of defense against bioterrorism for the general population, as they can be for the relatively small military population. However, if suitable vaccines can be made available, they have several potential uses: control of a smallpox epidemic and prevention of a global pandemic, postexposure prophylaxis against anthrax (with antibiotics), and preexposure prophylaxis in first-responders at high risk, laboratory workers, and health-care providers.

Top Threats

Smallpox and anthrax, which pose the greatest risk for causing large numbers of casualties in the event of an effective release by a terrorist group, are at the top of the list of threat agents. Licensed vaccines against both anthrax and smallpox that protect against aerosol transmission are available. An existing licensed plague vaccine is protective against flea-transmitted disease but not against aerosol challenge in animal experiments or against pneumonic plague. This vaccine is in limited supply, and the manufacturer has recently ceased production.

The Department of Defense Joint Vaccine Acquisition Program has several experimental vaccines in development. These vaccines will be further developed and tested with the intent of obtaining products licensed by the U.S. Food and Drug Administration.

Smallpox

One vaccine in development that is of great importance to civilian biodefense is the vaccinia virus vaccine made in cell culture. A new national stockpile of vaccinia vaccine is urgently needed to respond to the possible threat of a deliberate release of smallpox virus. Even though such release is unlikely, the consequences of being unprepared would be a global catastrophe. An unchecked epidemic in today's unvaccinated, densely packed urban populations linked by rapid air travel could kill millions. The only possible course of action would be to mount a global effort to control the spread and eradicate the disease using vaccinia virus vaccine. The number of deaths due to secondary and subsequent spread of this highly contagious virus would be determined by the rapidity of the public health response, the effectiveness of a vaccination campaign, and, most importantly, the availability of vaccine.

Low Supply

The national stockpile (fewer than 7 million doses of vaccinia virus vaccine) is insufficient to meet national and international needs in this scenario. The stockpile is also deteriorating and has a finite life span. The vaccine was made using the traditional method of scarifying and infecting the flanks and bellies of calves and harvesting the infected lymph. No manufacturer exists today with the capability to manufacture calf lymph vaccine by the traditional method. Replacing the stockpile will require the development and licensure of a new vaccine using modern cell-culture methods. This development program, which will include process development, validation of a new manufacturing process, and extensive clinical testing, will be expensive and may take several years.

Obstacles to the development of the vaccine include the lack of satisfactory stocks of vaccinia immune globulin necessary for managing complications of vaccination. Clinical testing cannot proceed without a supply of vaccinia immune globulin. As part of the development effort, the problems associated with manufacture of sufficient quantities of vaccinia immune globulin will have to be addressed and solved. The Department of Defense program is moving ahead with development of a cell-culture vaccine by using a cloned strain of vaccinia derived from another strain. Both civilian and military requirements could be met by a combined and expanded development effort using either the cloned strain or one of the licensed vaccinia strains. The development costs will undoubtedly be high, as for any new biologic product, but the cost of preparedness is insignificant when weighed against the costs of an unchecked smallpox epidemic.

Anthrax

Anthrax is the second threat that requires a major research and development effort to meet civilian needs. A covert attack, which exposes an urban population to an anthrax spore aerosol, is thought by some to be the most likely scenario for a bioterrorism attack. If the release is detected or the first cases are rapidly diagnosed, rapid action can save many lives. Providing the exposed population with antibiotics followed by vaccination could be lifesaving for exposed persons who would otherwise become ill with untreatable inhalation anthrax in the subsequent few weeks. Prophylactic antibiotics alone will prevent disease in persons exposed to antibiotic-susceptible organisms, but incorporating vaccination into the treatment regime can greatly reduce the length of treatment with antibiotics. Without vaccination, antibiotics must be continued for 60 days; if effective vaccination can be provided, this can be reduced to 30 days. Vaccination of persons affected by an attack will also face the issue of environmental contamination of urban areas after an attack. Stockpiling a vaccine capable of inducing protective immunity with two doses could be extremely valuable in reducing the impact of a terrorist release of anthrax.

The current anthrax vaccine manufactured by Bioport (formerly the Michigan Department of Public Health Laboratory) is an alum-adsorbed, partially purified culture filtrate of *Bacillus anthracis* with a high protective antigen content. The schedule for administration is 0, 2, and 4 weeks and 6, 12, and 18 months. This vaccine is safe and efficacious and is being used by the armed forces to protect personnel against the use of anthrax as a weapon. Immunization of rhesus monkeys followed by a high-dose aerosol challenge has convincingly demonstrated the capability of this vaccine to protect against aerosol challenge with *B. anthracis* spores. The multiple dose requirement, however, is a drawback for civilian use.

Studies in progress may find ways to allow modification of the schedule. Vaccine supply is limited, as is production capacity. As a result, at least for the immediate future, the armed forces will require the entire available supply. This vaccine is made by a method developed before the advent of molecular biology and requires dedicated facilities because *B. anthracis* is a spore-forming organism. In addition to having a multiple-dose requirement, the vaccine is not highly purified and contains multiple extraneous proteins. The characteristics of the vaccine and the constraints on the present method of manufacturing argue strongly against procuring large amounts for civilian use when the technology and the science base exist to rapidly develop a second-generation, improved anthrax vaccine.

Need for a New Vaccine

Anthrax depends on two toxins (lethal factor and edema factor) for virulence. A protein called protective factor is an essential component of both toxins. The protective factor content is the basis for the effectiveness of the current vaccine. A vaccine based on purified protective factor made by recombinant technology has been protective in animals. Use of a modern adjuvant with purified recombinant protective factor should make it possible to have a very effective two-dose vaccine. A recent report of the Institute of Medicine Committee on Research and Development to Improve Civilian Medical Response to Chemical and Biological Terrorism makes a strong case for a major research and development effort leading to an improved second-generation vaccine.

Questions regarding the ability of existing anthrax vaccines to protect against anthrax strains engineered to contain additional virulence genes have been raised in Russia. Research is needed to address this and related questions about the pathogenesis of anthrax and protective immunity.

The value of vaccinating law-enforcement and emergency response personnel, who must respond to threats (real or otherwise), depends on the nature of their work and the immediacy of the threat. Laboratory personnel who must work with unknown materials and with high concentrations of known infectious materials must be vaccinated. These are additional justifications for moving ahead with a vigorous development program for anthrax and smallpox vaccines.

The Campaign to Vanquish Polio

By the United Nations Foundation

Polio all but disappeared from the American landscape in the decades following the successful testing of the Salk vaccine in 1954. The same, however, was not true in all parts of the world. Even as smallpox was relentlessly tracked and thwarted in poor and remote regions, polio continued to paralyze and kill in similar areas. All that may soon change. In the selection that follows, the United Nations Foundation explains how a worldwide partnership of organizations is attempting to wipe polio from the face of the earth. The strategy, it explains, is much the same as that employed in the successful eradication of smallpox: to vaccinate repeatedly wherever the virus still lurks. The World Health Organization, one of the partners in the campaign, has set up laboratories around the world to check for the presence of the disease. Even where no polio case has been seen in years, children continue to be vaccinated just to be sure. According to the United Nations Foundation, the campaign has met with considerable success already. As of 2001, it says, cases of polio had been cut by 99 percent to just under five hundred. Organizers hope to declare the world free of polio by 2005. The United Nations Foundation is a nonprofit organization that raises money and makes grants in support of the United Nations and its aims. It has an international board of directors, headed by former United States Senator Timothy Wirth.

L aunched in 1988, the Global Polio Eradication Initiative—coordinated by the World Health Organization (WHO)—is working to make polio eradication a reality. The global polio partnership—the largest public health initiative in history—is a remarkable public-private enterprise on track to certify the world polio-free in 2005.

United Nations Foundation, "End Polio Now," www.unfoundation.org, August 12, 2002. Copyright © 2002 by the United Nations Foundation. Reproduced by permission.

The UN Children's Fund (UNICEF) provides the oral polio vaccine. The U.S. Centers for Disease Control and Prevention (CDC) and the WHO offer technical expertise. With 1.2 million members in 159 countries, Rotary International has raised approximately $500 million for polio eradication and provided tens of thousands of volunteers in the field. The Initiative also includes private foundations such as the UN Foundation and the Bill and Melinda Gates Foundation, national governments, development banks, humanitarian organizations and corporate partners.

The success of the eradication drive depends on current efforts in 10 Asian and sub-Saharan African countries, many of which are affected by conflict or are global poliovirus reservoirs—countries with large, dense populations and intense virus transmission. And as long as polio is endemic in any nation, no one is completely safe. Every child must be vaccinated; every part of the globe must be declared polio-free. WHO estimates that the final eradication push will cost $1 billion with a current funding gap of $275 million. By investing in eradication efforts, the international community will eventually save $1.5 billion annually in immunization and health costs.

For all of these reasons, the United Nations Foundation is doing all that it can to help make the final push for polio eradication a success.

Campaign Modeled on Smallpox Eradication

Many of the principles being used for the certification of the eradication of polio were first established during the successful United Nations–led effort to end another terrible infectious disease—smallpox.

Until its eradication in 1979, smallpox was a global scourge. Smallpox epidemics killed 20 to 40 percent of people who contracted the disease. Survivors were disfigured and often blinded. In 17th and 18th-century London, one-third of the population bore smallpox scars and two-thirds of blind people had lost their sight to the disease.

When the World Health Organization began its 12-year eradication campaign in 1967, smallpox still afflicted as many as 15 million people each year. About two million of these died; millions more were left disfigured or blind.

Costs and benefits? Smallpox eradication cost $200 million for the 33 countries where the disease was endemic, plus $100 million from international donors. Once it was possible to stop all preventive measures and to close treatment centers, the economic benefits were great. It is estimated that the United States—the largest international donor—realizes in savings the total of all its contributions every 26 days. Thus far, eradication has also spared the global community of some 350 million new smallpox victims and some 40 million deaths from the disease.

Elements of the Plan

There are five final steps the world must take to eradicate polio. They reflect the same strategy that was so successful in eliminating the disease in the Western Hemisphere, where the last case caused by the wild polio virus occurred in Peru in 1991. Each step must be taken to achieve world-wide eradication:
• Routine Immunization
Maintain high levels of coverage through routine immunization programs everywhere—in both polio-free and polio-endemic countries. As the level of routine immunization coverage increases, the circulation of wild poliovirus diminishes. To eradicate rather than simply control the disease, far more aggressive action is required.
• Mass Immunization
Conduct mass immunization campaigns in polio endemic nations to complement routine immunization. The aim of these National Immunization Days (NIDs), in which all children under five receive oral polio vaccine, is to interrupt the circulation of the virus.
Generally, two rounds, about one month apart, for three consecutive years are needed to interrupt transmission of the polio virus. The idea is to catch children who are not immunized, or only partially so, and to boost the immunity of those already immunized. Thus the virus is deprived of human hosts.
Oral vaccine can be administered by non-health personnel; volunteers, notably members of Rotary International, have been crucial to the success of immunization days.
• Surveillance
Establish a surveillance system that reports suspected cases of polio rapidly. The effort requires virologists, epidemiologists, clinicians, and immunization staff, as well as a global network of lab-

oratories. Without surveillance, the wild poliovirus might continue to circulate undetected in isolated areas. In collaboration with national governments, WHO has established a system of more than 125 high-quality laboratories where stool samples—collected from all possible polio cases—are tested for the presence of the wild virus.

• Mop-up Campaigns

When few or no cases of polio are occurring, conduct door-to-door immunization in high-risk areas where the virus is known or suspected to be still circulating. These "mop-up" efforts are most often needed in places with few health services, overcrowding, high population mobility, poor sanitation, and low rates of routine immunization. In Peru, for example, after the last reported case of polio in 1991, nearly two million children were immunized in a one-week mop-up effort.

• Certification

A 13-member global commission established by WHO stands ready to certify the complete eradication of polio. This group of experts examines the data and assesses the quality of each country's surveillance system before issuing a decision. It will certify that the world is free of polio only after three years have elapsed since the last confirmed case of the disease. Once this rigorous process of certification is completed—and only then—will the world's nations be able to halt their programs of routine immunization against polio. The disease will be no more.

Success to Date

With only 483 polio cases reported globally in 2001, efforts to eradicate the disease have driven the incidence of polio to its lowest point in history. This represents a more than 99% reduction since 1998, when polio paralysed more than 350,000 children in 125 countries.

Highlights from the 2001 Campaign include:

• The number of polio endemic countries has decreased from 30 at the beginning of 2000 to 10.

• More than 575 million children under five years of age were vaccinated in 94 countries.

• Despite ongoing conflict, the Democratic Republic of Congo has immunized more than 11 million children during National Immunization Days, resulting in a reduction in the number of confirmed polio cases from 603 to zero in just 12 months.

There are ten global priority countries that are the focus of the final phase of polio eradication. They are (in order of highest to lowest transmission): India, Pakistan, Nigeria, Afghanistan, Niger, Somalia, Egypt, Angola, Ethiopia and Sudan. Each of these countries has accelerated immunization activities and other strategies for ridding their communities of polio. Other challenges for certifying the world polio-free in 2005 include:

• Maintaining political commitment in the face of a disappearing disease;

• Delivering doses of vaccine to children in conflict-affected countries; and

• Closing the US $275 million funding gap for eradication efforts.

Vaccinating Children in War Zones

The UN Foundation has committed more than $28 million as well as a $50 million contribution from the Bill and Melinda Gates Foundation to support the final push for global polio eradication. With this funding, WHO and UNICEF have vaccinated millions of children against polio in the war-torn Democratic Republic of Congo (DRC)—one of the highest priorities in the global effort to eradicate polio. During the three rounds of the Congo's immunization campaign in 1999, volunteer vaccinators reached an estimated 80% of the 10 million children under five years in the country. Secretary-General Kofi Annan paved the way for the vaccinations of Congolese volunteers to safely conduct their work. These "Days of Tranquility" enabled more than 75,000 volunteer vaccinators in 16,000 health stations to deliver the polio vaccine to Congolese children.

Another UN Foundation–funded project being implemented by UNICEF is working to administer polio vaccine to approximately 7.6 million children and support or establish polio surveillance activities in five other war-afflicted countries: Afghanistan, Liberia, Sierra Leone, Somalia and Sudan.

A Global Partnership

The UN Foundation is proud to be working with the United Nations, its key agencies and leaders from the private sector, like Rotary International and the Bill and Melinda Gates Foundation, to do all that we can to help eradicate this disease once and for all. . . .

UNICEF, the world's leading agency for children, is a founding member of the international coalition to eradicate polio. Along with other eradication partners, UNICEF helps organize and carry out National Immunization Days and other activities central to the success of the campaign.

Opposition to Polio Vaccinations

By John Donnelly

The international campaign to eradicate polio achieved great success in its first few years, but going the last mile has proven difficult. Stiff opposition to the vaccination program has arisen in various places. Nowhere has it been stronger than in the predominantly Muslim territories of Nigeria, located in the northern section of that West African country. The trouble seems to have begun with rumors that the vaccine was laced with chemicals intended to sterilize the children who receive it. The following selection explains that Nigeria's Islamic leaders took the rumors seriously, largely because of U.S. involvement in the polio eradication campaign. Their opposition stalled the drive to inoculate millions of Nigerian children against polio. The disease immediately began making a comeback, and health officials expressed fears it would spread to neighboring countries. Attempts to settle the controversy were renewed early in 2004. Meanwhile, Nigeria has reported that more than three hundred children contracted polio in 2003. Reporter John Donnelly, whose story follows, is Africa correspondent for the *Boston Globe*.

Batakaye, Nigeria—In this village of 3,000 people, 12 cars, one college graduate, and no telephones, the final push to erase polio from the earth hit a dead end.

The poliomyelitis virus zigzagged down one alley to the next several months ago, almost surely carried along in a fetid ribbon of water polluted with human waste. Children drank from it, splashed in it, rubbed their dirty hands in it, and that was the virus' opportunity. It infected four of the village's youngest residents, who lost the use of one or two limbs.

The virus thrived here in part because of the usual obstacles to

John Donnelly, "Muslims' Fears Pose Barrier to Fighting Polio in Nigeria," *Boston Globe*, January 18, 2004. Copyright © 2004 by the Globe Newspaper Company. All rights reserved. Reproduced by permission of Copyright Clearance Center.

better health care: internal political struggles, misspent money, alleged corruption. But an unusual factor came into play in the hamlets along the fault line between Christians and Muslims in West Africa: Local Muslim clerics told villagers to reject the polio vaccine because it was part of an American plot.

Muslim leaders in hundreds of northern Nigerian communities such as Batakaye limited or halted door-to-door polio immunization last year [2003]. They told millions of faithful in this Muslim-dominated region that the American government had tainted the vaccine with either infertility drugs or HIV, the virus that causes AIDS—statements later proved false by independent laboratory tests.

Some leaders admitted in interviews late last year that they never believed such a thing. But they remained silent, they said, in order to stop anything associated with the United States.

They vowed to preach against polio vaccinations as long as the United States pays for them, even though it puts their own children at risk.

"People believe that America hates Muslims, and so whatever comes from the United States, no matter how good it is, people will reject it," said Sheik Muhammed Nasir Muhammed, the chief imam at the second largest mosque in Kano, the Muslim political center in northern Nigeria.

Last Places Are Toughest

The global fight to eradicate polio has been defined by the World Health Organization (WHO) as one of its two greatest public health challenges, the other being the AIDS epidemic.

"We are on the verge (of) removing polio from the face of the earth. We are on the last mile," said Dr. Lola Mabogunje, a pediatrician who is leading Kano's polio eradication team.

But the polio battle, down to its last 667 cases worldwide, faces its hardest task since the eradication campaign started in 1988, when the virus was transmitted in 125 countries and infected 370,000 children. Nearly half of the remaining cases are in Nigeria and neighboring Niger.

This month, the World Health Organization convenes a meeting in Geneva of health ministers and local officials from the last six countries where polio is still transmitted—Nigeria, Niger, India, Afghanistan, Pakistan and Egypt. The goal is to win a commitment to end virus transmission . . . by the end of 2004.

"The last places are going to be the toughest," said Bruce Aylward, who leads WHO's polio fight. "But we have a very strong motivation: This is an opportunity to get something finished. The international health community made a promise a long time ago, and we aim to keep it."

Partners in Fight Against Polio

The partnership involves a variety of powerful players, ranging from U.S. and European governments to Rotary International to UN organizations such as UNICEF and WHO. They hope to make polio the second disease afflicting humans to be eradicated; the first was smallpox.

But privately, many leading the polio effort worry that they won't stop transmission by the end of this year, and that could spell deeper trouble ahead. Funding has been cut in recent years, which was a factor in the cancellation of door-to-door immunization efforts in about 100 countries last year. Millions of children didn't receive the vaccine and are unprotected if the virus spreads more widely.

Secondly, groups know that the longer they hold such intensive immunization efforts in a country, the more difficult they become. Organizers tire of huge efforts needed to reach every child under age 5. Residents become suspicious about why international groups care so much about a disease that seems barely to affect them, while killer diseases, such as measles and malaria, receive far less attention.

In northern Nigeria's Kano state, organizers have held 20 polio immunization rounds in the past five years. Before last year, the rounds reached well below 80 percent of the children, the minimum needed to stop the virus from spreading. Last year, the efforts fell apart, largely because of the politically driven doubts about the vaccine's safety. The virus not only infected dozens of children here, but also spread into southern Nigeria, as well as Ghana, Burkina Faso, Chad, Togo, Benin, and Cameroon.

Leaders in northern Nigeria have seen their political influence wane during the nearly five years of rule by President Olusegun Obasanjo, a Christian from the south. Officials in his administration say the north is using the embarrassment over the polio campaign for political gain.

Handling the funds has been problematic. The European Commission decided last fall to give 12.9 million euros (roughly $14 million) through a third party, the WHO, instead of to the Nigerian government because of questions on how its money was spent earlier. The decision delayed the release of the money, halting immunization rounds last fall.

Asked about the European decision, Dr. Dere Awosika, head of Nigeria's immunization program, angrily denied any financial impropriety. During the interview, a representative of the European Union, Gerald Moore, was sitting in the room. Moore confirmed the EU is giving money for polio immunizations, but acknowledged that he knew of no other cases where the EU used a third-party channel because of concerns over spending. Hearing this, Awosika buried her head in her hands.

Anti-American Sentiments

On top of those problems come the anti-American feelings. Mabogunje, the Kano state polio team leader, has met with several Muslim clerics seeking their help.

"What most of them are worried about now is this gulf between the Americans and the Islamic world," she said. "To them, almost all the difficulties are caused by some Americans. It's the only language people seem to know."

But she said she would try to challenge the anti-Americanism. "Let's agree, for instance, that the Americans are waging a new war against fertility. Do they ask children, 'Which of you are Muslim, and which of you are Christian?' No, they don't. Then how can you say this is aimed against Muslims?"

Aylward, the head of polio efforts at the WHO, said the vaccine itself is not made or manufactured by a U.S. company. Most of the batches, produced by a French pharmaceutical company, are produced in Europe, he said.

Substantial U.S. Funding

The U.S. Centers for Disease Control and the Agency for International Development are major funders of the global eradication effort, giving $120 million in 2003; in Nigeria, the two agencies gave about $7 million.

Some Muslim leaders said that the U.S. funding makes them

suspicious, and a minority still believe the vaccine is unsafe.

Datti Ahmed, a Muslim doctor who is president of Nigeria's Supreme Council for Sharia Law, said that he doubts the validity of independent tests on the vaccine, which were examined by the WHO, a university lab in Lagos, and by a Muslim pathologist, Abdulmumini Hassan Rafindadi, in three laboratories in northern Nigeria.

"A lot of money is being spent by interested parties to make sure they got the results they want," he said.

He also believes the United States has a hidden agenda when it promotes infertility drugs. "Just look at the Internet," Ahmed said. "There's strong proof that the U.S. government, dating back to 35 years ago, with Kissinger and Nixon, believed that population is the most important factor for U.S. hegemony in the world. Since they cannot rapidly increase the U.S. population, the only way for them to dominate is to depopulate the Third World. This is the motive, as far as we are concerned."

Asked Sheik Muhammed, the chief imam at Waje Central Mosque: "How do you deal with an enemy? Muslims, we hate America. Everything is aggravated now. How can we trust this nation, especially when it helps buy the polio vaccine and then puts drops of the vaccine into our children's mouths?"

Stricken Children

In the village of Batakaye, about 10 miles south of Kano, parents, all Muslims, said they would welcome those drops.

Mallam Ibrahim Wada, 52, the community leader, said that because the disease has crippled four children—three of whom were just a year old when they were infected last May—everyone realizes the vaccine's value.

Wada said opinions on the United States are divided. He said many people are angry about the wars in Iraq and Afghanistan, but nearly everyone in his small village also is aware of the U.S. record of aid to poor countries.

Standing next to him was Abdul Kareem Sha'aibu, 38, a farmer, who held in his arms his son, Kamzullahi, nearly 2. Kamzullahi's left leg and right arm became partly paralyzed from polio in May.

The father has devoted himself to the son's care, taking him every week for physical therapy in a hospital about five miles away.

"What happened was an act of God," Sha'aibu said, as a crowd of more than 50 villagers gathered around the door of his mud hut. "When they come around with the vaccine again, all of our children will take it. They see Kamzullahi, and the other three children. But I haven't given up on my child. I am optimist he will walk again, God willing."

He smiled broadly. "I am optimistic that my son will be someone important, the leader of this village someday, polio or no polio," he said.

The father, still smiling, lowered his son to the ground. The boy's legs buckled, and his body sank to the ground, where he sat silently at his father's feet.

Enlisting Vaccines to Battle Cancer

By the National Cancer Institute

In 1971, President Richard Nixon declared a "war on cancer." Hopes ran high for a time that the nation's second-leading cause of death might be eliminated through research. Yet, more than thirty years later, the goal remains elusive. According to the biotech firm Genentech, one in three Americans alive at the beginning of the twenty-first century will develop cancer in their lifetimes, and half of those people will die within five years of diagnosis. Although great progress has been made in the response to cancer, the standard treatment continues to rely heavily on radiation and chemotherapy. Both of these have powerful side effects, and once the treatment has been completed the chance of a recurrence of the disease remains considerable. However, the National Cancer Institute (NCI) says that cancer vaccines have the potential to change that. In the selection that follows, the NCI explains how, unlike most vaccines, this new class is mainly therapeutic. That is, cancer vaccines are being used, experimentally, to actually fight the disease in progress. What's more, the NCI reports, they appear to be a promising avenue for prevention of recurrence. At present, however, no cancer vaccine has been approved for general use, and none yet shows the capacity to ward off an initial outbreak. Nevertheless, oncologists and companies with an interest in the battle against cancer are vigorously pursuing the potential of vaccines. The National Cancer Institute is a governmental body established by the 1937 Cancer Act. Based in Bethesda, Maryland, it operates as part of the National Institutes of Health.

For many years, the treatment of cancer was primarily focused on surgery, chemotherapy, and radiation. But as researchers learn more about how the body fights cancer on its own, therapies are being developed that harness the body's defense system

National Cancer Institute, "Treating Cancer with Vaccine Therapy," www.cancer.gov, December 3, 1999.

in the fight against cancer. The body's defense system, called the immune system, consists of a network of specialized cells that fight infection and disease. Therapies that use the immune system to fight cancer are called biological therapies.

Cancer vaccines are an emerging type of biological therapy that is still experimental. At this time, the Food and Drug Administration (FDA) has not approved any cancer vaccines for use as a standard treatment, but many vaccines are now being tested against a variety of cancer types in ongoing clinical trials.

A vaccine is a substance that is designed to stimulate the immune system to launch an immune response against the specific target contained by the vaccine. For instance, the flu vaccine is a common vaccine. The flu vaccine contains pieces of the flu virus, and stimulates the immune system to make cells that fight the flu virus. The flu vaccine only works if the vaccine is given at least two weeks before exposure to the flu. The immune system needs those two weeks to gear up and make the immune cells and substances that can attack the flu virus when it first shows up in your nose or throat. By preparing ahead of time, your immune system can be ready to get rid of the viruses as soon as they enter your body and before they have time to make you sick. Because the flu changes from year to year, each year you need a new flu vaccine. But the immune system is still able to protect you against last year's flu type. This type of a vaccine is a preventive vaccine—it stimulates a long-lasting (years or even a lifetime) immune response that prevents you from getting sick.

A Different Type of Vaccine

Cancer vaccines, however, are different. Cancers can vary widely among types of cancer and among individuals. Because of this variation, the number of different cancer types, and the unpredictability of who might get cancer, preventive cancer vaccines are not yet possible. Current cancer vaccines are therapeutic, used to treat rather than prevent cancer, and given after a person already has cancer. Therefore, the goal of a cancer vaccine is not to prevent disease, but rather to get the immune system to attack existing cancerous cells. Fighting an established cancer is a difficult task, so most vaccines are not used alone, but in combination with additional substances that help stimulate the immune response in general, called cytokines or adjuvants.

The Immune System

The immune system is made up of a network of immune cells that are generated in the bone marrow from a very basic type of cell called a stem cell. From stem cells, many different types of immune cells are generated. The cells of the immune system circulate through the body in the blood or in a system of channels similar to blood vessels, called the lymph system, or congregate in special areas called the lymph nodes, which store immune cells. Lymph nodes are distributed throughout the body.

Some immune cells have general functions. Macrophages and phagocytes patrol the body, eating dead cells, debris, viruses, and bacteria. Dendritic cells are more stationary and monitor the surrounding environment from one spot, like the skin. Other cells recognize and are activated by one single substance. These cells are called T and B lymphocytes, and the single substance one particular lymphocyte recognizes (for instance a protein on the surface of a virus, or a substance contained in a cancerous cell) is called its antigen. When a lymphocyte recognizes its antigen and is activated, the lymphocyte makes many identical copies of itself, each recognizing the same antigen. T and B lymphocytes are called specific cells because they recognize only one substance while the other immune cells can recognize many different substances and are called non-specific cells.

T Lymphocytes (T Cells)

There are two main types of T cells:
  • Killer T cells can recognize and kill cells that contain the antigen they recognize.
  • Helper T cells release chemical messengers called cytokines that recruit other immune cells to the site of attack, and help killer T cells do their job.

B Cells and APCs

• *B lymphocytes (B cells)*
  B cells are also specific for one antigen, and produce antibodies, proteins that have a main trunk and two branching arms, against that antigen. The antibodies from a B cell specific for a tumor cell can attach to the tumor cell and through several indirect mechanisms lead to the death of the cancer cell.

• *Antigen presenting cells*

Antigen presenting cells (APCs) sample their surrounding environment, eating whatever they come across. Then, they display little bits of everything they have eaten on the outside of their cell. Lymphocytes meeting an APC can look at the APC cell surface and see if their antigen is present. If their antigen is present, the T cell is activated by the APC. In this way, APCs perform precisely as the name implies; they capture and present antigens to T cells. Dendritic cells are a special type of APC that are particularly good at turning on T cells.

How Immune Cells Work Together

All of the cells of the immune system can communicate with and influence what the others do. They communicate either by direct contact of molecules on their cell surfaces, or by releasing chemicals into their environment that the other cells can sense and respond to.

B cells and T cells work together by giving off chemical messengers, called cytokines, that help turn on surrounding lymphocytes. B cells can also sometimes help T cells become activated and multiply by direct contact.

APCs work together with T cells to help the T cells become activated. Antigen presentation by APCs is more powerful than if the T cells see antigens on their own, because APCs have extra molecules on their surfaces that powerfully activate the T cells. A T cell activated by an APC with its extra activating molecules will make more copies of itself and be more effective than a T cell activated without an APC, for instance by a tumor cell.

Cancer Vaccine Strategies

Not too many years ago, researchers thought that the immune system constantly patrolled for cancer cells, actively preventing cancer. Therefore, cancer represented a breakdown of the immune system. In a broken-down immune system, anti-tumor immune responses were not effective. Researchers have more recently begun to realize that this is not the case, and have proposed a more likely reason that anti-tumor immune responses are difficult to generate.

Our immune system has the job of knowing the difference between our own normal cells and bacteria-infected cells, virus-infected cells, or cancerous cells. To keep us healthy, the immune system must be able to "tolerate" normal cells and to recognize and attack abnormal ones. To the immune system, a cancer cell is different in very small ways from a normal cell. Therefore, the immune system largely tolerates cancer cells rather than attacking them. Although tolerance is essential to keep the immune system from attacking normal cells, tolerance of cancer cells is problematic. Cancer vaccines must not only provoke an immune response, but stimulate the immune system strongly enough to overcome this tolerance.

In general, research has shown that the most effective antitumor immune responses are achieved by stimulating T cells, which can recognize and kill tumor cells directly. Most current cancer vaccines try to activate T cells directly, try to enlist APCs to activate T cells, or both. Some new ways in which researchers are attempting to better activate T cells are:

• Altering tumor cells so molecules that are normally only on APCs are now on the tumor cell. These molecules are capable of giving T cells a stronger activating signal than the original tumor cells.

• Testing more cytokines and adjuvants to determine which are best at calling APCs to areas they are needed.

• Using dendritic cells and other APCs as the cancer vaccines. These cells go into the body carrying antigen and ready to activate T cells.

Types Under Study

A cancer vaccine can be made either of whole tumor cells or of substances contained by the tumor, called antigens. For a whole cell vaccine, tumor cells are taken out of the patient(s), and grown in the laboratory. Then the tumor cells are treated to make sure that 1) they can no longer multiply, and 2) there is nothing present that could infect the patient. When whole tumor cells are injected into a person, an immune response against the antigens on the tumor cells is generated. There are two types of whole cell cancer vaccines.

• An autologous whole cell vaccine is made with your own whole, inactivated tumor cells.

• An allogenic whole cell vaccine is made with someone else's whole, inactivated tumor cells or several people's tumor cells combined.

Antigen vaccines are not made of whole cells, but of one or more substances (called antigens) contained by the tumor. One tumor can have many antigens. Some antigens are common to all cancers of a particular type, and some antigens are unique to an individual. A few antigens are shared between tumors of different types of cancer. There are many ways to deliver the antigens in an antigen vaccine.

• Proteins or pieces of protein from the tumor cells can be given directly as the vaccine.

• Genetic material coding for those proteins can be given (RNA or DNA vaccine).

• A virus can be enlisted to help deliver the antigen. Viruses used in this way are called viral vectors, and do not make people sick or carry any diseases. These viruses can be engineered in the laboratory so that when they infect a human cell, the cell will make and display the tumor antigen on its surface. The virus is capable of infecting only a small number of human cells—enough to start an immune response, but not enough to make a person sick.

• Viruses can also be engineered to make cytokines or display proteins on their surface that help activate immune cells. These can be given alone or with a vaccine to help the immune response.

• Occasionally, antibodies themselves are used as antigens in a vaccine. An antibody to a tumor antigen is administered, then the B cells of the immune system make antibodies to that antibody that also recognize the tumor cells. This is called an anti-idiotype vaccine and is different from another type of biological therapy called passive antibody therapy.

APC vaccines are made of the cells that are best at turning on T cells to kill tumor cells, the antigen presenting cells (APCs). The most common type of APC used is the dendritic cell. Cancer vaccines can be made of dendritic cells that have been primed, or grown in the presence of, tumor antigens in the laboratory. Dendritic cells (or APCs) primed with antigen carry the tumor antigens on their surface and when injected, are ready to strongly activate T cells to multiply and to kill tumor cells.

Supplemental Boosters

Cancer vaccines also often have added ingredients to help boost the immune response in general. One type of added ingredients are cytokines, chemical messengers that recruit other immune cells to the site of attack, and help killer T cells do their job. Another type of added ingredient is called an adjuvant. Adjuvants are substances derived from a wide variety of sources, from bacteria to simple sea creatures to the laboratory chemical shelf, that researchers have found can help call immune cells to an area where they are needed. In some cases, cytokines and adjuvants are added to the cancer vaccine mixture, in other cases they are given separately.

Researchers don't know right now if whole cell vaccines are best or if antigen vaccines are best. They also don't know what the best delivery method is, or what the best vaccination schedule is. That is why clinical trials are being performed—to determine the best vaccine type, delivery, and schedule that will produce the best anti-tumor activity results against tumors. . . .

Appropriate Uses

In studies using laboratory animals, cancer vaccines show the most potential promise in preventing cancer from recurring (coming back) after the primary tumor has been eliminated by surgery, radiation, or chemotherapy. When the immune system has to detect and fight a smaller number of cancerous cells, it is more likely to be successful. In contrast, shrinking existing tumors using vaccine therapy is more difficult. When the immune system is matched against a large number of tumor cells, it is more likely to be overwhelmed and ineffective—an outnumbered army.

It may be appropriate to consider experimental cancer vaccines for advanced cancers once all other therapies have been exhausted when standard therapy is no longer effective or in combination with other therapies, such as the cytokine IL-2 (Interleukin-2). In some patients with melanoma and renal cell cancers, IL-2 therapy has caused large tumors to shrink. Many current cancer vaccine clinical trials are testing vaccines in combination with other therapies such as IL-2. It is also possible that newer and more potent vaccine strategies could cause advanced cancers to shrink.

Future of Cancer Vaccines

When cancer vaccines are studied in laboratory animals, cancer vaccines that stimulate the immune system can cause tumors to recede. But in humans, the situation is more complicated. Tumors have learned to evade the immune system, and the immune system is not fighting tumors effectively. Researchers are looking for ways to counteract this evasion and learning how to best activate the immune system to recognize tumor cells. Even in animal studies of cancer, which are much simpler than human situations, a cancer vaccine alone is not likely to work against very advanced cancer. In humans, cancer vaccines seem to be more effective at eliminating small tumors, usually those that would be too small to detect with X-rays. Studies using cancer vaccines alone currently have not shown a great deal of benefit. However, there have been some encouraging studies using cancer vaccines against melanoma, and future vaccines may prove more effective than those that have been tested in the past.

Vaccine therapy research is still in very early stages, and researchers have much work to do to show clear evidence of benefit. Ongoing trials seek to find the most promising situations and the optimal vaccine makeup for cancer vaccines to work. Only when trials provide evidence of effective uses of vaccines for specific cancers will the FDA consider them for approval as standard treatment.

A New Frontier: DNA Vaccines

By Robert G. Whalen

Until recently, vaccines were typically created from weakened or killed examples of the pathogen they are intended to protect against. For instance, the varicella vaccine protects against chicken pox by introducing a live virus, suitably weakened, into the human body. There, it provokes an immune reaction which stands ready to repel not only the weakened version but any wild viruses of the same type. A novel approach to the development of needed vaccines uses DNA, the code for all life. In the following selection, medical researcher Robert G. Whalen explains the promise of new technology that allows specific DNA to be synthesized so as to stimulate an immune response for protection against disease. He suggests that recent results obtained in animal models indicate that this new technology may revolutionize the vaccination of humans. Protective immunity against various diseases has been established over long periods in animals. These new DNA vaccines, he says, also hold promise for being safer, less expensive, and easier to produce and administer than conventional vaccines. This could, he suggests, mean a breakthrough in underserved areas of the world, where vaccines are hard to come by. Robert G. Whalen is director of research at the French National Center for Scientific Research. His previous work at the Pasteur Institute in Paris, France, concerned gene expression in muscle tissue and led to the study of DNA for immunization.

What if one day an Ebola-infected traveler makes it to the boarding lounge and embarks on an airplane? As pointed out by David Heymann, director of the World Health Organization's new Division of Emerging Diseases, the virus would spread to far corners of the world with dramatic consequences.

Robert G. Whalen, "DNA Vaccines for Emerging Infectious Diseases: What If?" *Emerging Infectious Diseases*, vol. 2, July–September 1996. Copyright © 1996 by the National Center for Infectious Diseases. Reproduced by permission.

This scenario has already been played out with human immuno-deficiency virus (HIV). Vaccines have traditionally been used as weapons against health threats. In the case of HIV infection, the basis for one has not yet been clearly delineated. For scientific, commercial, and practical reasons vaccines cannot solve all the problems posed by emerging infectious organisms. However, novel and powerful methods for vaccine research, and possibly for vaccines themselves, hold some promise in our efforts to curb emerging disease threats. These methods involve the deliberate introduction of a DNA plasmid [nonessential bit of bacterial or viral DNA] carrying a proteincoding gene that . . . expresses an antigen causing an immune response. This procedure, known as a DNA vaccine, is perhaps better described as DNA-mediated or DNA-based immunization, with the understanding that the objective is not to raise an immune response to the DNA itself.

Various Methods

This method is conceptually sound and experimentally straight-forward; however, its most novel aspect is that it works at all! It was not expected that pure plasmid DNA could be taken up by cells, after parenteral [non-oral, as by injection] introduction in a simple saline solution, to levels allowing expression of enough protein to induce an immune response. A more radical method of introducing DNA involves the bombardment of DNA-coated gold particles. When applied to the skin, these particles produce good immune responses with much less DNA than is required by other routes, such as intramuscular or intradermal needle injection. More esoteric still is the application of pure DNA solution (as nose drops) to the nasal membranes, which has been reported to work but is perhaps too inefficient for further consideration.

DNA vaccines have distinct advantages: They can be manufactured far more easily than vaccines composed of an inactivated pathogen, subcellular fraction, or recombinant protein. Since almost all plasmids can be manufactured in essentially the same way, substantial economies of scale can be achieved. DNA is very stable and resists temperature extremes; consequently, the storage, transport, and distribution of DNA-based vaccines are more practical and less expensive. In addition to the commercial, there are vaccine research and development considerations. It is now possible to change the sequence of an antigenic protein, or to add heterologous epitopes [special antigens derived from other species], by simply introducing mutations to the plasmid DNA. The immunogenicity of the modified protein can be directly assessed after injecting the plasmid DNA. This simple method could increase considerably our understanding of the immune response to antigens.

Easy and Inexpensive

In addition, both in vaccine research and in actual use, DNA-mediated immunization is the great leveler among researchers around the world. It is easy to use because once the protein coding sequences are cloned into a suitable expression vector, the direct introduction of the plasmid vector (into mice for example) allows experimental assessment of the immune response and its consequences, without further experimental steps such as the preparation of a recombinant protein as antigen.

Because it is so straightforward and requires only simple molecular biologic techniques, the method should be practical in many laboratories around the world. It would be unrealistic to deny that certain diseases are not of great interest to large pharmaceutical firms. Moreover, even when triumphs over disease are achieved, as in the case of hepatitis B virus (HBV) infection, marketing strategies can exclude the vaccine from regions where it would do the most good. DNA-mediated immunization can be used in countries that cannot implement more complicated and expensive strategies.

What if DNA vaccine research could be carried out worldwide by a generic technology, where human creativity adds substantial value to the work? . . .

Animal Test of DNA Vaccines

Various experimental models of DNA vaccination have been reported. Most of the pathogens studied have been viruses, which is consistent with the method used: Since the genes transferred by the plasmids require the host cellular machinery to be expressed, DNA-based immunization most resembles a virus infection. However, genes from other microorganisms have also been used with success. The types of polypeptides expressed are often the envelope proteins of viruses, but various proteins have been used. Indeed, it is not obvious what aspects of a protein produce an effective immune response by this unusual method of antigen delivery. . . .

The crucial point, however, is the ability of DNA-based immunization to protect animals from infection upon challenge, and this has been demonstrated in several model systems, particularly with influenza and rabies viruses, as well as *Mycoplasma pulmonis* and *Plasmodium yoelii*. . . .

Targeting the Vaccines

A successful vaccine must confer protective response to the recipient, and therefore, the limits of the immune response must be known. This knowledge can be purely empirical, as in the case of the first polio vaccines for which the precise protective epitopes [antigens] were not known. Such knowledge is not required when using a killed or attenuated viral preparation. In contrast, for recombinant vaccines a single protein should induce an immune response that will provide sterilizing immunity; this is also true for DNA vaccines and represents a major conceptual limitation in the use of this approach for vaccination. Although mixtures of individual proteins or their genes can be envisioned, in the case of recombinant protein vaccines this would be prohibitively complicated and expensive. For DNA vaccines this is far easier to imagine since the injected material is always DNA, and no matter what genes are carried by the plasmid, the production process is the same.

The only human vaccine that uses a recombinant protein as its basis is that against HBV, which has been used for nearly 10 years. Such a high-tech vaccine was possible because empty viral particles, from the plasma of persons chronically infected with HBV, could be purified and used to induce humoral [circulating] immunity against the so-called surface antigen [on the outside of HBV] that would protect against infection. . . . The envelope proteins of viruses are always good targets for inducing protective immunity.

However, this rationale clearly breaks down in the case of a virus, such as HIV, which mutates so rapidly, apparently in response to immune pressure. The fundamental knowledge required to determine what would comprise a potential HIV vaccine is still lacking, and therefore, it is unlikely that a vaccine can be developed until further basic research provides more insight. Thus HBV and HIV illustrate two extremes in vaccine development: With HBV a simple antibody response to a single antigen neutralizes the virus, whereas with HIV some form of cytotoxic [infected-cell-killing] immune response is probably necessary. DNA-mediated immunization has a role to play in further research. . . .

Worst-Case Response

Let us take the most provocative scenario to illustrate what can perhaps be done, in principle and in practice, in the face of a rampantly infectious viral disease. When preventive measures against an agent like Ebola virus are needed on an emergency basis, speed is imperative. The filoviruses Ebola and Marburg are extremely pathogenic, causing a fulminating febrile hemorrhagic disease [massive bleeding]; they grow fast, kill most cells, and the infected person bleeds to death, usually within 48 hours of infection. . . .

If Ebola or Marburg, or a related filovirus, escaped a restricted ecologic niche, the following scenario might unfold. If the emerged virus is found (by serologic testing) to be one of the existing, characterized ones, existing cloned genes could be used. Otherwise, a virus isolate would need to be obtained, and the genes would need to be cloned. Cloning can be accomplished easily since related genes are available for probes in molecular cloning experiments. . . .

Rapid Response

The molecular method needed to rapidly go from a virus isolate to the vaccinating plasmid vector should represent only a relatively minor bottleneck to the development of an urgently needed vaccine, at least compared with any other approach used before. It is not surprising that Bernard Dixon, writing in *Bio/Technology*, has called DNA vaccines "the third vaccine revolution."

This review poses questions about DNA vaccines and suggests that the answers lie in new methods of research and development. If DNA-mediated immunization were used in all countries that have expertise in molecular biology, novel vaccines would be developed. Ultimately, a major goal of the DNA vaccine approach for public health might well be to bring vaccine development within the reach of researchers working on infectious disease problems in which there is no great commercial interest. If DNA vaccines come into widespread use for public health applications, vaccines for many diseases could be produced rapidly since, in the end, the product is simply a DNA plasmid.

What if such a method were used for human vaccination? The cost of production and delivery of vaccines would be reduced, thus allowing vaccines to reach areas of the world somewhat deprived of preventive public health measures, particularly the recent biotechnologic methods. If new infectious diseases appear in the future, as they surely will, perhaps these new tools will be used to combat them more effectively.

Today's research method can be tomorrow's vaccine. DNA vaccines will be within the means of many more populations and countries since full GMP [Good Manufacturing Process] production technology will be both simpler than technology for other products and far more available to research scientists. A little more than 2 years stood between the first published description of a DNA vaccine and the beginning of the first clinical trial, which indicates that the necessary infrastructure for producing DNA vaccines was rapidly put in place. But more importantly, this short time span bodes well for the ability of public health agencies all over the world to bring scientific research to bear on diseases relevant to their own situation and to disease prevention.

New Delivery Systems: Vaccines You Can Eat

By Mandy Redig

Vaccines can only protect if they are administered in a timely way. Sadly, many children in the developing world never get inoculated. In part, that's because transporting and administering vaccines to children in poor and remote areas of the world represents a huge challenge. Many vaccines have to be preserved at precise temperatures, or they lose their power to immunize. It takes at least some medical training to be able to administer an injection. The following selection tells of an innovative strategy for getting vaccines to the poorest, most forbidding parts of the world. To do this, Dr. Charles Arntzen and his colleagues are working on an entirely new delivery system. Instead of culturing vaccines from bacteria or animal cells, they are using DNA to make antigens—the proteins that stimulate an immune response—grow in food plants such as bananas and potatoes. Scientists use gene-splicing techniques to shift the desired antigen from the germ into the plant. The so-called transgenic plant then reproduces the antigen over and over. Early tests in animals, and a few trials with people, show promising results. However, as student journalist Mandy Redig tells it, there are many questions yet to be dealt with before the edible vaccine can become a staple of public health in the world's poorest countries. At the time she authored this article, Redig was a biochemistry and creative writing student at the University of Arizona.

Mandy Redig, "Banana Vaccines: A Conversation with Dr. Charles Arntzen," *Journal of Young Investigators*, vol. 7, March 2003. Copyright © 2003 by Mandy Redig and *JYI*. All rights reserved. Reproduced by permission.

s Archimedes could attest, inspiration can strike anywhere. Legend has it that the ancient Greek thinker discovered the mathematical laws governing buoyancy in a bathhouse while idly watching soap float. The nature of scientific research has changed since the third century B.C., but the spirit of observational inquiry that led to Archimedes's principle is still active.

When Dr. Charles Arntzen of Arizona State University visited Thailand in 1992, he was not expecting a moment of scientific "eureka" that would redirect his career. However, after observing a young Thai mother soothing her fussy infant with bits of banana, this plant molecular biologist was struck with an idea that is both startling and ingenious. What if, in addition to quieting her child, the mother could also administer a life-saving vaccine—*in the banana*?

From Vision to Reality

Arntzen's vision is well on its way to becoming reality, thanks to a combination of dedication and applied biotechnology. As the president emeritus of the Boyce Thompson Institute for Plant Research, founding director of the Arizona Biomedical Institute, and member of the President's Council of Advisors on Science and Technology, Arntzen is well equipped to handle the challenge he has undertaken. His breakthrough lies in forging a link between green plants, foreign DNA, and vaccines.

Vaccination stands as one of modern medicine's greatest success stories. Early experiments by Edward Jenner and Louis Pasteur taught physicians they could prevent disease merely by exposing a patient to a weakened or inactivated pathogen. While his protocols violate today's clinical trials regulations, Dr. Jenner was able to prevent children from getting smallpox—even when he deliberately exposed them to it—after first inoculating them with the pus from cowpox.

Today, most new vaccines contain a specific protein or set of proteins from a pathogen of interest and not the pathogen itself. A protective immune response can result from this more limited (and inherently less risky) exposure. Though materially different from those developed by Jenner and Pasteur, modern vaccines, including Arntzen's, still build upon the same fundamental principle: If the immune system is trained to recognize a pathogen prior to infection, the disease can be prevented when the actual pathogen is encountered.

Disease prevention via an edible vaccine is great news for people around the globe. The problem with current vaccination protocols—and the passion behind Arntzen's research—is that what works in the developed world is often much more difficult to deliver in the developing world, or simply too costly to purchase. A vaccine that requires a sterile syringe, refrigeration prior to injection, and repeated booster shots is difficult to implement in many countries. Unfortunately, this often means that the people who most need a vaccine cannot get it. In a discussion of his work, Arntzen points out that "each year diarrhea kills about two and one-half million children under the age of five." He persuasively uses such horrendous statistics to champion his cause. In his own words, "It's hard to be pro-infant mortality."

While Arntzen's edible vaccine is likely to win approval from children everywhere, there are actually significant medical advantages to this route of administration. An oral vaccine incorporated into a plant bypasses the need for sterile syringes, costly refrigeration, or multiple injections. Furthermore, since many of the developing world's most deadly diseases—cholera, rotavirus, and *E. coli* infection, to name a few—enter the body through the gastrointestinal tract, a vaccine that is ingested may actually provide the best protection because it mimics the natural route of infection.

Splicing Genes into Plants

The trick with an edible vaccine is convincing a plant to express the genes of a foreign organism. Fortunately, Arntzen's prior work prepared him to face this challenge. As a biochemist, his career focused on unraveling the means by which photosynthetic membranes in plants capture solar energy. "What we've done for the last ten years is try to change the cellular machinery of a plant by adding a new gene, cause that gene to make a new protein, and coax the new protein into folding to the desired shape so that it accumulates. I took knowledge about plant proteins under normal circumstances and used that for something new." That something new was vaccine development.

When Arntzen started investigating the vaccine issue in the early 1990s, scientists were already using genetically engineered yeast to produce proteins for injection vaccines. Arntzen's experience with green plants led him to consider other options. He remembers thinking at the time, "Would it be possible to use a higher plant instead of a lower plant, something we already know is an agricultural crop? Can we take a potato or tomato and turn it into a green factory?"

Indeed, modern technology enables Arntzen to insert specific genes from a foreign organism into the genome of a green plant. Progeny plants will then produce the foreign protein. If the foreign protein happens to be an immunity-inducing pathogen protein, an edible vaccine is in the making.

Yet the challenges of science are not the only obstacles Arntzen faces. This type of project requires a multidisciplinary approach, incorporating the skills of many types of basic and clinical scientists as well as experts in product regulation and distribution. Says Arntzen, "No biochemist can make progress in moving something forward on his own. I need linkages with people who do immunology. I need people in vaccine development. I also have increasingly found that I have to understand the regulatory environment."

In fact, satisfying regulatory policies has been one of the most painstaking elements of Arntzen's work. He is determined to demonstrate that his vaccine passes the rigorous requirements of the Food and Drug Administration, thereby silencing any critics who would accuse him of "dumping" experimental technology on the world's poor. Indeed, an interview with Arntzen reveals him to be passionate and articulate in explaining the rationale behind his work. His ideas involve sophisticated science and technology, but his motives are grounded in a genuine concern and humanitarian interest.

Opposition to Modifying Food

Not everyone agrees with him, though. In an interview with Nova and PBS in October 2000, Dr. Jane Rissler, a senior scientist with the Union of Concerned Scientists, expressed the opinion that in the context of genetically modified foods, "It's a ploy to convince relatively well-to-do people in the industrialized world to approve of this technology. It's playing on the guilt of relatively well-off people, that somehow if they don't approve of this technology by agreeing to buy the products, the result will be people dying of starvation in the developing world."

While directed at genetically modified foods in general and not specifically edible vaccines, her comments do strike at the heart of the debate over genetically modified organisms (GMOs) that has also stirred up controversy between the United States and Europe. Some scientists feel GMOs are safe while others do not. In a 2000 interview with PBS, Jeremy Rifkin, president of the Foundation on Economic Trends, recalls the time in 1983 when the United States government approved the release of the first GMO, a bacteria that prevents frost from forming on agricultural crops: "All of our regulations had been set up in an era in which physics and chemistry ruled. It seemed to me that we needed to have a thorough and thoughtful global discussion on the potential environmental implications of reseeding the earth with genetically modified organisms."

Critics of GMO technology argue that not enough testing has been done (or is even possible) to ensure that genetically altered organisms will not have negative environmental consequences. Arntzen recognizes these concerns and much of his time is spent working to first ensure that his work meets rigorous standards of integrity and then to translate that information to the public. He says, "To a large extent I rely on the regulatory side [agencies] to help in the education and acceptance. I have to be constantly alert to those issues because it's always something that can always rise up." In fact, Arntzen's protocols take such concerns into consideration. As a result, the genetically altered vaccine-producing plants are not grown freely, thereby minimizing the risk that such genes would be unintentionally incorporated into other species.

Promising Human Trials

From an efficacy perspective, Arntzen's most recent clinical trials are particularly exciting. Human volunteers who enrolled in a study at the University of Maryland at Baltimore started producing antibodies against Norwalk virus (which causes acute bouts of diarrhea) after eating Arntzen's creations—genetically engineered potatoes. Negotiations are in progress to start clinical trials abroad with the International Vaccine Institute in Korea, a new center funded in large part by the Bill and Melinda Gates Foundation. Clinical trials of cholera vaccines are also planned to take place there as well as in Vietnam and Cambodia, regions where cholera is still a serious medical concern.

In addition, during a recent scientific conference held at the Flinn Foundation's Phoenix office, tentative connections were made with company representatives from Egypt and India. This meeting, organized by Arizona Biodesign Institute on behalf of the Production of Vaccines from Applied Crop Sciences (ProVACS) Center, highlighted technical advances in plant-based vaccines. Arntzen, the keynote speaker at the meeting, said, "We intend to visit India. They're willing to fund clinical trials there—we could send vaccine materials to them and they're interested in developing the product."

For now, all such clinical trials will involve modified potatoes or tomatoes. Both products can be easily freeze-dried, transported, and reconstituted. Since many target countries have a long history of herbal medicine, Arntzen is interested in working within already-existing ideas. "Our goal is not to make the decision for how we want (the freeze-dried dose) introduced," he said. "We want to work with them."

Banking on Bananas

In the meantime, Arntzen is still working on the banana vaccine. His original, utopian vision was of a communal banana tree where villagers could dose themselves. Unfortunately, this scenario does not adequately address the concerns related to any vaccination protocol-efficacy, quality control, and dosage regulation. As a result, Arntzen's current efforts focus on tomatoes and potatoes, which have shorter growing seasons, are easier to manipulate in an experimental setting, and can be freeze-dried in controlled doses. Practicality hasn't inhibited his idealism, however. To this day he keeps a jar of Gerber's baby food—banana, of course—on the corner of his desk for inspiration.

Arizona's sunny skies and warm weather are known to attract people from all over the world—who can resist playing golf in short sleeves in December? Arizonans are fortunate that warm weather is also good for growing plants. A combination of ASU's offer of the Florence Ely Nelson Presidential Endowed Chair and greenhouse opportunities brought Arntzen to Phoenix. He sounds remarkably like a winter tourist when he exclaims, "The weather is perfect!" Yet unlike the tourists, Arntzen is excited about greenhouse horticulture, not golf. In its own way, a functional edible vaccine would indeed be a hole-in-one.

CHRONOLOGY

430 B.C.

Plague devastates ancient Athens, claiming among its tens of thousands of victims the famed Greek leader Pericles. The historian Thucydides wrote a contemporaneous account, making this perhaps the oldest epidemic on record.

A.D. 550

A text attributed to the Hindu physician Dhanwantari describes mixing fluid from an infected cow's udder with the blood of a healthy person. Some believe this was an early form of vaccination. Skeptics, however, note that there is no indication whether the subject survived.

1715

Scottish physician Peter Kennedy recommends collecting fluid from the sores of a smallpox victim and scratching it into the skin of a healthy person. The technique, called variolation, sometimes works but often just infects the healthy person with full-blown smallpox.

1716

Lady Mary Wortley Montagu, wife of Britain's ambassador to the Ottoman court, observes the practice of variolation with powdered smallpox, and later applies it to her own son.

1721

Boston-based doctor Zabdiel Boylston performs the first known variolation in America.

1742

A Chinese medical text is published containing advice on how to prevent smallpox by blowing dried scabs from a smallpox victim up the nose of an uninfected person. The method, a form of variolation, carries great risk but sometimes confers immunity.

1798

English physician Edward Jenner publishes a careful study of the effectiveness of vaccinating people against smallpox by deliberately infecting them with cowpox, a related animal disease generally harmless to humans.

1813

U.S. Congress passes a bill enabling the first national smallpox vaccination campaign. The bill is repealed in 1822 after poor vaccination procedures lead to a smallpox outbreak in North Carolina.

1881

French scientist Louis Pasteur develops the first vaccine against anthrax. It is used to immunize livestock.

1882

German medical researcher Robert Koch, employing a novel staining technique, identifies the bacterium responsible for tuberculosis.

1885

Pasteur develops a rabies vaccine.

1890

German physician Emil von Behring develops novel method of extracting antitoxins, which leads eventually to vaccines against diphtheria and tetanus.

1896

British medical researcher Almroth Wright develops a vaccine against typhoid fever, the disease that killed President Lincoln's son.

1921

French physicians test a vaccine against tuberculosis in humans. It comes to be known as BCG.

1927

Though variable in its effectiveness, the BCG vaccine goes into general use.

1953

Jonas Salk announces that he has developed a killed-virus vaccine against polio.

1955

Tests confirm the Salk vaccine safe and effective; mass production gets under way.

1963

An oral polio vaccine developed by Albert Sabin replaces the injected Salk vaccine. The first measles vaccine is licensed.

1967

The World Health Organization launches its global smallpox eradication program by mass vaccination.

1971

Three vaccines, against measles, mumps, and rubella, are combined in what becomes known as the MMR vaccine.

1977

Last known case of smallpox is reported in East African nation Somalia.

1980

World Health Organization officially certifies that smallpox has been eradicated.

1982

Hepatitis B vaccine becomes available.

1988

World Health Organization launches campaign to rid the world of polio.

1990

At World Summit for Children, nations agree on a global campaign to greatly reduce the incidence of childhood measles through vaccination.

1994

The Pan-American Health Organization declares that the Americas have been freed of all cases of polio, thanks to vaccination.

1995

U.S. Food and Drug Administration approves first chicken pox vaccine.

2000

The western Pacific region is declared polio free as eradication campaign continues.

2001

World Health Organization renews measles-reduction campaign, sets target of halving disease by 2005.

2003

Polio eradication campaign hits a major snag as Muslim leaders in northern Nigeria object to vaccination of children on suspicion that the vaccine is contaminated.

2004

Polio vaccinations resume in Nigeria, although resistance continues in some Muslim regions.

FOR FURTHER RESEARCH

Books

Paul F. Basch, *Vaccines and World Health: Science, Policy, and Practice.* New York: Oxford University Press, 1994.

Barry Bloom, ed., *The Vaccine Book.* Boston: Academic Press, 2002.

Mark Caldwell, *The Last Crusade: The War on Consumption, 1862–1954.* New York: Atheneum, 1988.

Stephanie Cave, *What Your Doctor May Not Tell You About Children's Vaccinations.* New York: Warner, 2001.

Jon Cohen, *Shots in the Dark: The Wayward Search for an AIDS Vaccine.* New York: W.W. Norton, 2001.

Robert Goldberg, *The Vaccines for Children Program: A Critique.* Washington, DC: American Enterprise Institute, 2003.

Christine Grady, *The Search for an AIDS Vaccine: Ethical Issues in the Development and Testing of a Preventive HIV Vaccine.* Bloomington: Indiana University Press, 1995.

Margaret O. Hyde and Elizabeth H. Forsyth, *Vaccinations: From Smallpox to Cancer.* London: Franklin Watts, 2000.

Lois M. Joellenbeck et al., eds., *The Anthrax Vaccine: Is It Safe? Does it Work?* Washington, DC: National Academies Press, 2002.

Stanley M. Lemon et al., eds., *Protecting Our Forces: Improving Vaccine Acquisition and Availability in the U.S. Military.* Washington, DC: National Academies Press, 2002.

Douglas B. Lowrie and Robert G. Whalen, *DNA Vaccines: Methods and Protocols.* Totowa, NJ: Humana, 2000.

William A. Muraskin, *Politics of International Health: The Children's Vaccine Initiative and the Struggle to Develop Vaccines for the Third World.* New York: State University of New York Press, 1998.

———, *The War Against Hepatitis B: A History of the International Task Force on Hepatitis B Immunization.* Philadelphia: University of Pennsylvania Press, 1995.

Paul Offit and Louis M. Bell, *Vaccines: What You Should Know.* 3rd ed. New York: John Wiley, 2003.

Stanley A. Plotkin and Walter A. Orenstein, eds., *Vaccines.* Philadelphia: Saunders, 2004.

Richard A. Rettig, *Military Use of Drugs Not Yet Approved by the FDA for CW/BW Defense: Lessons from the Gulf War.* Santa Monica, CA: RAND, 1999.

Frank Ryan, *The Forgotten Plague: How the Battle Against Tuberculosis Was Won—and Lost.* New York: Little, Brown, 1993.

Peter Stern, Peter Beverley, and Miles W. Carroll, eds., *Cancer Vaccines and Immunotherapy.* New York: Cambridge University Press, 2000.

Kathleen Stratton et al., eds., *Immunization Safety Review: Measles-Mumps-Rubella Vaccine and Autism.* Washington, DC: National Academies Press, 2001.

Kathleen R. Stratton, Jane S. Durch, and Robert S. Lawrence, eds., *Vaccines for the 21st Century: A Tool for Decision-Making.* Washington, DC: National Academies Press, 1997.

Periodicals

AIDS Weekly, "AIDS Vaccine to Be Tested on Humans," April 12, 2004, p. 37.

David Bjerklie, "Fewer Shots in Store for Baby," *Time,* January 20, 2003, p. 146.

David Brown, "U.S. Soldier's Death Is Tied to Vaccines," *Washington Post,* November 19, 2003, p. A19.

Daily Trust, "But What Is a Safe Vaccine?" April 28, 2004.

Christine Gorman, "Who Needs Shots?" *Time*, April 12, 2004, p. 78.

Ben Harder, "The Vaccinia Dilemma," *Science News*, April 5, 2003.

James G. Hodge and Larry Gostin, "School Vaccination Requirements: Historical, Social, and Legal Perspectives," *Kentucky Law Journal*, Spring 2002, pp. 831–90.

Leon Jaroff et al., "Vaccine Jitters," *Time*, September 13, 1999, p. 64.

Sasha Nemecek, "Granting Immunity," *Scientific American*, March 2000, p. 15.

Anahad O'Connor, "Chickenpox Vaccine Found to Fade in a Year," *New York Times*, February 24, 2002, p. F7.

Joannie Schrof, "Miracle Vaccines," *U.S. News & World Report*, November 23, 1998, p. 56.

Thom Shanker, "Defense Dept. Halts Anthrax Vaccinations," *New York Times*, December 24, 2003, p. A18.

Rachel Sobel, "A Tailor-Made Vaccine," *U.S. News & World Report*, March 13, 2000, p. 53.

TB & Outbreaks Week, "Health Officials Pledge Renewed Global Efforts to Fight Tuberculosis," April 13, 2004, p. 56.

———, "Muslim Nigerian State Won't Join Immunization Campaign," April 13, 2004, p. 43.

John Travis, "Here's the Skinny on Painless Vaccines," *Science News*, September 11, 1999, p. 164.

Vaccine Weekly, "Danish Study Finds No Link Between Childhood Vaccinations and Diabetes," April 21, 2004, p. 18.

David B. Weiner and Ronald C. Kennedy, "Genetic Vaccines," *Scientific American*, July 1999, p. 50.

Internet Sources

CBS News, "More Smallpox Vaccine Concerns," May 27, 2003. www.cbsnews.com/stories/2003/03/31/eveningnews/main547073.shtml.

Sabin Vaccine Report, "Sabin Vaccine Institute Convenes 8th

Colloquium at Cold Spring Harbor: Making Vaccines for the
Developing World: Access to and Deployment of New Tech-
nologies," Spring 2002. www.sabin.org/PDF/SVR_No1_
Vol5_02.pdf.

United Press International, "U.S. Eyes New, Safer Smallpox Vaccine," April 15, 2004. http://washingtontimes.com/upi-break
ing/20040415-074643-2870r.htm.

Web Sites

Allied Vaccine Group, http://vaccine.org. The Allied Vaccine
Group is a group of provaccine organizations dedicated to presenting the facts about vaccines in a straightforward fashion
on the Web. Its members include the American Academy of
Pediatrics and the National Network for Immunization Information.

American Academy of Family Physicians (AAFP), www.aafp.org.
The American Academy of Family Physicians is the national
association of family doctors. With more than 93,700 members,
it is one of the nation's largest medical organizations. The AAFP
site includes recommended vaccination schedules and detailed
information on a wide variety of vaccine-related issues.

American Academy of Pediatrics, www.cispimmunize.org. The
academy represents fifty-seven thousand physicians serving
infants, children, and young adults. Their "Immunizations Initiative" site contains a wealth of information on infectious diseases, vaccines, risks, and recommendations. It includes a
"Frequently Asked Questions" section.

Centers for Disease Control, www.cdc.gov/node.do/id/0900f3ec
8000e2f3. The Centers are the U.S. government's official disease prevention agencies. Their "Vaccines and Immunizations" page offers a wide variety of topics, including vaccination tips for travelers, safety and adverse events data, a parent's
guide to childhood immunizations, and public awareness event
information.

FamilyDoctor.org, http://familydoctor.org. A site operated by the
American Academy of Family Physicians for the general public. A "Vaccines" section under "Healthy Living" includes information about specific vaccines, such as polio, chicken pox,

and smallpox, as well as general information about vaccine safety and shortages.

National Network for Immunization Information, www.immuniza tioninfo.org. The network is a collaboration of several medical organizations, including the Infectious Diseases Society of America, the American Academy of Pediatrics, the American Nurses Association, and the American Academy of Family Physicians, among others. The site offers specific information on numerous vaccines and allows users to look up school vaccination requirements by state.

The Vaccine Page, http://vaccines.org. Operated by PATH, the Program for Appropriate Technology in Health, this site offers a wealth of international vaccine information. It includes links to professional journals containing vaccine information and a section for parents.

World Health Organization (WHO), "Immunization, Vaccines and Biologicals," www.who.int/vaccines. Another highly international site, this one includes information about the WHO's global vaccine initiatives. It also contains information about vaccines in development. The World Health Organization is the UN's health division.

INDEX